Deep Learning: Theory, Architectures and Applications in Speech, Image and Language Processing

Edited by

Gyanendra Verma
National Institute of Technology Raipur, Raipur, India

&

Rajesh Doriya
National Institute of Technology Raipur, Raipur, India

Deep Learning: Theory, Architectures and Applications in Speech, Image and Language Processing

Editors: Gyanendra Verma and Rajesh Doriya

ISBN (Online): 978-981-5079-21-0

ISBN (Print): 978-981-5079-22-7

ISBN (Paperback): 978-981-5079-23-4

First published in 2023.

need for a court order if at any point you breach any terms of this License Agreement. In no event will any delay or failure by Bentham Science Publishers in enforcing your compliance with this License Agreement constitute a waiver of any of its rights.

3. You acknowledge that you have read this License Agreement, and agree to be bound by its terms and conditions. To the extent that any other terms and conditions presented on any website of Bentham Science Publishers conflict with, or are inconsistent with, the terms and conditions set out in this License Agreement, you acknowledge that the terms and conditions set out in this License Agreement shall prevail.

Bentham Science Publishers Pte. Ltd.
80 Robinson Road #02-00
Singapore 068898
Singapore
Email: subscriptions@benthamscience.net

BENTHAM SCIENCE

CONTENTS

FOREWORD

Machine Learning proved its usefulness in many applications in Image Processing and Computer Vision, Medical Imaging, Satellite imaging, Remote Sensing, Surveillance, *etc.*, over the past decade. At the same time, Machine Learning, particularly Artificial Neural Networks has evolved and demonstrated excellent performance over traditional machine learning algorithms. These methods are known as Deep Learning.

Nowadays, Deep Learning has become the researcher's first choice in contrast to traditional machine learning due to its apex performance on speech, image, and text processing. Deep learning algorithms provide efficient solutions to problems ranging from image and speech processing to text processing. The research on deep learning is getting enriched day by day as we witness new learning models.

Deep learning models significantly impacted speech, image, and text-domain and raised the performance bar substantially in many standard evaluations. Moreover, new challenges are easily tackled by utilizing deep learning, which older systems could not have handled. However, it is challenging to comprehend, let alone guide, the learning process in deep neural networks; there is an air of uncertainty about exactly what and how these networks learn.

This book aims to provide the audience with a basic understanding of deep learning and its different architectures. Background knowledge of machine learning helps explore various aspects of deep learning. By the end of the book, I hope that the reader understands different deep learning approaches, models, pre-trained models, and gains familiarity with implementing various deep learning algorithms using multiple frameworks and libraries.

Dr. Shitala Prasad
Scientist, Institute for Infocomm Research, A*Star
Singapore 138632
Singapore

PREFACE

Machine Learning proved its usefulness in many applications in the domain of Image Processing and Computer Vision, Medical Imaging, Satellite imaging, Remote Sensing, Surveillance, *etc* ., over the past decade. At the same time, Machine Learning methods themselves have evolved, particularly deep learning methods that have demonstrated significant performance over traditional machine learning algorithms.

Today's Deep Learning has become researchers' first choice in contrast to traditional machine learning due to its apex performance in many applications in the domain of speech, image, and text processing. Deep learning algorithms provide efficient solutions to problems ranging from vision and speech to text processing. The research on deep learning is getting enriched day by day as we witness new learning models.

This book contains two major parts. Part one includes the fundamentals of Deep Learning, theory, and architecture of Deep Learning. Moreover, this part provides a detailed description of the theory, frameworks, and non-conventional approaches to deep learning. It covers foundational mathematics that is essential in understanding the framework. Moreover, it covers various kinds of models found in practice.

Chapter 1 contains the basic operating understanding, history, evolution, and challenges associated with deep learning. We will also cover some basic concepts of mathematics and the hardware requirements for deep learning implementation, and some of its popular software frameworks. We will start with neural networks, which focus on the basics of neural networks, including input/output layers, hidden layers, and how networks learn through forward and backpropagation. We will also cover the standard multilayer perceptron networks and their building blocks. Moreover, we will include a review of deep learning concepts in general and deep learning in particular to build a basic understanding of this book. Chapters 2–7 are based on applying artificial intelligence to medical images with various deep learning approaches. It also covers the application of Deep Learning in lung cancer detection, medical imaging, and COVID-19 analysis.

The second part, chapters 8–10, is dedicated to sentiment analysis using deep learning and machine learning techniques. This book section covers the experimentation and application of deep learning techniques and architectures in real-world applications. It details the salient approaches, issues, and challenges in building ethically aligned machines. An approach inspired by traditional Eastern thought and wisdom is also presented.

The third part, Chapters 11–15, is miscellaneous and covers the different artificial intelligence approaches used to explain the machine learning models that enhance transparency between the user and the model. A review and detailed description of the use of knowledge graphs in generating explanations for black-box recommender systems and elaborative education ecosystems for sustainable quality education is provided. Reinforcement learning is a semi-supervised learning technique for portfolio management.

Gyanendra Verma
National Institute of Technology Raipur
Raipur, India

&

Rajesh Doriya
National Institute of Technology Raipur
Raipur, India

List of Contributors

Aqib Ali Sayed	Amity School of Engineering and Technology, Amity University Mumbai, Maharashtra 410206, India
Abdul Jabbar Perumbalath	School of Computer Science, Mahathma Gandhi University,Kottayam, Kerala, India
Anil Verma	Department of Computer Science and Engineering, Lovely Professional University, Jalandhar, Punjab, India
Aman Singh	Department of Computer Science and Engineering, Lovely Professional University, Jalandhar, Punjab, India
Archana Mathiazhagan	School of Computing, SASTRA Deemed University, Thanjavur 613401, India
Babita Panda	School of Electrical Engg., KIIT University, Bhubaneswar, India
Chellapilla Vasantha Lakshmi	Dayalbagh Educational Institute, Agra, India
Chellapilla Patvardhan	Dayalbagh Educational Institute, Agra, India
Divya Anand	Department of Computer Science and Engineering, Lovely Professional University, Jalandhar, Punjab, India
Elakkiya Rajasekar	School of Computing, SASTRA Deemed University, Thanjavur 613401, India
Gyanendra Verma	Department of Information Technology, National Institute of Technology, Raipur, India
Harshawardhan Tiwari	Jyothy Institute of Technology, Pipeline Rd, near Ravi Shankar Guruji Ashram, Thathaguni, Karnataka, India
Harshee Pitroda	Department of Computer Engineering, NMIMS University, Mukesh Patel School of Technology Management & Engineering, Mumbai, India
Ishani Saha	Department of Computer Engineering, NMIMS University, Mukesh Patel School of Technology Management & Engineering, Mumbai, India
Jay Prajapati	Department of Data Science, SVKM's NMIMS, Mumbai, Maharashtra, India
Jayalakshmi Ramachandran Nair	Bharathidasan University, Department of Sciences, St. Claret College, Bengaluru, Karnataka, India
Jaykumar Suraj Lachure	Department of Information Technology, National Institute of Technology, Raipur, India
Mayank Gupta	Department of Computer Science and Engineering, Punjab Engineering College, Chandigarh, India
Muhamed Ilyas Poovankavil	PG and Research Department of Computer Science, Sullamussalam Science College, Areekode, Malappuram Dt, Kerala, India
Manisha Tiwari	Department of Computer Engineering, NMIMS University, Mukesh Patel School of Technology Management & Engineering, Mumbai, India

Natarajan Balasubramanian School of Computing, SASTRA Deemed to be University, Thanjavur, Tamilnadu 613401, India

Nehha Seetharaman Amity School of Engineering and Technology, Amity University Mumbai, Maharashtra 410206, India

Poonam Saini Department of Computer Science and Engineering, Punjab Engineering College, Chandigarh, India

Parth Kalkotwar Dwarkadas J. Sanghvi College of Engineering, Mumbai, India

Prajwal Sethu Madhav Jyothy Institute of Technology, Pipeline Rd, near Ravi Shankar Guruji Ashram, Thathaguni, Karnataka, India

Priyanka Prashanth Kumar Jyothy Institute of Technology, Pipeline Rd, near Ravi Shankar Guruji Ashram, Thathaguni, Karnataka, India

Rakesh Kumar Dhaka ITM University, Gwalior, India

Rajkumar Narayanan Department of Sciences, St. Claret College, Bengaluru, Karnataka, India

Rajalakshmi Elangovan School of Computing, SASTRA Deemed University, Thanjavur 613401, India

Rishika Vij Department of Veterinary Physiology & Biochemistry, Dr. GC Negi College of Veterinary & Animal Science, Palampur, Himachal Pradesh, India

Rajesh Doriya Department of Information Technology, National Institute of Technology, Raipur, India

Saleena Thorayanpilackal Sulaiman PG and Research Department of Computer Science, Sullamussalam Science College, Areekode, Malappuram Dt, Kerala, India

Sampurna Panda ITMUniversity,Gwalior, sampurnapanda, India

Sanay Shah Dwarkadas J. Sanghvi College of Engineering, Mumbai, India

Saurav Tiwari Dwarkadas J. Sanghvi College of Engineering, Mumbai, India

Sindhu Nair Dwarkadas J. Sanghvi College of Engineering, Mumbai, India

Siba Panda Department of Data Science, SVKM's NMIMS, Mumbai, Maharashtra, India

Sumathy Pichai Pillai Department of Computer Science & Applications, Bharathidasan University, Tiruchirappalli, Tamil Nadu, India

Srishti Sakshi Sinha Department of CSE, Pondicherry University, Puducherry, India

Sukrati Chaturvedi Dayalbagh Educational Institute, Agra, India

Sushila Ratre Amity School of Engineering and Technology, Amity University, Mumbai, Maharashtra 410206, India

Trupthi Muralidharr Jyothy Institute of Technology, Pipeline Rd, near Ravi Shankar Guruji Ashram, Thathaguni, Karnataka 560082, India

Vatsal Khandor Dwarkadas J. Sanghvi College of Engineering, Mumbai, India

Uma Vijayasundaram Department of Computer Science, Pondicherry University, Puducherry, India

## CHAPTER 1

Deep Learning: History and Evolution

Jaykumar Suraj Lachure[1,*], **Gyanendra Verma**[1] and **Rajesh Doriya**[1]

[1] National Institute of Technology Raipur, Raipur, India

Abstract: Recently, deep learning (DL) computing has become more popular in the machine learning (ML) community. In the field of ML, the most widely used computational approach is DL. It can solve many complex problems, cognitive tasks, and matching problems without any human performance or interface. ML cannot handle large amounts of data and DL can easily handle it. In the last few years, the field of DL has witnessed success in a range of applications. DL outperformed in many application domains, *e.g.*, robotics, bioinformatics, agriculture, cybersecurity, natural language processing (NLP), medical information processing, *etc.* Despite various reviews on the state of the art in DL, they all concentrated on a single aspect of it, resulting in a general lack of understanding. There is a need to provide a better beginning point for comprehending DL. This paper aims to provide a more comprehensive overview of DL, including current advancements. This paper discusses the importance of DL and introduces DL approaches and networks. It then explains convolutional neural networks (CNNs), the most widely used DL network type and subsequent evolved model starting with LeNET, AlexNet with the Letnet-5, AlexNet, GoogleNet, and ResNet networks, and ending with the High-Resolution network. This paper also discusses the difficulties and solutions to help researchers recognize research gaps for DL applications.

Keywords: Convolution neural network, Deep learning applications, Deep Learning, Image classification, Machine Learning, Medical image analysis.Natural Language Processing.

INTRODUCTION

In the last decade, machine learning (ML) models [1 - 3] have been widely used in every field and have been applied in versatile applications like classification, image/video retrieval, text mining, multimedia, anomaly detection, attack detection, video recommendation, image classification, *etc.* Nowadays, deep learning (DL) is frequently employed in comparison to other machine learning methods. DL stands for representative learning. The unpredictable expansion of

---

* **Corresponding author Jaykumar Suraj Lachure:** National Institute of Technology Raipur, India; E-mail: jaykuamrlachure@gmail.com

DL and distributed learning necessitates ongoing study. Deep and distributed learning studies are continuing to emerge as a result of unanticipated advances in data availability and huge advancements in hardware technologies such as High-Performance Computing (HPC). DL is a Neural Network (NN) that outperforms its predecessors. DL also employs transformations and graph technology to create multi-layer learning models. In fields such as Natural Language Processing (NLP), data processing, visual data processing, and audio and speech processing, the most recent DL techniques have achieved extraordinary performance. The representation of input data is often what determines the success of an ML approach. A proper data representation outperforms a poor data representation. Thus, for many years, feature engineering has been a prominent study topic in ML. This method helps to build features from raw data. It also involves a lot of human effort and is quite field-specific. These are the scale-invariant feature transform (SIFT), histogram of oriented gradients (HOG), and bag of words (BoW).

The DL algorithms automatically extract features, and this helps researchers extract discriminative features with minimal human effort and field knowledge. A multi-layer data representation architecture extracts low-level features at the first layer, while the last layer extracts high-level features. Artificial Intelligence (AI) is the basis of all technology, including ML, DL, and NLP, *etc.*, which processes data for particular applications, much like in the human brain's basic sensory regions. The human brain can automatically derive data representation using different scenes. This procedure's output is the classified objects, while the input is the incoming scene information. This mimics the human brain's workings. Thus, it accentuates DL's key advantage.

Due to its significant success, DL is presently one of the most important research fashions in ML. Architectures, issues, computational tools, the evolution matrix, and applications are all significant elements in DL. In DL networks, convolutional neural networks (CNN) are widely employed. CNN automatically finds key features, making it the most widely used. Therefore, we delved deep into CNN by showing its core elements. From the AlexNet network to the GoogleNet with high-resolution network, each uses the most prevalent CNN topologies.

Several deep learning models have solely dealt with one application or issue in recent years, such as examining CNN architectures or deep learning. There are different applications like autonomous machines, deep learning for plant disease detection and classification, deep learning for security and malicious attack detection, and so on. Table **1** shown below provides a few domains and applications of DL. Prior to diving into DL applications, it is important to grasp the concepts, problems, and benefits of DL. Learning DL to address research gaps and applications takes a lot of time and research. Our proposal is to conduct an extensive review of DL to provide a better starting point for a comprehensive grasp of DL.

Table 1. Different Domains of DL and Applications.

Internet &Cloud	Medicine & Biology	Media & Entertainment	Security & Defense	Autonomous Machines	Agriculture
Image Classification	Cancer Cell Detection	Video Captioning	Face Detection	Pedestrian Detection	Crop Recommendation
Speech Recognition	Diabetic Grading	Video Search	Video Surveillance	Lane Tracking	Leaf Disease Detection
Language Translation	Drug Discovery	Real Time Translation	Satellite Imagery	Recognize Traffic Sign	Fruit Classification
Language Processing	Drug-Drug Interaction	Recommendation	Malicious Attack	Object Detection	Smart Irrigation
Sentiment Analysis	Drug-protein Interaction	Image/ video Retrieval	Firewall Security	Object Tracking	Leaf Identification

For our review, we focused on open challenges, computational tools, and applications. This review can also be a springboard for further DL discussions.

The review helps individuals learn more about recent breakthroughs in DL research, which will help them grow in the field. In order to deliver precise alternatives to the field, researchers would be given greater autonomy. Here are our contributions:

- This review aids researchers and students in gaining comprehensive knowledge about DL.
- We will describe the historical overview of neural networks.
- We discuss deep learning approaches using Deep Feedforward Neural Networks, Deep Backward Neural Networks, and CNN, as well as their concepts, theories, and current architectures.
- We describe the different CNN architectures like AlexNet, GoogleNet, and ResNet.
- We describe deep learning models that use auto-encoders, long short-term memory, and a deep belief network architecture.

The rest of the paper is organized as follows: A description of neural networks and its fundamental structure is given in Section 2. Section 3 provides the different neural network architectures. Section 4 discusses the detailed study of CNN and its components, with different architectures of CNN models. Section 5 discusses the different DL models with a time-series base and a deep belief network. Section 6 concludes with the discussion of DL.

OVERVIEW OF THE NEURAL NETWORK

Over the years, many people have contributed to the development of neural networks [2, 4, 5]. Given the current spike in interest in DL, it's not surprising that credit for substantial advancements is being contested. The following is an overview of the most significant contributions in an objective manner. McCulloch and Pitts developed the first mathematical neuron model in 1943. However, this model does not attempt to replicate the biophysical mechanism of an actual neuron. Intriguingly, this model omitted education. Hebb developed the concept of physiologically driven learning in neural networks in 1949. Hebbian learning is an unsupervised neural network learning technique. Rosenblatt introduced the Perceptron in 1957. A perceptron is a single-layer based neural network that can be used to classify a perceptron. It uses the Heaviside activation function in the current ANN language. Widrow and Hoff introduced the delta-learning rule for learning a perceptron. To update the neurons' weights, the delta-learning rule uses gradient descent. It is a back propagation algorithm variation. To train neural networks, Ivakhnenko invented the Group Method of Data Handling (GMDH) in 1968. These networks were the first feedforward multilayer perceptron deep learning networks. In 1971, the first 8-layer deep GMDH net was used with the number of layers. Each level contains units per layer that could be learned rather than predetermined.

A perceptron cannot learn XOR since it is not linearly separable. In 1974, the error back propagation (BP) algorithm was proposed for weighted learning in a supervised manner. Fukushima introduced the Neocognitron in 1980. The Neocognitron is viewed as a deep neural network in the same vein as the deep GMDH networks (DNN). The D-FFNNs (Deep Feedforward Neural Networks) are the ancestors of this network, and it has a similar design. In 1982, Hopfield developed the Hopfield Network, which is also known as a content-addressable memory neural network. Recurrent neural networks are similar to Hopfield networks. In the given example, backpropagation resurfaced in 1986, and this learning technique can build meaningful internal representations for broad neural network learning tasks.

Terry Sejnowski created NETtalk in 1987. That programme improved over time in pronouncing English words. In 1989, the back propagation (CNN) first did handwritten digit learning. Hochreiter studied a basic issue in 1991 when training a deep learning network *via* backpropagation. According to his research, backpropagation signals either drop or rise without limits. In the event of a decline, the network depth is proportionate. also called the "vanishing or bursting gradient issue." Pre-training Recurrent Neural Network (RNN) unsupervised to speed up future supervised learning was suggested in 1992 as a partial solution. The RNN investigated contained over 1000 layers. In 1995, Wang and Terman introduced oscillatory neural networks.

Image and audio segmentation, as well as time series production, are examples of applications. In 1997, Long Short-Term Memory (LSTM) was proposed by Hochreiter and Schmidhuber, which is a supervised model for learning recurrent neural networks (RNNs). LSTM networks avoid decaying error signals between layers.

It was integrated with backpropagation to improve learning at CNN in 1998. It was therefore created to classify handwritten numbers on checks using LeNet-5, which typically contains a 7-level convolutional network. The greedy layer-wise approach was used to train the model and was demonstrated by Hinton *et al.* in 2006. The third wave of neural networks popularised the phrase "deep learning."

In 2012, CNN, with a GPU, AlexNet, beat LeNet5 to win the ImageNet Large Scale Visual Recognition Challenge. In 2014, Goodfellow *et al.* introduced generative adversarial networks. Two neural networks battle in the fashion of a game mode. Overall, this creates a generative model that can produce fresh data. This is the evolution of the Hopfield network to CNN and other CNN architectures that have been replaced over the years.coolest machine learning idea in 20 years, according to Yann LeCun. With deep neural networks, Yoshua Bengio, Yann LeCun, and Geoffrey Hinton won the Turing Award in 2019.

THE NEURAL NETWORK'S BASIC STRUCTURE

Artificial Neural Networks (ANNs) are basic mathematical models based on how the brain works [6]. However, the models discussed below are not biologically realistic. Instead, these models analyse the data. The different neural models are explained as follows:

ARTIFICIAL NEURON MODEL WITH FFNN

Any neural network starts with a neuron model (Fig. **1**) depicts an artificial neuron model. In a neuron model, the basic input, x, is feed with weighted w and bias b to summarized [7]. Assume that the input vector Rn and the weight vector w are both vectors, with n equal to the input dimension N. The bias term is not always existing and might be remove. They are added together to create the an activation function argument, giving the neuron model's output:(z)=wTx+b. Only the argument of provides a linear discriminant function. The activation function is identified as transfer or unit function or transforms z nonlinearly.

$$y = \phi(z) = \phi(\mathbf{w}^T\mathbf{x} + b) \tag{1}$$

The ReLU activation function is termed as a rectifier and most widely used in DNNs. The softmax function:

$$y_i = \frac{e^{x_i}}{\sum_j^n e^{x_j}} \tag{2}$$

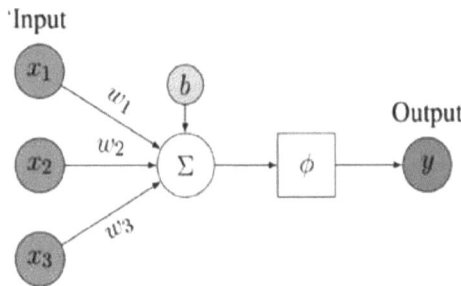

Fig. (1). Artificial Neuron Model.

The softmax maps an n-dimensional x to an n-dimensional y. Therefore, y represents the probability for each of the n elements. It is sometimes used as the last layer in a network. The activation function uses the Heaviside step function in the perceptron model. The neurons must be connected in NN. A feedforward arrangement in its simplest form is shown in Fig. (2) and Fig. (3)., which illustrate the shallow and deep architecture of NN.

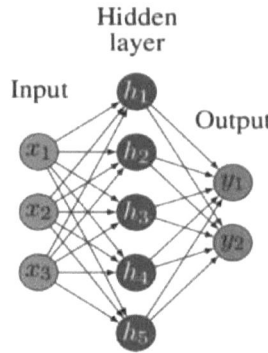

Fig. (2). Shallow Architecture of NN.

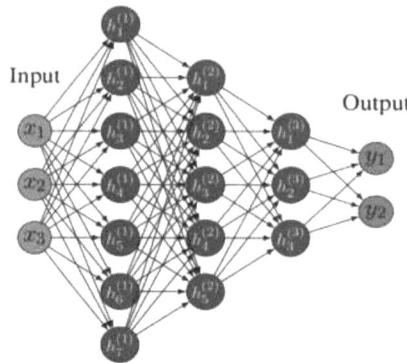

Fig. (3). Deep Architecture of NN.

Generalized deepness of a network in NN is the sum of non-linear revolutions between the layers that are separated, whereas hidden layer width is the number of hidden neurons. Fig. (**2**) has a single hidden layer, whereas Fig. (**3**) has a three number of hidden layers. The depths for the shallow and deep architectures of NN are two and four. Debatable, however, topologies with two layers are called "shallow" and those with more than two hidden layers are typically called "deep" in Feedforward Neural Networks (FFNN).

The activation functions of a feedforward neural network (FNN) might be linear or non-linear. The NN lacks any cycles that would permit direct input. How an MLP gets its output from its input.

$$f(\mathbf{x}) = \varphi^{(2)}\left(W^{(2)}\varphi^{(1)}\left(W^{(1)}\mathbf{x} + \mathbf{b}^{(1)}\right) + \mathbf{b}^{(2)}\right) \tag{3}$$

Equation (3) illustrates the neural network's discriminant function. An optimization method to find the optimal parameters for training data sets with a cost function or an error function is being developed.

Recurrent Neural Networks: The RNN family has 2 subclasses that are able to be identified by their characteristics of signal processing [8]. The first type is composed of Finite Recurrent Networks (FRN), whereas the second type is composed of Infinite Impulse Recurrent Networks (IIRN). However, an FRN comes under a directed acyclic graph (DAG) type that may be unrolled and replaced by a FNN, whereas an IIRN comes under a directed cyclic graph (DCG) that cannot be unrolled.

Hopfield Network: A Hopfield Network is an example of a FRN. It is a network of McCulloch-Pitts neurons that is entirely connected. For a

McCulloch-Pitts neuron, the activation function is as:

$$s = \text{sgn}(x\_i) = \begin{cases} +1 & \text{for } x\_i \geq 0 \\ -1 & \text{for } x\_i < 0 \end{cases} \tag{4}$$

The activation neuron of the function is as:

$$x_i = \text{sign}\left(\sum_{j=1}^{N} w_{ij} x_j - \theta_i\right) \tag{5}$$

$$w_{ij} = \sum_{k=1}^{P} t_i(k) t_j(k) \tag{6}$$

xiis updated synchronously or asynchronously with the xj.wijis updated weight for updating the xi value for sign value.

Boltzmann Machine: It uses a noisy Hopfield network with a probabilistic-based activation function. From Eq. 7, it is shown that probability is updated with an update from Eq. 5. This model is significant as it was one of the first to use hidden units. The contrastive-divergence algorithm is used to train Boltzmann Machines.

$$p(s_i = 1) = \frac{1}{1 + \exp(-x_i)} \tag{7}$$

Boltzmann Machines are two-layered neural networks with visible and hidden layers.

The edges between the two layers are undirected within the graph, which implies information could flow in both directions. The network is completely connected, which means every neuron is connected to another through undirected edges Fig. (4) shows how to transform the Boltzmann machine into an RBM [9]. RBM is a basic structure used in many applications and for creating different networks. (Table 2) provides the usage of models and their working nature, not the comparison. Each model in the table performs differently for different domains.

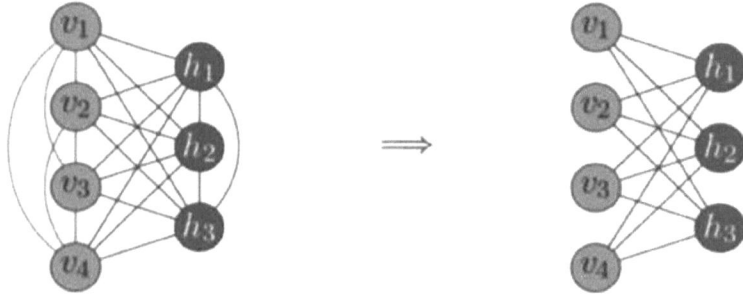

Fig. (4). Conversion of Boltzmann Machine to Restricted Boltzmann machine (RBM).

Table 2. Deep Learning Models and its Learning Algorithms.

Model	Unsupervised	Supervised
Multilayer Perceptron	No	Yes
Deep Belief Network	Yes	Yes
Restricted Boltzmann Machine	Yes	Yes
Convolutional Neural Network	Yes	Yes
Recurrent Neural Network	No	Yes
Convolutional Deep Belief Network	Yes	Yes
Autoencoder	Yes	No
Deep Boltzmann Machine	No	Yes
Long short-term memory	No	Yes

DEEP LEARNING NEURAL NETWORK

The neural network consists of deep layers of neurons [10]. The neurons must constantly learn to tackle tasks or to apply in different ways to produce better results. It learns every time based on new updated information. A deep neural network uses multiple layers of nodes to extract high-level functions from incoming data [1, 4]. It means changing data into something more creative and abstract. The Deep Forward Neural Networks (DFNN) are explained as below:

A Deep Forward Neural Network

A FNN contains a set of neurons and a hidden layer for any continuous function. The reason for adopting an FFNN with multiple hidden layers is that it uses the universal approximation theorem, which does not explain how to learn such a network. A related concern is that the network's diameter can grow exponentially. Unexpectedly, the universal approximation theorem holds for FFNN with a limited number of hidden neurons and numerous hidden layers. So DFFNNs are employed instead of shallow FFNNs for learnability. Approximating an unknown function f* is:

$$y = f^*(x) \approx f(x, w) \approx \phi(x^T w) \tag{8}$$

Here, f is a function with a specific family that is reliant on the parameters θ, and φ is a non-linear activation function with a single layer. For deep hidden layers, φ has the form is as below:

$$\phi = \phi^{(n)}\left(\ldots \phi^{(2)}\left(\phi^{(1)}(x)\right)\ldots\right) \tag{9}$$

In place of assuming the precise family functions from f, D-FFNNs learn Eq. 9 function by approximating it with φ, which is approached by the n separate hidden layers.

CNN Architecture and its Components

A CNN [4, 11 - 13] is a special type of FFNN that uses a combination of convolution layers, ReLU, and pooling layers. These layers are usually combined with several layers of FNN. In traditional ANN, each neuron in a layer is linked to all the neurons in the next layer. Each connection is a parameter in the network, and each connection is how the network works. In CNN, there could be different variables that are not fully connected layers. This significance cuts down on the number of parameters and reduces the operations in the network. All the connections between neurons and local receptive fields use a set of weights, and we call this set of weights a kernel, or core.

Kernel: All the neurons that attach to their local receptive fields will share the same kernel. The neurons' calculations results will be stored in a matrix called the activation map. Weight sharing refers to the fact that CNNs can share their weight. Consequently, different kernels will produce different activation maps, and hyper-parameters can be used to change the number of kernels in the map. The number of weights in a network is proportional to the kernel *i.e.* to the size of the local receptive field. Fig. (5) shows the typical CNN architecture with 3-channel input. Each channel was connected with a convolution layer, pooling, and then again, convolution, pooling, and merge. The merge layer connects with the fully connected layer (FC) to provide the decision using the softmax function.

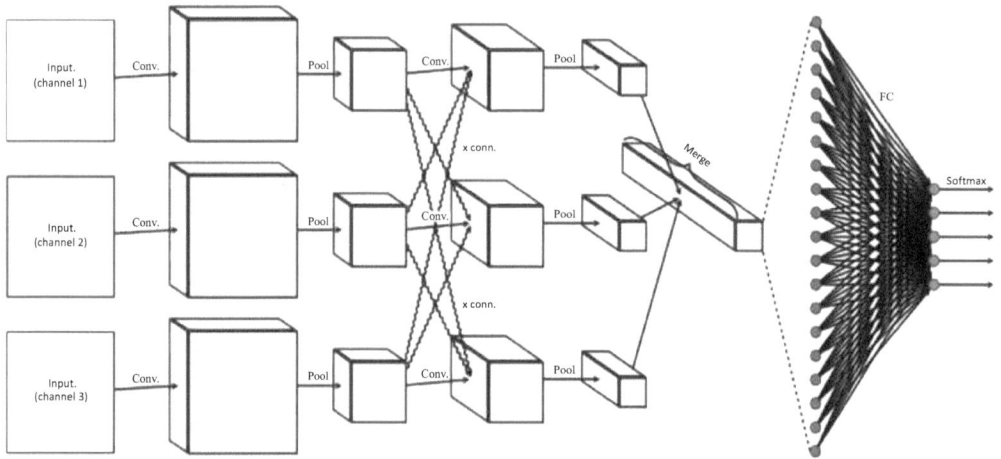

Fig. (5). Typical CNN with 3-Channel input.

The softmax equation is given in eq. 10, where it is calculated to provide the classification based on their threshold values.

$$y_i = \frac{e^{x_i}}{\sum_j^n e^{x_j}} \quad \frac{\partial y_i}{\partial j} = y_i\left(\delta_{ij} - y_j\right) \tag{10}$$

The different layers in CNN models are explained as follows:

- **Convolution layer:** A convolution layer is a critical component of a convolutional neural network's architecture. A convolutional layer, like a hidden layer in a conventional neural network, seeks to convert the input to a higher level of abstraction. On the other hand, the convolutional layer, rather than relying on total connectivity to perform calculations between the input and hidden neurons, takes advantage of local connectivity. A convolutional layer slides at least one kernel across the input, convoluting each region. The results are stored in activation maps, which are the outputs of the convolutional layer.
- **Pooling layer:** It is frequently sandwiched between two layers of convolution. By retaining as much information as possible, pooling layers attempt to minimise the input dimension. Additionally, a pooling layer can impart spatial invariance to the network, hence increasing generality. The zero padding, stride, pooling window size, and hyperparameters of a pooling layer. The pooling layer, like the kernel of a convolutional layer, scans the whole input using the specified pooling window size. By pooling with a stride of 2, a window size of 2, and zero

padding, the input dimension is halved. Min-pooling, averaging, and more sophisticated methods such as stochastic pooling and fractional max-pooling are examples of pooling procedures. Max pooling is the most commonly used pooling technique, as it efficiently captures picture invariance. Max-pooling is used to get the extreme value from each sub-window.

- **Fully connected layer:** The smallest unit in FFNN is a completely connected layer. Between the penultimate and output layers of a normal CNN, a fully connected layer is frequently added to represent non-linear interactions between input features. However, the numerous criteria given have been questioned recently, posing the possibility of overfitting. It has been used in some CNN architectures instead of linear layers.

DIFFERENT CNN ARCHITECTURE

CNN is a common FFNN model that was designed to recognise visual patterns directly from group or pixel images with minimal preprocessing [11, 14]. An image database, ImageNet, was proposed for object recognition research. An annual software challenge called the ImageNet Large Scale Visual Recognition Challenge (ILSVRC) tests software's ability to detect and classify objects and scenes. Below, we discuss the CNN architectures of ILSVRC's main competitors.

LeNet-5

In 1998, LeNet-5 used a 7-level convolutional network developed by LeCun *et al.* to classify digits. For processing higher resolution images, it requires a large number of convolutional layers; therefore, processing resources are restricted to computing in Fig. (**6**).

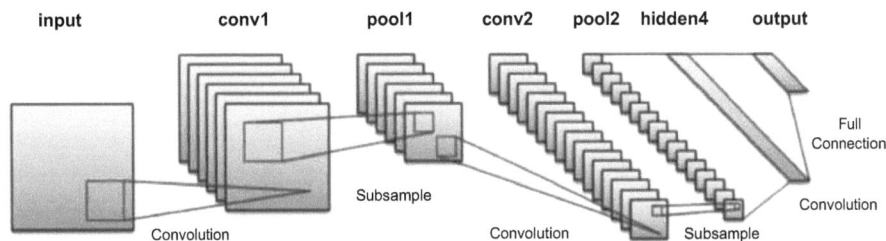

Fig. (6). LetNet-5 Architecture.

AlexNet: In 2012, AlexNet surpassed all previous opponents, by cutting the topmost-5 errors from 26% to 15.3%. The AlexNet network was deeper, featured more filters per layer, and stacked convolutional layers were used than in LeNet5. Convolutions, max-pooling, dropout, data-augmentation, ReLU activations, and SGD with momentum were used in AlexNet in Fig. (**7**). Every fully connected layer and convolutional layer had a ReLU activation function. For the first 6 days, AlexNet was trained on 2 Nvidia Geforce GTX 580 GPUs. In addition, the SuperVision group designed AlexNet by Geoffrey Hinton and Ilya Sutskever.

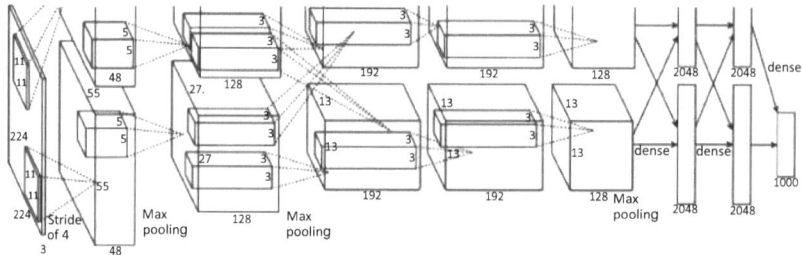

Fig. (7). AlexNet Architecture.

GoogleNet/Inception

The ILSVRC 2014 competition was won by GoogLeNet (Inception V1). The challenge organizers were now forced to evaluate this near-human performance. It turns out that beating Google's accuracy requires some human instruction. Using ensemble mode, a human expert achieved a top-5 error rate of 5.1 percent for a single model and 3.6 percent for multi-models.

The network employed a LeNet-inspired CNN, but it included a new element called an inception component. There was also RMSprop and batch normalization. This module uses numerous minor convolutions to reduce the number of parameters. Their architecture uses a 22-layer deep CNN with 4 million parameters instead of 60 million (AlexNet).

VGGNet

VGGNet was the runner-up at ILSVRC 2014 and was developed by Zisserman and Simonyan. VGGNet uses 16 convolutional layers with a fine and reliable design. Only 3x3 convolutions, but many filters, and the programme ran for 2–3 weeks on four GPUs continuously. It is now the most commonly used method for extracting features from images or photos. The VGGNet weight configuration is open source and is now being utilised in many other applications and challenges. VGGNet has 138 million parameters, which can be difficult to manage in Fig. (**8**).

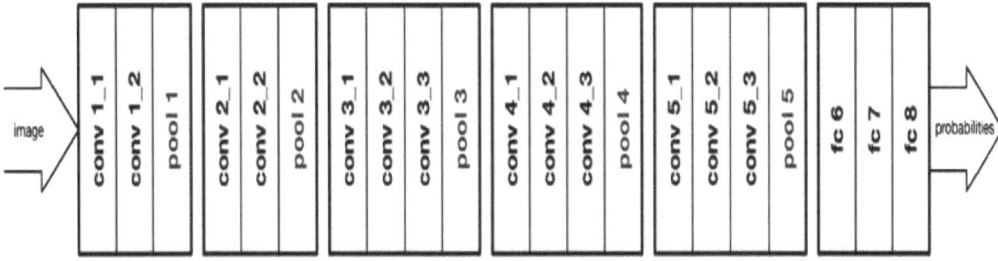

Fig. (8). VGGNet Architecture.

ResNet

Finally, Kaiming *et al.* proposed and developed a novel architecture with "skip connections" and significant batch-normalization at ILSVRC 2015 called the Residual Neural Network (ResNet).

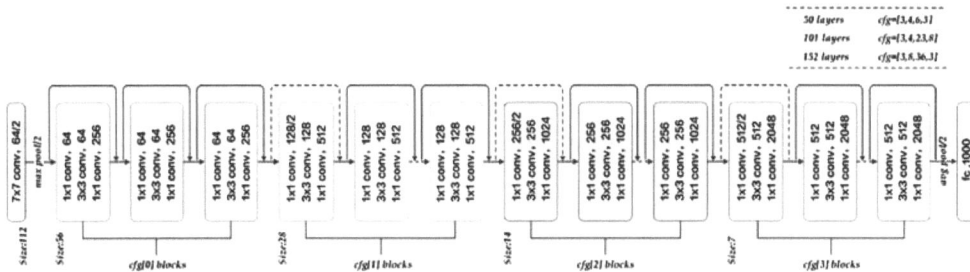

Fig. (9). ResNet Architecture.

These skip connections, also called gated units or gated recurrent units, are closely related to recent successful RNN elements. They trained a NN with 152 layers that was less complex than the VGGNet. Using this dataset, it achieves a top-5 error rate of 3.57%. GoogleNet has inception components, while ResNet has residual connections.

UNSUPERVISE NEURAL NETWORK ARCHITECTURE

Deep Belief Network

A DBN is a model that combines different forms of NN [1, 15]. DBN is a hybrid of RBM and Deep Feedforward Neural Networks (D-FFNN). The RBM serve as the input, and the D-FFNN serve as the output. RBMs are commonly stacked, which means they are used sequentially. Because RBM and D-FFNN are independent networks with two different learning techniques, this enriches the

DBN. RBMs are commonly used to unsupervised initialise a model. A supervised technique is used to fine-tune the settings. These two stages of DBN training are discussed in greater detail below in Fig. (**10**).

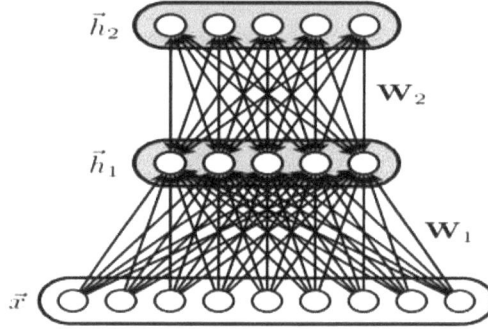

Fig. (10). Deep Belief Network.

Autoencoder

It is an unsupervised NN model for feature selection or dimension reduction [1, 3, 16]. An autoencoder's input and output layers have the same size, symmetrically. An input pattern x is learned to a new encoding, which provides an output pattern identical to the input pattern, *i.e.,* (c). So the encoding c can replicate x. Autoencoders are built similarly to DBN. Interestingly, the original autoencoder only pre-trained the first half of the network with RBM and then unrolled the network, creating the second half. Pre-training is followed by fine-tuning, as in DBN. Fig. (**11**) shows the typical denoising autoencoder. Autoencoders are unsupervised learning models because they don't need labels.

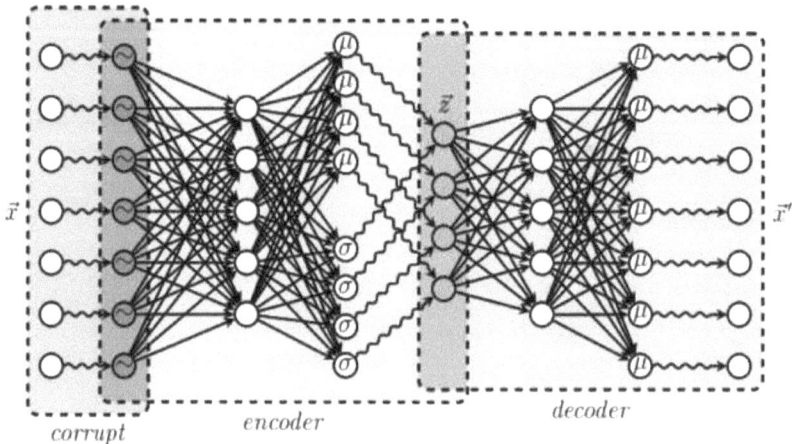

Fig. (11). Denoising Autoencoder.

The model has been used to reduce dimensionality successfully. When given enough data, autoencoders can produce a superior 2-dimensional representation of array data. PCAs use linear transformations, whereas autoencoders use non-linear transformations. This usually results in improved performance. Some of these models are called sparse autoencoders, denoising autoencoders, or variational autoencoders, and there are many different types of them.

LSTM

In 1997, Hochreiter and Schmidhuber proposed LSTM networks. LSTM is an RNN variant that can alleviate RNN faults, such as long-term dependencies [3, 8]. LSTM also prevents gradients from disappearing or bursting. In 1999, an LSTM with a forget gate was introduced. As a result, unlike DFNs, LSTM with feedback links became the standard LSTM network structure. They can also process data sequences as opposed to single data pieces. As a result, LSTMs are excellent for evaluating voice or video data. Fig. (**12**) shows a typical LSTM with a forget gate, input gate, and output gate all connected by a single flip-flop.

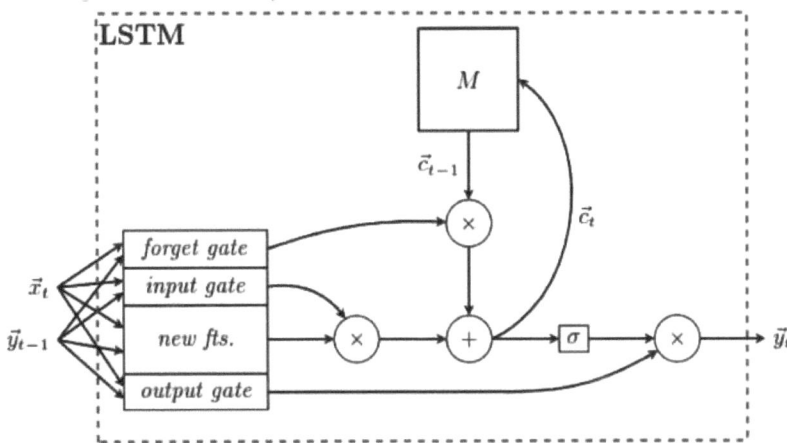

Fig. (12). Long Short Term Memory.

CONCLUSION

In this paper, we gave an overview of the history of neural networks and deep learning models. The basic models of artificial neural networks like the shallow FNN and deep FNN are discussed. The brief details of neural network models like RNN with Hopfield, Boltzmann machine, and RBM are studied. The architecture of DFNN, with a special example of CNN is discussed. The application of different models like Lenet-5, Alexnet, VGG group, GoogleNet/Inception, ResNet has been discussed. In this study, we gave an overview of deep learning models such as Deep Feedforward Neural Networks, Convolutional Neural Networks,

Deep Belief Networks, Autoencoders, and Long Short-Term Memory Networks in this study. These models could be the main architecture of deep learning today. As a result, a fundamental understanding of these concepts is essential for being prepared for future AI breakthroughs.

CONSENT FOR PUBLICATION

Not applicable.

CONFLICT OF INTEREST

The authors declare no conflict of interest, financial or otherwise.

ACKNOWLEDGEMENT

Declared none.

REFERENCES

[1]   Q. Zhang, L.T. Yang, Z. Chen, and P. Li, "A survey on deep learning for big data", In: *Inf. Fusion*. vol. 42, no. October 2017, pp. 146–157, 2018.
[http://dx.doi.org/10.1016/j.inffus.2017.10.006]

[2]   M. Shyu, S. Chen, and S.S. Iyengar, "A survey on deep learning techniques", *Strad Res.,* vol. 7, no. 8, 2020.
[http://dx.doi.org/10.37896/sr7.8/037]

[3]   S. Dargan, M. Kumar, M.R. Ayyagari, and G. Kumar, "A survey of deep learning and its applications: A new paradigm to machine learning", *Arch. Comput. Methods Eng.,* vol. 27, no. 4, pp. 1071-1092, 2020.
[http://dx.doi.org/10.1007/s11831-019-09344-w]

[4]   F. Emmert-Streib, Z. Yang, H. Feng, S. Tripathi, and M. Dehmer, "An introductory review of deep learning for prediction models with big data", *Front. Artif. Intell.,* vol. 3, no. February, p. 4, 2020.
[http://dx.doi.org/10.3389/frai.2020.00004] [PMID: 33733124]

[5]   J. Schmidhuber, "Deep learning in neural networks: An overview", *Neural Networks,* vol. 61, pp. 85-117, 2015.
[http://dx.doi.org/10.1016/j.neunet.2014.09.003] [PMID: 25462637]

[6]   F. Emmert-Streib, "A heterosynaptic learning rule for neural networks", *Int. J. Mod. Phys. C,* vol. 17, no. 10, pp. 1501-1520, 2006.
[http://dx.doi.org/10.1142/S0129183106009916]

[7]   Y. Bengio, P. Lamblin, D. Popovici, and H. Larochelle, "Greedy layer-wise training of deep networks", *Adv. Neural Inf. Process. Syst.,* no. 1, pp. 153-160, 2007.
[http://dx.doi.org/10.7551/mitpress/7503.003.0024]

[8]   Y. Ming, "Understanding hidden memories of recurrent neural networks", *2017 IEEE Conf. Vis. Anal. Sci. Technol. VAST 2017 - Proc.,* 2018pp. 13-24

[9]   G. E. Hinton and R. R. Salakhutdinov, "Reducing the dimensionality of data with neural networks," Science (80-.)., vol. 313, no. 5786, pp. 504–507, 2006.
[http://dx.doi.org/10.1126/science.1127647]

[10]   A. Mayr, G. Klambauer, T. Unterthiner, M. Steijaert, J.K. Wegner, H. Ceulemans, D.A. Clevert, and S. Hochreiter, "Large-scale comparison of machine learning methods for drug target prediction on

ChEMBL", *Chem. Sci. (Camb.),* vol. 9, no. 24, pp. 5441-5451, 2018.
[http://dx.doi.org/10.1039/c8sc00148k] [PMID: 30155234]

[11]   L. Alzubaidi, "Review of deep learning: Concepts", In: *CNN architectures, challenges, applications, future directions* vol. 8. Springer International Publishing, 2021no. 1, .

[12]   M. Kwabena Patrick, A. Felix Adekoya, A. Abra Mighty, and B.Y. Edward, "Capsule networks – a survey, J. King Saud Univ. -", *Comput. Inf. Sci.,* vol. 34, no. 1, pp. 1295-1310, 2019.
[http://dx.doi.org/10.1016/j.jksuci.2019.09.014]

[13]   M.Z. Alom, "A state-of-the-art survey on deep learning theory and architectures", *Electron.,* vol. 8, no. 3, 2019.
[http://dx.doi.org/10.3390/electronics8030292]

[14]   G. Litjens, "A survey on deep learning in medical image analysis", In: *Med. Image Anal..* vol. 42, no. December 2012, pp. 60–88 2017.
[http://dx.doi.org/10.1016/j.media.2017.07.005]

[15]   L. Deng, "A tutorial survey of architectures, algorithms, and applications for deep learning", *APSIPA Trans. Signal. Inf. Process.,* vol. 3, pp. 1-29, 2014.
[http://dx.doi.org/10.1017/ATSIP.2013.99]

[16]   M. Alfarhood, and J. Cheng, "Deep learning-based recommender systems", *Adv. Intell. Syst. Comput.,* vol. 1232, no. 1, pp. 1-23, 2021.
[http://dx.doi.org/10.1007/978-981-15-6759-9_1]

## CHAPTER 2

Application of Artificial Intelligence in Medical Imaging

Sampurna Panda[1], Rakesh Kumar Dhaka[1] and Babita Panda[2,*]

[1] *ITM University, Gwalior, India*

[2] *School of Electrical Engineering, KIIT University, Bhubaneswar, India*

Abstract: The emergence of the Internet of Things (IoT) and Artificial Intelligence (AI) applications in many industries is due to recent developments in technology and connectivity. This paper outlines various industry initiatives in healthcare that utilize machine learning techniques. To meet this rising demand, considerable investment is required to develop new medical imaging algorithms, such as those that can be used to diagnose disease diagnostic systems errors, which can yield ambiguous medical treatments. Early disease in imaging is usually predicted by machine learning and deep learning algorithms. Imaging tools use machine learning and deep learning techniques to analyze early disease. Medical imaging is on the cutting edge of deep learning techniques, specifically the application of convolution neural networks. The supervised or unsupervised algorithms are applied to a dataset containing specific instances, and then the predictions are displayed. Machines and deep learning approaches are excellent for data classification and automated decision-making.

Keywords: Artificial Intelligence, Deep Learning, Internet of Things (IoT), Machine Learning, Neural Network.

INTRODUCTION

The computer system's machine learning algorithm is essential to improve its ability to make accurate predictions and make decisions. The area of study that teaches computers how to study without requiring them to be explicitly programmed is known as machine learning [1]. Deep learning is a group of machine learning, which enables systems to gain an understanding of the world in terms of a pinpoint of ideas [2]. The growing performance of neural networks propelled the growth of deep learning in computer vision.

---

* **Corresponding author Babita Panda:** School of Electrical Engineering, KIIT University, Bhubaneswar, India; E-mail: pandababita18@gmail.com

Gyanendra Verma & Rajesh Doriya (Eds.)

MACHINE-LEARNING

Machine learning describes methods that enable computers to learn on their own and solve problems. A mathematical model should be trained so that it can be fed with useful input data and then produce valuable results. Fig. (**1**) shows the Pictorial visualization of Machine Learning.

Fig. (1). Pictorial visualization of Machine Learning.

Machine learning models are provided with training data and optimized to yield accurate predictions. To put it simply, the models are developed with the goal of delivering predictions for new data with an unseen level of certainty. To estimate the generalization ability of a model, you use a separate dataset called the validation set and apply the model's predictions to that dataset as a form of feedback for tuning the model. The model is evaluated using test data against which it has been trained and fine-tuned to see how it will perform with unseen data. It is possible to roughly categorize machine learning methods according to how the models' input data is utilized during training. An agent is a built-in reinforcement learning through trial and error, while one is optimizing a particular objective function. The computer is assigned the task of learning on its own without guidance.

Fig. (**2**) shows the relationship between artificial intelligence (AI), Machine learning (ML), Artificial Neural Network(ANN), and Convolutional Neural Network(CNN). In a nutshell, grouping is the quintessential use case. Most of the today's machine learning is working with real-time algorithms, such as supervised learning. Here, a set of already labeled or annotated images is given to the computer. Then, it is challenged to assign correct labels to new, previously unseen datasets that are constructed according to the learned rules. This consists of a collection of input-output examples.

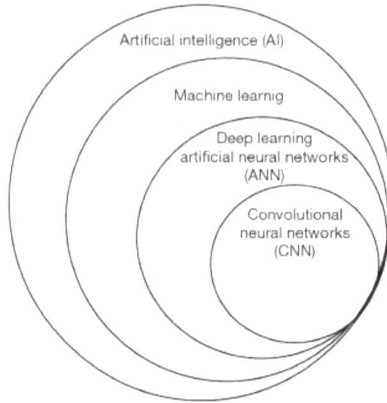

Fig. (2). Relation of AI with ML, ANN, CNN.

There are various machine learning techniques. Fig. (**3**) shows the different types of machine learning techniques available. In this section, different machine learning techniques are described, each with its process, advantages, and disadvantages.

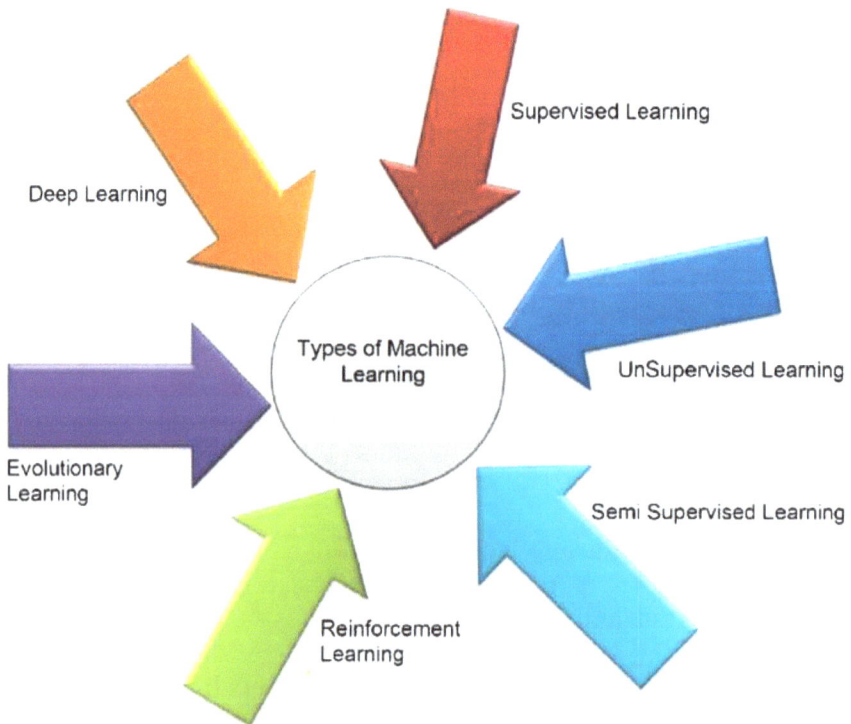

Fig. (3). Different types of machine learning techniques.

Supervised Learning

In case of supervised learning, the model is trained to perform certain data processing task. The labels such as "classify" are applied to the images after performing the Image annotation which estimates the amount of malignancy based on the severity of skin lesions [3]. When applied to machine learning, this describes a scenario in which a predicted output variable (y) is computed based on a vector of input variables (x). By postulating that the input and output conform to a functional relationship, called the predictive model, in Fig. (1), it is assumed that the algorithm succeeds. Supervised learning, where the predictive model is discovered by training on data with examples where both x and y are known, is known as discovery learning. I is composed of n variables (called features), so x Rn For simplicity, we are only concerned with the case of scalar outputs. Fig. (4) shows the basics of supervised machine learning, where the output is expressed as a function of the input.

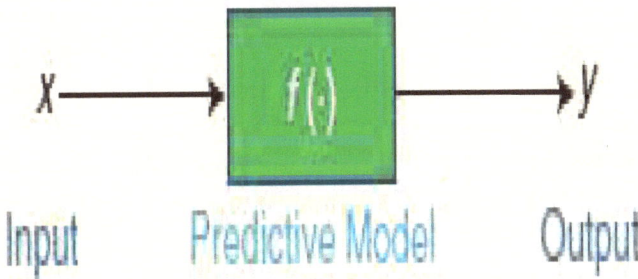

Fig. (4). Supervised machine learning output is a function of input.

Unsupervised Learning

Decisions will be made autonomously without requiring data to be processed. There are no labels that can be used for predictions made on the system. Feature learning enables us to obtain the hidden pattern using unsupervised learning. Unsupervised learning techniques are used to divide the input space into clusters. There is no way to identify these clusters earlier. Group formation is predicated on similarity. Fig. (5) shows the basics of unsupervised machine learning, where the output is expressed as a function of the input.

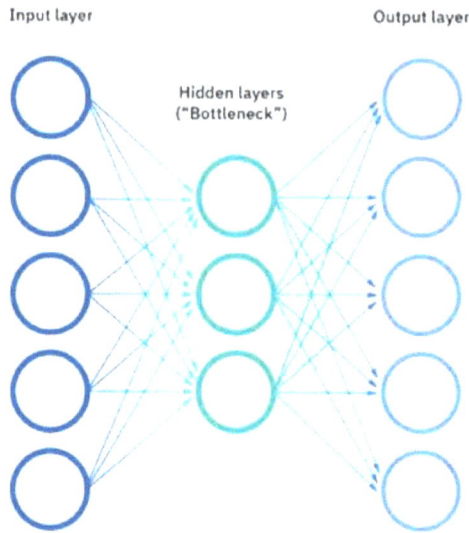

Fig. (5). Unsupervised machine learning output is a function of input.

Semi-supervised Learning

Semi-supervised learning supposes that the training data is incomplete. This type of training is typically utilized with appropriately trained data that aims to improve performance where a number of missing results are present. For training commitment, this type of algorithm is employed on unmarked data. The semi-supervised learning algorithm is trained on both labeled and unlabelled data.

Active Learning

Training tags only appear a limited number of times in Active learning. It is utilized to help add tags to aid in the attainment of objectives. Example: For example, a budget functions in an organization.

Reinforcement Learning

Reinforcement learning is applicable to real-world tasks that need guidance to successfully complete the goal, like driving a vehicle or playing a video game.

Evolutionary Learning

Biological research uses biospheres as learning tools for identifying and forecasting the lifespan of biological organisms, as well as projecting the chances of having offspring. Using the knowledge of fitness, we can use this model to guess how to adjust the result.

Introduction to Deep Learning

Deep learning is a branch of machine learning concerned with the construction of neural networks as deep as those found in the human brain that is inspired by biological neural networks.

Neural networks are the most popular machine learning method in this phase, where they are used for learning and prediction. A group of diverse algorithms is employed. The aim of these is to create a general system capable of dealing with various kinds of problems and giving predictions. This graph features numerous processing layers stacked on top of one another, comprising various linear and nonlinear conversions.

When it comes to developing AI, deep learning should be the primary focus. The artificial neural network built by a deep learning algorithm is composed of multiple layers. Input, hidden layers, and an output layer make up an artificial neural network (ANN). When a signal is sent across a network, and a choice is made on what to do with it, the input layer, which receives the signal, and the output layer, which makes the decision, are shown in the picture below in Fig. (**6**). The input and output layers of a deep neural network are separated by several hidden layers.

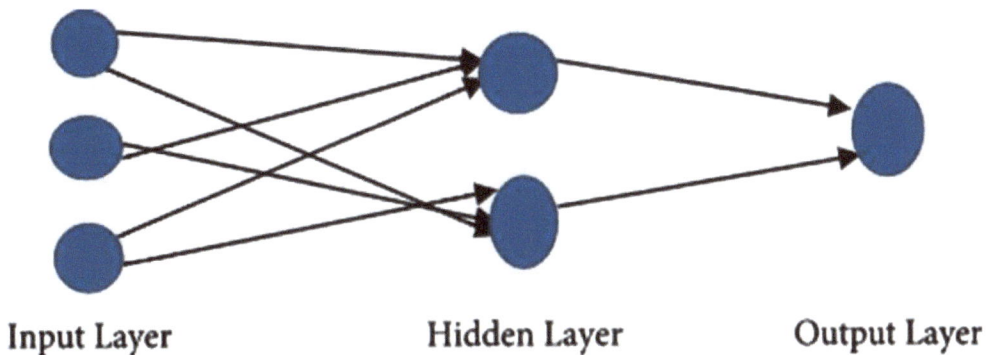

Input Layer   **Hidden Layer**   **Output Layer**

Fig. (6). Artificial neural network (ANN) model.

The difference between deep learning and machine learning is shown in Figs. (7, 8 and 9). The classic machine learning technique consists of 4 stages, while the deep learning technique has three stages.

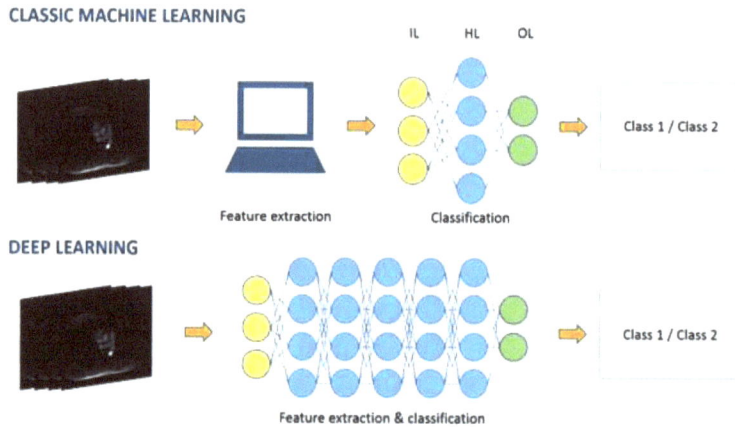

Fig. (7). Traditional Machine Learning vs. Deep Learning.

Though they delivered on their promises, ML architecture increases the chance of failure in training dataset convergence and overfitting. They are also time-consuming and require larger datasets for training.

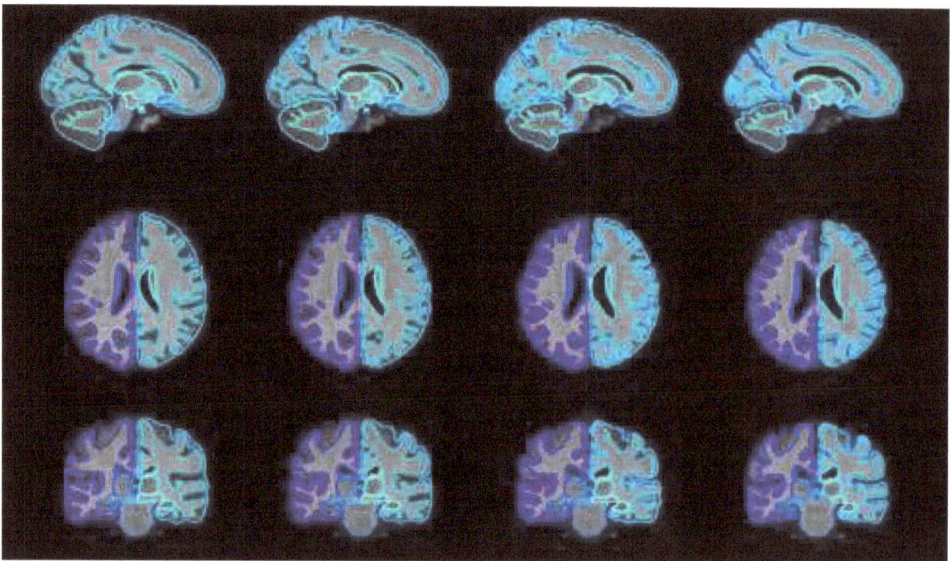

Fig. (8). Traditional Machine Learning vs. Deep Learning.

Today, illness diagnosis can be an extremely challenging mission in medical disciplines. Medical inspection and evaluation are important tasks to comprehend the accurate diagnosis of patients. A large amount of data concerning medical evaluation, a statement about the patient, treatment, supplements and prescriptions, appear from the healthcare sector. The main problem is that the reports appear to have a symbiotic relationship caused by management errors in data management [4, 5].

APPLICATION OF ML IN MEDICAL IMAGING

Medical imaging is highly effective in using machine learning algorithms to study specific diseases. Non-mathematical solutions are incapable of accurately representing certain entities in medical image processing, such as lesions and organs. The pixel-based investigation was used to search for diseases in medical images. The usage of pixel analysis in machine learning in medical imaging is another instance of machine learning-based feature extraction. It may be more effective to use an interactive method rather than a simple feature-based classifier for a particular issue [6]. It's difficult to probe the properties of the image because of its low contrast. Pixel-based machine learning does not require feature calculation and segmentation [7]. Pixel analysis is used to enhance the targeted low-contrast medical images. Histogram equalization is the most efficient technique for contrast improvement (HE), which is intended to modify histogram-based contrast enhancement techniques using homomorphic image filtering (MHFIL).

Histogram modification is used in the first phase to improve the global contrast. Homomorphic filtering in the second phase is additionally used for image sharpening. This experiment investigates ten chest X-ray images that have certain low contrast. Using a minimum values approach across all ten images yields the MH-FIL. Radiologists bear the main responsibility for medical image clarification, with image analysis and quality assignments having equal importance. CAD has been developed for several years using computer-aided design.

Today's machine learning techniques need to focus on constructing and organizing a relationship between unstructured, raw data and stories. By having such a large amount of data, the implementation of machine learning techniques in healthcare will yield major benefits. Although useful in helping physicians perform close to perfect diagnoses, identifying the best medications for patients, and reducing the number of patients who wind up on expensive medications, currently, machine learning has limited capabilities [8, 9].

DEEP LEARNING IN MEDICAL IMAGING

The goal of this technique is to help computers find features that allow them to identify and characterize data that may apply to a given issue. This concept is fundamental to several machine learning algorithms. Increasingly detailed models are stacked on top of each other, which transmute input images into outputs. Convolutional neural networks are the better model type for image analysis (CNNs). The CNNs utilize a number of filter layers to process the input. The medical field frequently employs deep learning methods to adapt itself with modern architecture by introducing them to various input formats, such as three dimensional data. Previously, the CNNs avoided dealing with the large volume of data because of how big 3D convolutions are, along with the additional constraints that came along with them. Fig. (**10**) shows one example of medical image analysis using deep learning.

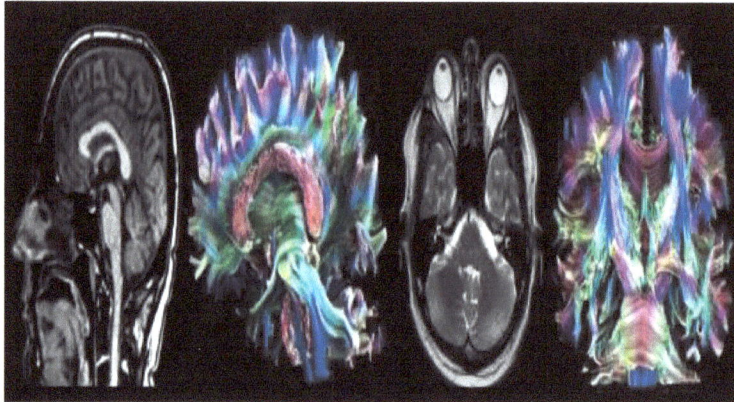

Fig. (9). Traditional Machine Learning vs. Deep Learning.

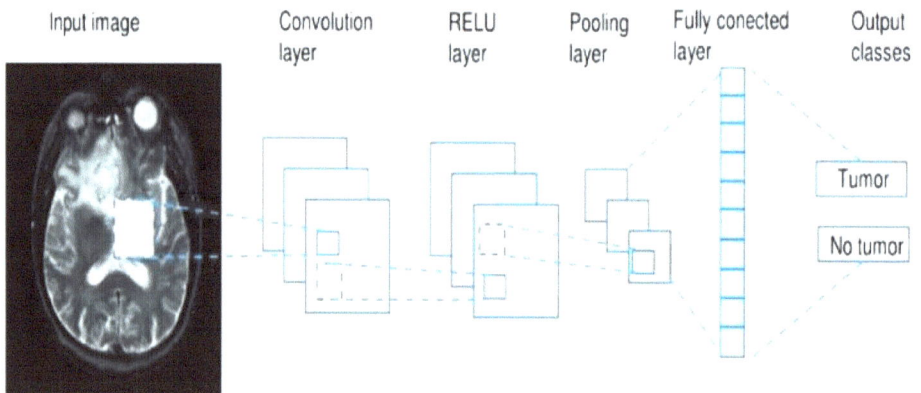

Fig. (10). Use of Deep Learning in medical imaging.

Image Classification

As one of the primary tasks in deep learning, the classification of medical images is focused on exploring clinical-related issues like earlier treatment for the patient. Multi-image input; single diagnostic (disease yes or no). It is common to see that the number of different diagnostic tests used by a medical imaging method or software application is typically minor compared to the number of test models and sample sets utilized in computer vision. As seen in [10], it seems the fine modification, or feature extraction, did better, achieving 57.6% accuracy in evaluating knee osteoarthritis compared to 53.4%. It seems that CNN feature extraction for cytopathology classification, as done by CNN feature extraction for cytology classification, yields accuracy levels between 69.1 percent and 70.5 percent [11].

Object Classification

The object classification is placed on small, focused sections of the medical image; for those patients with a greater level of interest, Projection into two or more classes is possible with these chunks. In order to obtain more accurate results, local facts, as well as global information, are critical. The results in three CNNs methods of deep learning can be used to correct an image with respect to objects of differing sizes. After applying these three methods, the final image features matrix can be calculated.

Organ or Region Detection

After classification, the next phase is object detection and localization. Segmentation is a critical step where we can focus on only the important objects and discard the irrelevant ones. As a way to challenge this issue, we have employed deep learning algorithms in order to perform 3D data parsing. In addition to this, the author used three separate 2D and 3D MRI image chunks in the image. Its purpose is to locate the various regions related to various diseases and focus on a specific one, such as the heart, the aortic arch, and the descending aorta [12, 13].

Data Mining

In the segmentation process, organs and substructures are extracted from medical images. It is utilized for quantitative assessments of the patient's clinical characteristics, for example, an examination of the heart or brain. Also, it is used in computer-aided design (CAD) for various functions. It is by recognizing the details that make up the subject of interest that one becomes able to define a digital picture. This is the combination of upsampling and downsampling architecture, where each layer up samples and downsamples a given data set. By incorporating the connection points of convolution and de-convolution samples of layers, it connected those two processes together [14 - 17].

The Sign-up Process

In the registration, multiple sets of data are used to calculate a new coordinate. Providing comparison or integration of data from multiple viewpoints, times, depths, sensors, *etc.,* is an important part of medical imaging [18 - 20].

Other Imaging Applications

(a) Image from an X-ray machine:

Chest X-rays are commonly utilized in the diagnosis of heart and lung illnesses, including tuberculosis, atelectasis, consolidation, pleural effusion, pneumothorax, and hypercardia. For mass screening, X-ray images are easily available, inexpensive, and dose-effective compared to other imaging modalities.

(b) Computerized tomography (CT):

CT creates cross-sectional images of the body using computers and rotary X-ray equipment. Soft tissues, blood arteries, and bones are all visible on CT scans. In addition to its ability to detect tiny lesions, CT is able to provide a more comprehensive evaluation. Nodules in the lungs can be detected using computed tomography (CT) scans. Lung cancer can be diagnosed at an early stage if malignant pulmonary nodules are found.

(c) Mammograph (MG):

In the world's female cancer population, breast cancer is the leading cause of mortality. MG is the most often used method for detecting breast cancer in its earliest stages. Breast illness identification is made easier by using low-dose x-ray imaging techniques like MG. Breast cancer detection by mammography screening is difficult due to the small size of lesions in the actual breast picture. The identification, segmentation, and classification of breast lesions from MG necessitate three phases.

(d) Histopathology:

Pathologists use a microscope to discover diseases like kidney cancer, lung cancer, breast cancer, and so on by looking at human tissue *via* a sliding glass Staining is a technique in histopathology that is employed to highlight and visualize a particular region of tissue. Staining with Hematoxylin and Eosin (H&E) produces dark purple nuclei and pink structures. Different diseases and cancer grading have relied heavily on H&E staining during the previous century. Digital pathology imaging is a relatively new imaging technology to emerge in the medical imaging market. Nucleus detection, classification, cell segmentation, and tissue segmentation are some of the tasks that may be performed using deep learning in the interpretation of histopathology pictures.

(e) Other images:

Procedures such as endoscopy allow for a detailed study of interior tissues and organs by inserting an endoscope (a solid tube) straight into the body. A wide range of internal organs can be studied *via* endoscopy, including the digestive system, respiratory system, urinary system, and female reproductive system. A nuclear imaging technology, Positron Emission Tomography (PET) makes use of the injection of certain radioactive tracers to reveal molecular-level activity in tissues.

CONCLUSION

Machine learning capabilities have been cultivated over the last few years. In current practice, machine learning methods are robust to real-world applications, and the structures clearly enhance this advantage. Previously, this pertains to the preparation of medical imaging, and in the future, it will make a significant advancement at a swift pace. Machines that use machine learning can have important inferences for medication administration. The patients will benefit from this research. It is a huge part of the machine learning solution as the machines are used to their fullest potential. The deep learning algorithm used in medical image analysis aids in classifying, categorizing, and enumerating disease patterns. It also opens the door to exploring the boundary of analytical goals, which then helps to generate prediction models for treatment. Scientists in the imaging field are weighing these issues to grant the use of deep learning in the healthcare sector. As deep learning is rapidly improving, it is increasingly being used in numerous other fields along with the healthcare sector.

CONSENT FOR PUBLICATION

Not applicable.

CONFLICT OF INTEREST

The authors declare no conflict of interest, financial or otherwise.

ACKNOWLEDGEMENT

This research received no specific grant from any funding.

REFERENCES

[1] L.G. Valiant, "A theory of the learnable", *Commun. ACM,* vol. 27, no. 11, pp. 1134-1142, 1984.
[http://dx.doi.org/10.1145/1968.1972]

[2] Andre Esteva, Brett Kuprel, Roberto A. Novoa, Justin Ko, Susan M. Swetter, and Helen M. Blau, "Dermatologist-level classification of skin cancer with deep neural networks." *nature* 542.7639 (2017): 115-118.

[3] Andre Esteva, Brett Kuprel, Roberto A. Novoa, Justin Ko, Susan M. Swetter, and Helen M. Blau, "Dermatologist-level classification of skin cancer with deep neural networks", *nature,* vol. 542, no. 7639, pp. 115-118, 2017.

[4] J. Schmidhuber, "Deep learning in neural networks: An overview", *Neural Netw.,* vol. 61, pp. 85-117, 2015.
[http://dx.doi.org/10.1016/j.neunet.2014.09.003] [PMID: 25462637]

[5] William Warwick, Sophie Johnson, Judith Bond, and Geraldine Fletcher, "A framework to assess healthcare data quality." *The European Journal of Social & Behavioural Sciences* (2015).

[6] K. Suzuki, "Pixel-based machine learning in medical imaging", *Int. J. Biomed. Imaging,* vol. 2012, p. 792079, 2012.
[PMID: 22481907]

[7] T.K. Agarwal, T. Mayank, and S. L. Subir, "Modified histogram based contrast enhancement using homomorphic filtering for medical images", *2014 IEEE International Advance Computing Conference (IACC),* 2014pp. 964-968
[http://dx.doi.org/10.1109/IAdCC.2014.6779453]

[8] D. Maddux, *The Human Condition in Structured and Unstructured Data.* Acumen Physician Solutions (2014).

[9] D. Page, *Challenges in Machine Learning from Electronic Health Records.* MLHC, 2015.

[10] J. Antony, "Quantifying radiographic knee osteoarthritis severity using deep convolutional neural networks", *Pattern Recognition (ICPR),* 2016
[http://dx.doi.org/10.1109/ICPR.2016.7899799]

[11] E. Kim, M. Corte-Real, and Z. Baloch, A deep semantic mobile application for thyroid cytopathology. *Medical Imaging 2016: PACS and Imaging Informatics: Next Generation and Innovations.* Vol. 9789. SPIE, 2016.

[12] C.W. Wang, C.T. Huang, and M.C. Hsieh, "Evaluation and comparison of anatomical landmark detection methods for cephalometricx-ray images: a grand challenge", *IEEE Trans. Med. Imaging,* vol. 34, no. 9, pp. 1890-1900, 2015.
[http://dx.doi.org/10.1109/TMI.2015.2412951] [PMID: 25794388]

[13]   B.D. De Vos, "2D image classification for 3D anatomy localization: employing deep convolutional neural networks", In: *Medical Imaging 2016: Image Processing*. vol. 9784, pp. 517-523. SPIE, 2016.

[14]   Ö. Çiçek, "3D U-Net: learning dense volumetric segmentation from sparse annotation", In: *International Conference on Medical Image Computing and Computer-Assisted Intervention* Springer., 2016.

[15]   X. Luo, D. Zhang, and X. Zhu, "Deep learning based forecasting of photovoltaic power generation by incorporating domain knowledge", *Energy,* vol. 225, p. 120240, 2021.
        [http://dx.doi.org/10.1016/j.energy.2021.120240]

[16]   M.I. Jordan, and T.M. Mitchell, "Machine learning: Trends, perspectives, and prospects", *Science,* vol. 349, no. 6245, pp. 255-260, 2015.
        [http://dx.doi.org/10.1126/science.aaa8415] [PMID: 26185243]

[17]   R. Kabilan, V. Chandran, and J. Yogapriya, "AlagarKarthick, Priyesh P. Gandhi, V. Mohanavel, Robbi Rahim, and S. Manoharan. Short-term power prediction of building integrated photovoltaic (bipv) system based on machine learning algorithms", *International Journal of Photoenergy*, p. (2021), 2021.

[18]   J-P. Lai, Y-M. Chang, C-H. Chen, and P-F. Pai, Lai, Jung-Pin, Yu-Ming Chang, Chieh-Huang Chen, and Ping-FengPai, "A survey of machine learning models in renewable energy predictions", *Appl. Sci. (Basel),* vol. 10, no. 17, p. 5975, 2020.
        [http://dx.doi.org/10.3390/app10175975]

[19]   N. Charles, M. Kabalan, and P. Singh, "Open source photovoltaic system performance modeling with python", In: *2015 IEEE Canada International Humanitarian Technology Conference (IHTC2015)* IEEE. pp. 1-4, 2015.
        [http://dx.doi.org/10.1109/IHTC.2015.7238046]

[20]   S. Salcedo-Sanz, L. Cornejo-Bueno, L. Prieto, D. Paredes, and R. García-Herrera, "Feature selection in machine learning prediction systems for renewable energy applications", *Renew. Sustain. Energy Rev.,* vol. 90, pp. 728-741, 2018.
        [http://dx.doi.org/10.1016/j.rser.2018.04.008]

## CHAPTER 3

Classification Tool to Predict the Presence of Colon Cancer Using Histopathology Images

Saleena Thorayanpilackal Sulaiman[1,*], **Muhamed Ilyas Poovankavil**[2] and **Abdul Jabbar Perumbalath**[3]

[1] *Sullamussalam Science College, Areekode, Malappuram, Kerala, India*

[2] *PG and Research Department of Computer Science, Sullamussalam Science College, Areekode, Malappuram Dt, Kerala – India*

[3] *School of Computer Science, Mahathma Gandhi University, Kottayam, Kerala, India*

Abstract: The proposed model compares the efficiency of CNN and ResNet50 in the field of digital pathology images. Deep learning methods are widely used in all fields of disease detection, diagnosis, segmentation, and classification. CNN is the widely used image classification algorithm. But it may show less accuracy in case of complex structures like pathology images. Residual Networks are a good choice for pathology image classification because the morphology of digital pathology images is very difficult to distinguish. Colon cancer is one of the common cancers, and it is one of the fatal diseases. If early-stage detection has been done using biopsy results, it will decrease the mortality rate. ResNet50 is selected among the variants as its computational complexity is moderate and provides high accuracy in classification as compared to others. The accuracy metric used here is the training and validation accuracy and loss. The training and validation accuracy of ResNet50 is 89.1% and 90.62%, respectively, whereas the training loss and validation loss are 26.7% and 24.33%, respectively. At the same time, for CNN, the accuracy is 84.82% and 78.12% and the loss is 36.51% and 47.33% .

Keywords: Colon cancer, CNN, H&E stained histopathology, ResNet50.

INTRODUCTION

There are nineteen different types of cancer that can affect a healthy person [1]. Among them, colon cancer is the third leading cancer in the US. Tumors inside of a patient's body are most commonly detected through medical imaging techniques, such as radiology. Different modalities like X-rays [2], CT scan, PET

---

[*] **Corresponding author Saleena Thorayanpilackal Sulaiman:** Sullamussalam Science College, Areekode, Malappuram, Kerala, India; E-mail: tssaleena@gmail.com

Gyanendra Verma & Rajesh Doriya (Eds.)

scan or MRI, *etc.,* can be used to find the position and rate of progress of cancer and thereby leading to classifying whether it is benign or malignant. But the confirmation can be done only through biopsy. So pathologists play a crucial role in disease diagnosis and treatment plan decision in case of cancer.

The workload of pathologists is very hectic as their number is very low as compared to their work.

Colon cancer originates from the large intestine, where the colon is the end of the digestive tract [3, 4]. The signs and symptoms showing for this cancer are very non-specific. So screening like colonoscopy in people of any age can reduce the mortality rate as this is a preventable and curable disease in the early stage. Pathological tests will be very beneficial in such situations.

Most colon adenocarcinomas are moderately differentiated, but some are poorly differentiated. So the classification may not be correct looking at histopathology images. So now, ancillary studies, or mainly ImmunoHistochemical staining is the prevalent method for the same [5 - 7]. It is a protein-based test that is very costly as compared with histopathology image analysis.

How colon cancer looks like and where it originated are shown in Fig. (**1**).

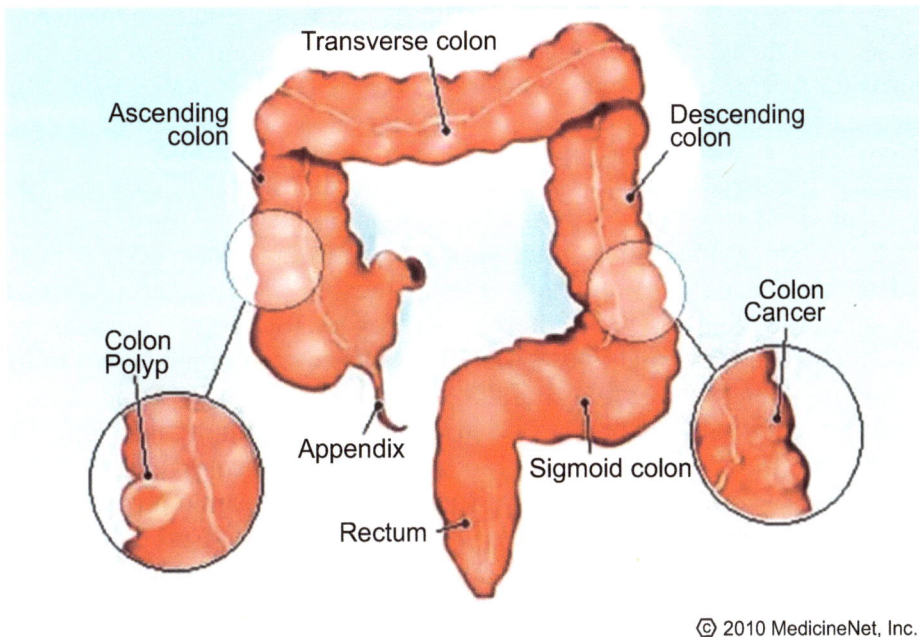

© 2010 MedicineNet, Inc.

Fig. (1). Colon cancer-affected region [1].

Deep learning algorithms are very effective in [8] stain normalization [9], segmentation, classification, grading, staging, prognosis, *etc.,* especially neural networks. Digital pathology can be used as a good sort of alternative to the conventional glass slide-keeping process. It is easy to transport and can store the image without physical damage. Convolutional Neural Network (CNN) is a powerful and accurate alternative to digital image analysis and image classification methods. Computer vision can identify and classify the region of cancer present in the histopathology images which are very difficult using the naked eye. First, we have to train the model with adequate data and the best network should be chosen on a trial-and-error basis. [10] Pacal *et al.* described various CNN algorithms applied in colon cancer for various applications. Recently published 135 papers have been reviewed in that paper. Recently published 135 papers have been reviewed in that paper. Digital images of H&E stained histopathology images are used as input for these algorithms. The size and shape of the nucleus, the shape of colorectal polyps, accumulation of irregular tissues, *etc.,* are some of the features to be considered for the detection and classification of colon cancer.

Even though CNN is a powerful tool in image classification, the classification of pathology images is more difficult due to its morphology. Different powerful pre-trained networks are available for image classification. Such networks are working with the principle of transfer learning, and most of them are trained with ImageNet; and their feature extraction ability and their weights can be applied to our local dataset to create our own models. Only the last dense layer will be changed, and all other layers will be kept untouched.

This paper comprises a comparison of the CNN algorithm with ResNet50 [11] using a dataset of colon cancer obtained from an online repository. ResNet50 is one of the efficient and widely used variants of Residual Networks. It is a pre-trained network that has been trained upon the ImageNet dataset. This study proves that the ResNet50 is more appropriate for such complex image classification. The CNN that is used here has four convolutional layers followed by a pooling layer. A similar kind of CAD has been developed for the classification of breast cancer [12], Gastric and Colonic Epithelial Tumors [13], and ten other kinds of cancers [14, 15]. Nucleus detection models are also developed for several cancers [16, 17]. Noise removal is the major part of the pre-processing technique that can improve the efficiency of the model. As we are using the processed data in this model, no such methods are used here.

As direct data collection is the most tedious and almost hard-to-reach step in AI, especially in the case of medical data, public repositories are a blessing to some extent. Among several repositories, TCGA is one of them. The Cancer Genome

Atlas (TCGA) is a renowned project funded by National Cancer Institute that started in 2005. It acts as a large public public repository for bio-specimen to connect researchers all over the world. They provide thousands of WSIs of biopsy as data of around 33 types of cancers [18]. Even though the WSI is new to the pathology field, they made tremendous changes in the conventional glass slide-keeping methods. It acts as a solution for storage, transportation, and even analysis of pathology data. But as each WSIs have several thousands of dimensions, multiple patches can be created from the same. The pathologists can manually label the image and crop the region of interest in any convenient size. In this work, the dataset has been obtained from the work of Borkowski *et al.* [19], where the dataset has been created by patchification of WSI images obtained from TCGA, which is of high-resolution images, as shown in Fig. (**2**).

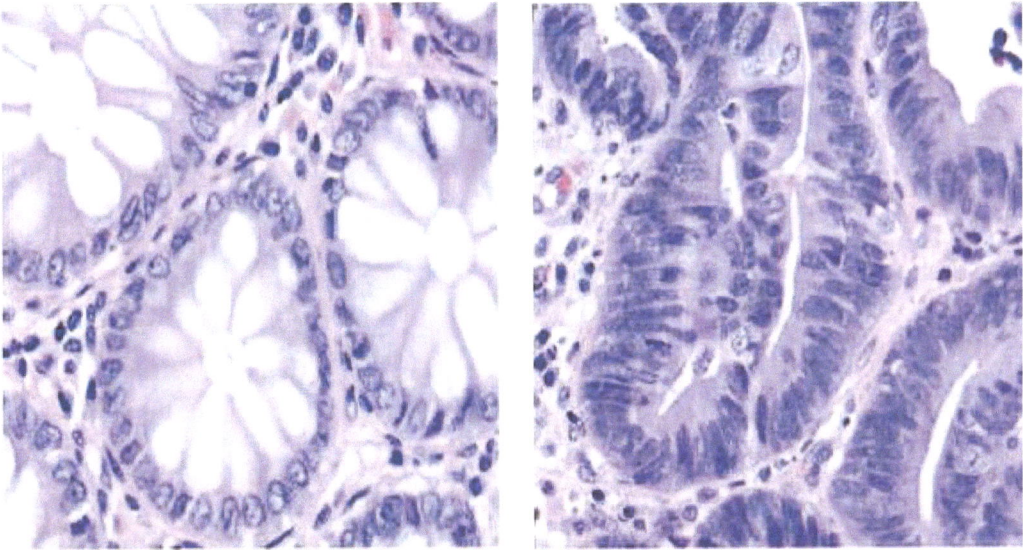

Fig. (2). Cross section of normal colon tissue(left),tissue affected with cancer [19].

METHODS AND PREPARATION

Dataset Preparation

Borkowski *et al.* [19] prepared a new dataset, LC25000, that contains lung and colon carcinoma images. It has five classes, each with 25000 images. These 25000 images are created from 750 lung tissues and 500 colon tissues. The original images of 1024 x 768 pixels were resized to 768 x 768 pixels, and data augmentation was performed using an Augmentor software package. Left/right rotations and vertical/horizontal flips were performed to augment the data.

Related Works

Due to the very high dimensionality nature of WSIs (maybe of 100k to 50k resolutions), it can not be directly fed to the CNN [20]. Also, Le Hou *et al.* have created around 1000 patches per image per scale, each with a size 500X500 and with 20X and 5X magnifications.

A total number of 1634 WSIs from TCGA have been taken for the creation of a dataset that included LUAD, LUSC, and normal tissues [21]. 512x512 non-overlapping patches have been taken from each slide, which ranges from tens to thousands of patches from each slide.

The difficulty in the pathology images to get annotated by pathologists is clearly described by Andrew J. Schaumberg *et al.* [22] in their paper. As a solution, they made use of social media, especially Twitter, to do the same. They managed to develop a dataset of 2,750 images with the help of pathologists from 8 countries, and it included diverse cases of images.

Different types of segmentation methods are thresholding, clustering, edge-based segmentation, region-based segmentation, ANN-based segmentation, and partial differential equation-based segmentation [23].

Francesco Bianconi *et al.* [24] compared how the color pre-processing on H&E stained digital images affects the classification performance. Staining problems, inbuilt noise artifacts from image acquisition tools, tissue preparation variations, *etc.,* will be adversely affecting the clarity of the image.

Meghana Dinesh Kumar *et al.* [25] performed a classification operation on the dataset KIMIA PATH960, which contains 20 different classes. It was a comparison operation using pre-trained networks, local binary patterns (LBP histogram), dictionary approach, or bag of visual words or BoVW. Among these, deep networks and LBP histogram requires extensive training, and the obtained accuracy was 94.72% and 90.62%, respectively. The third method, BoVW, performed better with an accuracy of 96.50%. AlexNet and VGG16 were used as pre-trained networks, and they might have performed well if the dataset had more samples in each class (here, 48 samples only). The leave-one-out method was used for cross-validation purposes except for the BoVWapproach.

AbtinRiasatian *et al.* [26] took thumbnails of 244 WSIs from TCGA and made the masks of these images and published them as publically available. As the WSI's maybe 50,000 X 50,000 or larger, they used thumbnails of them which are of 1X magnification. A segmentation approach has been experimented with using [27]U-Net and various backbone networks MobileNet, VGG16, Efficient Net-B3,

ResNet50, ResNext101, and DenseNet121. Among these, EfficientNet-B3 and MobileNet secured almost 99% sensitivity and specificity. The results were compared with different hand-crafted algorithms such as Improved FESI [20], TissueLoc [21], Histomics-TK, and Otsu binarization which is nearly 80% of sensitivity. Five-fold cross-validation, Jaccard index, and Dice coefficient were the other performance metrics used.

Two publically available ML platforms, cloud-based "Google Auto ML" and computer-based "Apple Create ML," have been discussed by Andrew *et al.* [28]. Both are classification models that distinguish colon and lung carcinomas. The presence or absence of the KRAS gene can predict whether the cancerous tissues respond to specific chemotherapy agents, which is now found with the help of complex molecular testing. Apple Create ML is specifically for Mac OS systems, and Google Auto ML is charging some amount for using their cloud.

A pre-trained network has been developed by Atsushi Teramoto *et al.* [29] for the classification of cytological images of NSCLC into 3 subtypes, Adeno, Squamous, and Small Cell, with 3 convolution layers, 3 pooling layers, and 2 fully connected layers. This was a novel method of NSCLC classification using cytology images. The feature map created in each layer was 256X256X32, 128X128X32, and 64X64X32, respectively, and 3-fold cross-validation was used for performance evaluation. The accuracy rate was adeno - 89.0%, squamous - 60.0%, and small cell - 70.3%.

Since the cancer subtypes are distinguished based on cellular-level morphological factors, the patch-level classifier will perform better than the image-level classifier [30]. But the complication that comes with classification is that the normal downsampling process may cause losing several pieces of information from the image, and also the ground truth labels of individual patches are unknown, as only the image-level ground truth label is given. So a novel Expectation-Maximization (EM) based method has been introduced by Le Hou *et al.* in which discriminative patches will be automatically located. The network was trained using the CAFFE toolbox on a single NVidia Tesla K40GPU.

A survey has been done by Deng *et al.* [31] on different deep learning techniques applied to histopathology images for classification, semantic/instance segmentation, stain normalization, *etc.* The convolution layer extracts the feature maps, whereas the pooling layer reduces the feature dimension, and the activation function handles the non-linearity of data. Stain normalization, getting information about the morphological structures, and grading/prognosis are the important steps discussed here. Several supervised [32], unsupervised [33], structure-preserving [34], and GAN [35] algorithms have been discussed related to stain separation and color normalization. The pathologists are identifying and classifying the tumors based on the spatial distribution and morphological features of cells and nuclei. The role of semantic segmentation and instance segmentation comes here. As manual segmentation is laborious and time-consuming, the deep network can contribute much towards this.

METHODOLOGY

Deep neural networks are a good option for image classification. Pathology image classification is still in its infant stage because of the complex structure of images. So transfer learning techniques will be the better choice in such a situation. Residual Networks, VGG16, Inceptionv3, EfficientNet, MobileNet, *etc.*, are some of the examples for them. In our work, we have used ResNet50 for the classification of colon cancer.

Convolutional Neural Network (CNN)

CNN has been the major algorithm used for image classification for the past decades. The architecture of CNN can be explained as follows [36]. Convolution layers along with the pooling layer and activation function, so the feature extraction job is in the finest model. the finest model. The number of layers that should be selected for building the model will purely depend upon the data. The 8 classification will be done at the final layer, which is called the fully connected layer or dense layer. As this is a binary classification model, it will have 2 outputs [37]. Fig. (**3**) explains the architecture of CNN.

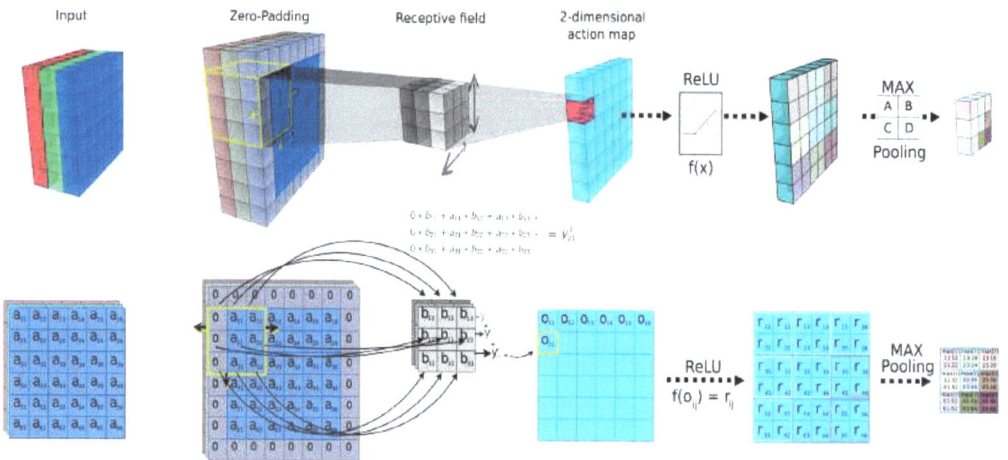

Fig. (3). Architecture of CNN [37].

The CNN model that is used here has four convolutional layers followed by a pooling layer. By mathematically speaking, convolution is a process that can be applied to two functions *f* and *g* and the result will be *(f*g)* and defines how much the shape of one has been affected by the other [38]or it is the integral of the product of the two functions after one is reversed and shifted. The integral is evaluated for all values of shift, producing the convolution function. Here the two functions are known as the image image matrix and filter matrix. The filter used here is a 3x3 matrix.

$$(f * g)(t) := \int_{-\infty}^{\infty} f(\tau)g(t - \tau)\, d\tau. \qquad (1)$$

Where *t* represents the amount of shift.

Pooling methods are used to reduce the dimensions of the feature map. Max-pooling is used here for this model. As the name suggests, this method selects the maximum element region of the feature map covered by the filter. The Max pooling method is depicted in Fig. (**4**).

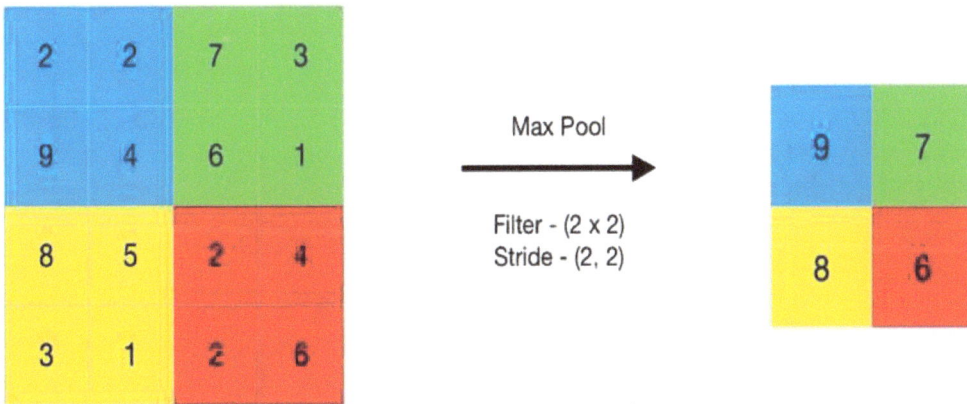

Fig. (4). Max pooling method [39].

In the second, third, and forth layer, *dropout* is used so that overfitting can be avoided. In this model, we have used 25% dropout that will randomly select and remove the neurons that may be useless towards the feature extraction. After four layers, a flattened layer and 2 dense layers were added. For all the layers except the output layer, the activation function used is *'relu'*. In the output layer, as this is a binary classification *'sigmoid'* is used.

ResNet50

Residual learning framework [40] as shown in Fig. (**5**) contributes to the deeper neural networks present now. Even though it is a more complex network, it is so easy to optimize. It got the 1st place on the ILSVRC 2015 classification task. It had 152 layers and ResNet-50 is one of the smallest versions of that. Residual Networks contain variants of networks like ResNet-18, ResNet-34, ResNet-50, ResNet-101, ResNet-110, ResNet-152, ResNet-164, ResNet-1202, *etc.* [41 - 43]. Skip connection or Identity Short Connection is the special feature in ResNet in which skipping of one or more layers occurs. The mathematical notation for this peculiarity is shown below,

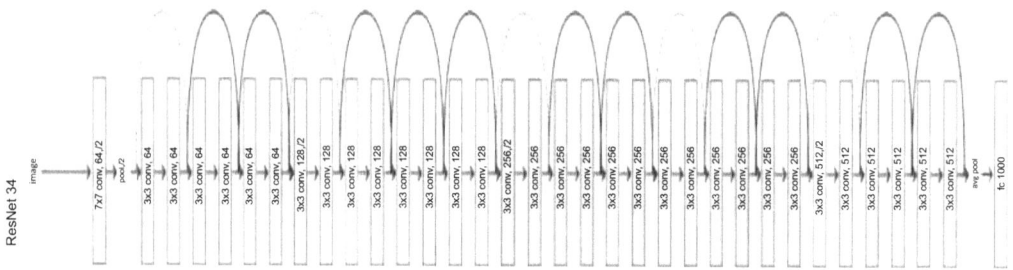

Fig. (5). Architecture of ResNet34 [44].

$$y = \mathcal{F}(x, \{W_i\}) + W_s x. \tag{2}$$

The layering structure of the same Residual Network is clearly defined. The same blocks are stacked one after the other to form a network. The name of the networks indicates the number of blocks present in Fig. (**6**).

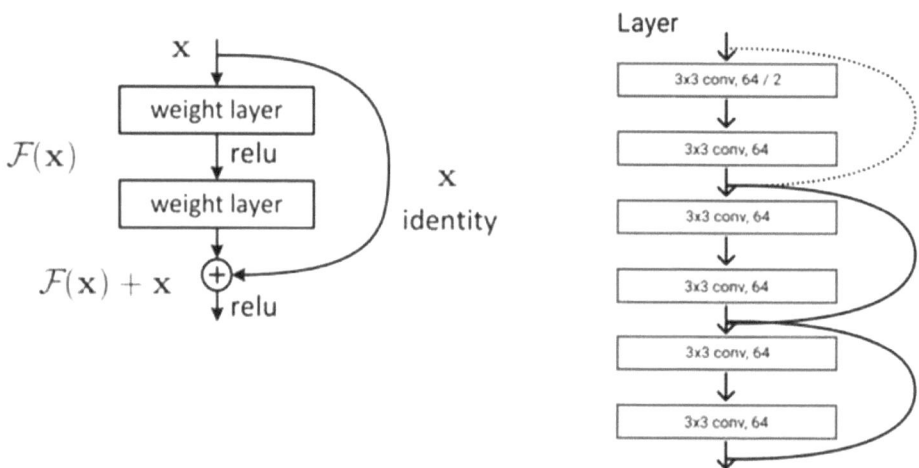

Fig. (6). A residual block(left) [42], Layer formation in ResNet [44].

TensorflowKeras has been used for the implementation. All the layers except the output layer freezed so that the training of those layers should not be taken place again. As the model is already trained on ImageNet [44], the weights of the model can be imported to our newly created model. Only a single flatten layer with an output layer is added here. As there are two classes(normal and cancerous), there exist two outputs so here binary classification is performed . The model has compiled with 'Adam' optimizer, binary cross-entropy, and a learning rate of 0.0001. The number of trainable parameters here is 200, 706 whereas in VGG16, there are only 50,178 parameters, which will be too less in number in normal CNN algorithms.

ResNet is a CNN architecture itself that overcame the 'vanishing gradient' problem, which makes the network deeper than CNN.

RESULTS

This model has used the feature extraction method and weights of the transfer learning method ResNet50. The accuracy metric used here is the training and validation accuracy and loss. The values are given as training and validation

accuracy of ResNet50 is 89.1% and 90.62%, respectively, whereas the training loss and validation loss are 26.7% and 24.33%, respectively. Whereas for CNN, the training and validation accuracy is 84.82% and 78.12%, respectively, whereas the training loss and validation loss are 36.51% and 47.33%, respectively.

CONCLUSION

Classification of pathology images is not as simple as other normal images due to their complex morphology and variety of tissue shapes. So the most powerful deep networks like ResNet have to be used to do this task. We have compared the efficiency of CNN and ResNet50 on the same dataset that we have obtained. Among them, ResNet50 shows more accuracy than the other. More accuracy can be obtained using more upper variants of ResNet. The classification itself is not much useful for real-time use. So segmentation tasks also can be applied with the same images with the help of pathologists. Also, different pre-processing methods can be applied to data to improve theresults.

CONSENT FOR PUBLICATION

The author hereby gives consent to the publication of the work. The Author warrants that this work has not been published before in any form, and the is not being concurrently submitted to and is not under consideration by another publisher.

CONFLICT OF INTEREST

The authors declare no conflict of interest, financial or otherwise.

ACKNOWLEDGEMENT

We gratefully acknowledge Andrew A. Borkowski for providing the colon image dataset, LC25000.

REFERENCES

[1]   https://www.medicinenet.com/colon_cancer/article.htm

[2]   S.K Lakshmanaprabu, SachiNandanmohanty, Shankar K, Arunkumar N, Gustavo Ramirez, "Optimal deep learning model for classification of lung cancer on ct images", Future Generation Computer Systems 92 (2019): 374-382.

[3]   R. Labianca, G.D. Beretta, B. Kildani, L. Milesi, F. Merlin, S. Mosconi, M.A. Pessi, T. Prochilo, A. Quadri, G. Gatta, F. de Braud, and J. Wils, "Colon cancer", *Critical Reviews in Oncology/Hematology,* vol. 74, no. 2, pp. 106-133, 2010.
[http://dx.doi.org/10.1016/j.critrevonc.2010.01.010] [PMID: 20138539]

[4]   M. Ahmed, "Colon cancer: A clinician's perspective in 2019", *Gastroenterology Research,* vol. 13, no. 1, pp. 1-10, 2020.
[http://dx.doi.org/10.14740/gr1239] [PMID: 32095167]

[5]   N. Coudray, P. S. Ocampo, T. Sakellaropoulos, N. Narula, M. Snuderl, D. Fenyö, A. L. Moreira, N. Razavian and A. Tsirigos (2018) "Classification and mutation prediction from non–small cell lung cancer histopathology images using deep learning", Nature Medicine vol. 24 1559–1567, October (2018). www.nature.com/naturemedicine

[6]   E. Thunnissen, K. van der Oord, and M. den Bakker, "Prognostic and predictive biomarkers in lung cancer. A review", *Virchows Arch.,* vol. 464, no. 3, pp. 347-358, 2014.
[http://dx.doi.org/10.1007/s00428-014-1535-4] [PMID: 24420742]

[7]   S. Zachara-Szczakowski, T. Verdun, and A. Churg, "Accuracy of classifying poorly differentiated non–small cell lung carcinoma biopsies with commonly used lung carcinoma markers", *Hum. Pathol.,* vol. 46, no. 5, pp. 776-782, 2015.
[http://dx.doi.org/10.1016/j.humpath.2015.02.001] [PMID: 25776027]

[8]   A.M. Khan, N. Rajpoot, D. Treanor, and D. Magee, "A nonlinear mapping approach to stain normalization in digital histopathology images using image-specific color deconvolution", *IEEE Trans. Biomed. Eng.,* vol. 61, no. 6, pp. 1729-1738, 2014.
[http://dx.doi.org/10.1109/TBME.2014.2303294] [PMID: 24845283]

[9]   R.R. Gharieb, G. Gendy, and A. Abdelfattah, "Image segmentation using fuzzy c-means algorithm incorporating weighted local complement membership and local data distances", *2016 World Symposium on Computer Applications & Research (WSCAR),* pp. 6-11, 2016.
[http://dx.doi.org/10.1109/WSCAR.2016.18]

[10]   I. Pacal, D. Karaboga, A. Basturk, B. Akay, and U. Nalbantoglu, "A comprehensive review of deep learning in colon cancer", *Comput. Biol. Med.,* vol. 126, p. 104003, 2020.
[http://dx.doi.org/10.1016/j.compbiomed.2020.104003] [PMID: 32987202]

[11]   D. Sarwinda, R.H. Paradisa, A. Bustamam, and P. Anggia, "Deep Learning in Image Classification using Residual Network (ResNet) Variants for Detection of Colorectal Cancer", *Procedia Comput. Sci.,* vol. 179, pp. 423-431, 2021.
[http://dx.doi.org/10.1016/j.procs.2021.01.025]

[12] V. Ojansivu, N. Linder, E. Rahtu, M. Pietikäinen, M. Lundin, H. Joensuu, and J. Lundin, "Automated classification of breast cancer morphology in histopathological images", *Diagn. Pathol.,* vol. 8, no. S1, p. S29, 2013.
[http://dx.doi.org/10.1186/1746-1596-8-S1-S29]

[13] O. Iizuka, F. Kanavati, K. Kato, M. Rambeau, K. Arihiro, and M. Tsuneki, "Deep Learning Models for Histopathological Classification of Gastric and Colonic Epithelial Tumours", *Sci. Rep.,* vol. 10, no. 1, p. 1504, 2020.
[http://dx.doi.org/10.1038/s41598-020-58467-9] [PMID: 32001752]

[14] L. Hou, R. Gupta, J.S. Van Arnam, Y. Zhang, K. Sivalenka, D. Samaras, T.M. Kurc, and J.H. Saltz, "Dataset of segmented nuclei in hematoxylin and eosin stained histopathology images of ten cancer types", *Sci. Data,* vol. 7, no. 1, p. 185, 2020.
[http://dx.doi.org/10.1038/s41597-020-0528-1] [PMID: 32561748]

[15] J.P. Vink, M.B. Van Leeuwen, C.H.M. Van Deurzen, and G. De Haan, "Efficient nucleus detector in histopathology images", *J. Microsc.,* vol. 249, no. 2, pp. 124-135, 2013.
[http://dx.doi.org/10.1111/jmi.12001] [PMID: 23252774]

[16] Macenko, Marc, Marc Niethammer, James S. Marron, David Borland, John T. Woosley, Xiaojun Guan, Charles Schmitt, and Nancy E. Thomas. "A method for normalizing histology slides for quantitative analysis." In 2009 IEEE international symposium on biomedical imaging: from nano to macro, pp. 1107-1110. IEEE, 2009.

[17] S.H.A. Kharofa, "Remove Noise from Medical Images", International Journal of Enhanced Research in Science, Technology & Engineering, ISSN: 2319-7463, Vol. 7 Issue 5, May-2018.

[18] https://www.cancer.gov/about-nci/organization/ccg/research/structural-genomics/tcga

[19] Borkowski, A. A., Bui, M. M., Thomas, L. B., Wilson, C. P., DeLand, L. A., and Mastorides, S. M. "Lung and colon cancer histopathological image dataset (LC25000)." arXiv preprint arXiv:1912.12142, 2019.

[20] L. Hou, D. Samaras, T.M. Kurc, Y. Gao, J.E. Davis, and J.H. Saltz, "Patch-based convolutional neural network for whole slide tissue image classification", *Proceedings of the IEEE conference on computer vision and pattern recognition,* pp. 2424-2433, 2016.
[http://dx.doi.org/10.1109/CVPR.2016.266]

[21] N. Coudray, P.S. Ocampo, T. Sakellaropoulos, N. Narula, M. Snuderl, D. Fenyö, A.L. Moreira, N. Razavian, and A. Tsirigos, "Classification and mutation prediction from non–small cell lung cancer histopathology images using deep learning", *Nat. Med.,* vol. 24, no. 10, pp. 1559-1567, 2018.
[http://dx.doi.org/10.1038/s41591-018-0177-5] [PMID: 30224757]

[22] A.J. Schaumberg, W. Juarez, S.J. Choudhury, L.G. Pastrián, B.S. Pritt, and M.P. Pozuelo, "Large-scale annotation of histopathology images from social media", *BioRxiv,* p. 396663.

[23] https://learnopencv.com/otsu-thresholding-with-opencv/

[24] F. Bianconi, J.N. Kather, and C.C. Reyes-Aldasoro, "Evaluation of colour pre- processing on patch-based classification of H&E-stained images", *European Congress on Digital Pathology,* pp. 56-64, 2019.
[http://dx.doi.org/10.1007/978-3-030-23937-4_7]

[25] M.D. Kumar, M. Babaie, S. Zhu, S. Kalra, and H.R. Tizhoosh, "A comparative study of CNN, BoVW and LBP for classification of histopathological images", *2017 IEEE Symposium Series on Computational Intelligence (SSCI),* pp. 1-7, 2017.

[26] A. Riasatian, M. Rasoolijaberi, M. Babaei, and H.R. Tizhoosh, "A Comparative Study of U-Net Topologies for Background Removal in Histopathology Images", *2020 International Joint Conference on Neural Networks (IJCNN),* pp. 1-8, 2020.
[http://dx.doi.org/10.1109/IJCNN48605.2020.9207018]

[27] O. Ronneberger, P. Fischer, and T. Brox, *"Unit: Convolutional Networks for Biomedical Image Segmentation", MICCAI 2015.,* pp. 234-241, 2015.

[28] A.A. Borkowski, C.P. Wilson, S.A. Borkowski, L.B. Thomas, L.A. Deland, S.J. Grewe, and S.M. Mastorides, "Comparing artificial intelligence platforms for histopathologic cancer diagnosis", *Fed. Pract.,* vol. 36, no. 10, pp. 456-463, 2019.
[PMID: 31768096]

[29] A. Teramoto, T. Tsukamoto, Y. Kiriyama and H. Fujita, "Automated Classification of Lung Cancer Types from Cytological Images Using Deep Convolutional Neural Networks", 2017.

[30] D.S. Le Hou, Y. Gao, and J. Saltz, "Patch-Based Convolutional Neural Network for Whole Slide Tissue Image Classification", *IEEE Computer Society Conference on Computer Vision and Pattern Recognition,* 2016.
[http://dx.doi.org/10.1109/CVPR.2016.266]

[31] S. Deng, X. Zhang, W. Yan, E.I.C. Chang, Y. Fan, M. Lai, and Y. Xu, "Deep learning in digital pathology image analysis: a survey", *Front. Med.,* vol. 14, no. 4, pp. 470-487, 2020.
[http://dx.doi.org/10.1007/s11684-020-0782-9] [PMID: 32728875]

[32] A.M. Khan, N. Rajpoot, D. Treanor, and D. Magee, "A nonlinear mapping approach to stain normalization in digital histopathology images using image-specific color deconvolution", *IEEE Trans. Biomed. Eng.,* vol. 61, no. 6, pp. 1729-1738, 2014.
[http://dx.doi.org/10.1109/TBME.2014.2303294] [PMID: 24845283]

[33] A. Janowczyk, A. Basavanhally, and A. Madabhushi, "Stain Normalization using Sparse AutoEncoders (StaNoSA): Application to digital pathology", *Comput. Med. Imaging Graph.,* vol. 57, pp. 50-61, 2017.
[http://dx.doi.org/10.1016/j.compmedimag.2016.05.003] [PMID: 27373749]

[34] A. Vahadane, T. Peng, A. Sethi, S. Albarqouni, L. Wang, M. Baust, K. Steiger, A.M. Schlitter, I. Esposito, and N. Navab, "NavabN. Structure-preserving color normalization and sparse stain separation for histological images", *IEEE Trans. Med. Imaging,* vol. 35, no. 8, pp. 1962-1971, 2016.
[http://dx.doi.org/10.1109/TMI.2016.2529665] [PMID: 27164577]

[35] A. Bentaieb, and G. Hamarneh, "Adversarial stain transfer for histopathology image analysis", *IEEE Trans. Med. Imaging,* vol. 37, no. 3, pp. 792-802, 2018.
[http://dx.doi.org/10.1109/TMI.2017.2781228] [PMID: 29533895]

[36] https://machinelearningmastery.com/review-of-architectural-innovations-for-convolutional-neural-networks-for-image-classification/

[37] www.antweb.org

[38] https://en.wikipedia.org/wiki/Convolution

[39] https://www.geeksforgeeks.org/cnn-introduction-to-pooling-layer/

[40] D. Sarwinda, R.H. Paradisa, A. Bustamam, and P. Anggia, "Deep Learning in Image Classification using Residual Network (ResNet) Variants for Detection of Colorectal Cancer", *Procedia Comput. Sci.,* vol. 179, pp. 423-431, 2021.
[http://dx.doi.org/10.1016/j.procs.2021.01.025]

[41] K. He, X. Zhang, S. Ren, and J. Sun, "Deep residual learning for image recognition", *Proceedings of the IEEE conference on computer vision and pattern recognition,* pp. 770-778, 2016.

[42] https://towardsdatascience.com/an-overview-of-resnet-and-its-variants-5281e2f56035

[43] https://towardsdatascience.com/understanding-and-coding-a-resnet-in-keras-446d7ff84d33

[44] W. Liu, J. Li, G. Zhao, L. Sun, H. Wang, W. Li, and B. Sun, "Improvement of CIFAR-10 Image Classification Based on Modified Res Net-34", *The International Conference on Natural Computation, Fuzzy Systems and Knowledge Discovery,* Springer: Cham, pp. 619-631, 2020.

[45] https://towardsdatascience.com/residual-network-implementing-resnet-a7da63c7b278

## CHAPTER 4

Deep Learning For Lung Cancer Detection

Sushila Ratre[1,*], **Nehha Seetharaman**[1] and **Aqib Ali Sayed**[1]

[1] *Amity School of Engineering and Technology, Amity University Mumbai, Maharashtra 410206, India*

Abstract: By detecting lung cancer in advance, doctors can make the right decision to treat patients to ensure that they live long and healthy lives. This research aims to build a CNN model using a pre-trained model and functional API that would classify if a person had lung cancer or not based on a CT scan. This research uses CT scan images as input for the prediction model from the LUNA16 [Luna Nodule Analysis 2016] dataset for experimenting by using ResNet 50 and VGG 16. ResNet50 showed slightly high accuracy on test data compared to VGG16, which is 98%.

Keywords: ResNet 50, VGG 16, CNN, Lung Cancer, Deep Learning.

INTRODUCTION

Lung cancer is considered the world's most lethal cancer, taking countless lives each year. This is the most common cancer in the world, as well as the most common cause of death. This cannot be ignored and leads to death if not treated on time. It is a state that causes cancerous cells to split uncontrollably in the lungs. This causes the growth of tumors that impair a person's ability to breathe. According to World Health Organization (WHO) in 2019, lung cancer was the second leading cause of death earlier than 70 years in a hundred and twelve countries and ranked third or fourth in a further 23 countries among 183 countries across the globe [1]. Propitiously, early detection of cancer can significantly enhance survival rates. Lung tumor identification is done using numerous imaging techniques such as Computed Tomography Scans (CT), Sputum Cytology, Chest Lung X-rays, and Magnetic Resonance Imaging (MRI). Discernment means classifying a tumor into two cancerous tumors or non-cancerous tumors. An artificial intelligence approach is being used in this research to identify anomalies in lung CT scans using tumor-specific characteristics.

---

[*] **Corresponding author Sushila Ratre:** Amity School of Engineering and Technology, Amity University Mumbai, Maharashtra 410206, India; E-mail: suratre@mum.amity.edu

Gyanendra Verma & Rajesh Doriya (Eds.)
All rights reserved-© 2023 Bentham Science Publishers

There are four main stages in non-small cell lung cancers [NSCLC], from stage 1 to stage 4. If cancerous cells are detected in Stage 1 in the lungs, and it has not di spersed outside to any other body part, then a person's survival rate is close to approximately five years. The tumor size should be less than 3 cm for Stage 1. Similarly, in stage 2, the size of the tumor is between 3-5 cm, and the survival rate is between 2-3 years [2]. The details regarding the stages and survival rate are given below in Table **1**.

Table 1. Stages of Lung Cancer [NSCLC].

S. No	Stage No	Size (In cm)	Dispersion	Rate of Survival (Approx.)
1	Stage 1	< 3 cm	Inside lung	5 Years
2	Stage 2	3-5 cm	Inside lung and nearby lymph nodes	3 Years
3	Stage 3	5-7 cm	Middle of the chest	1-2 Years
4	Stage 4	>7 cm	Both lungs and distant organs	0-6 Months

From (Fig. **1**), we can identify the location and position of the tumor that CT scan images can easily capture. Researchers can prepare a dataset according to the stages of lung cancer to train their model in the future.

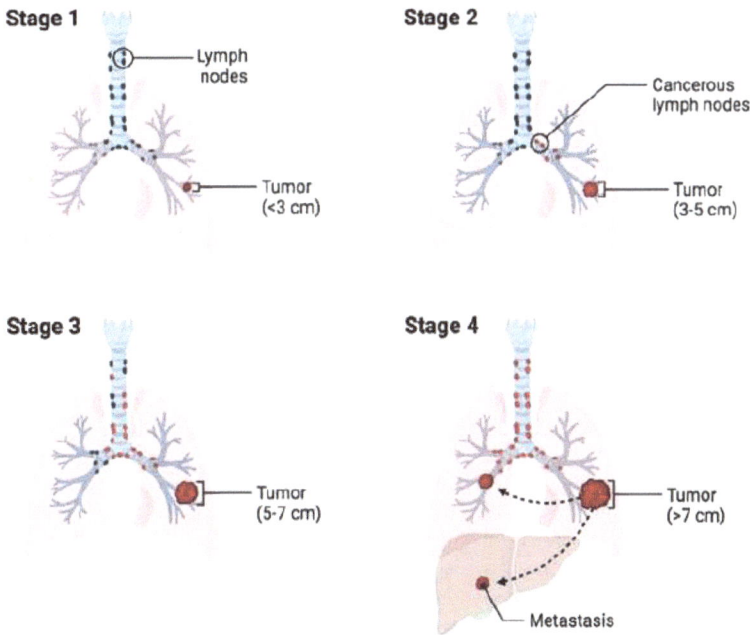

Fig. (1). Types of Stages of Non-Small Cell Lung Cancers [3].

According to the Global survey from the Source [4]: GLOBOCAN 2020, the new lung cancer cases is 2,206,771, and the death rate is very high, *i.e.,* 1,796,144. It is the motivation behind these research activities. Research has considered a total of 36 types of cancers, and lung cancer is the second deadliest disease for humans.

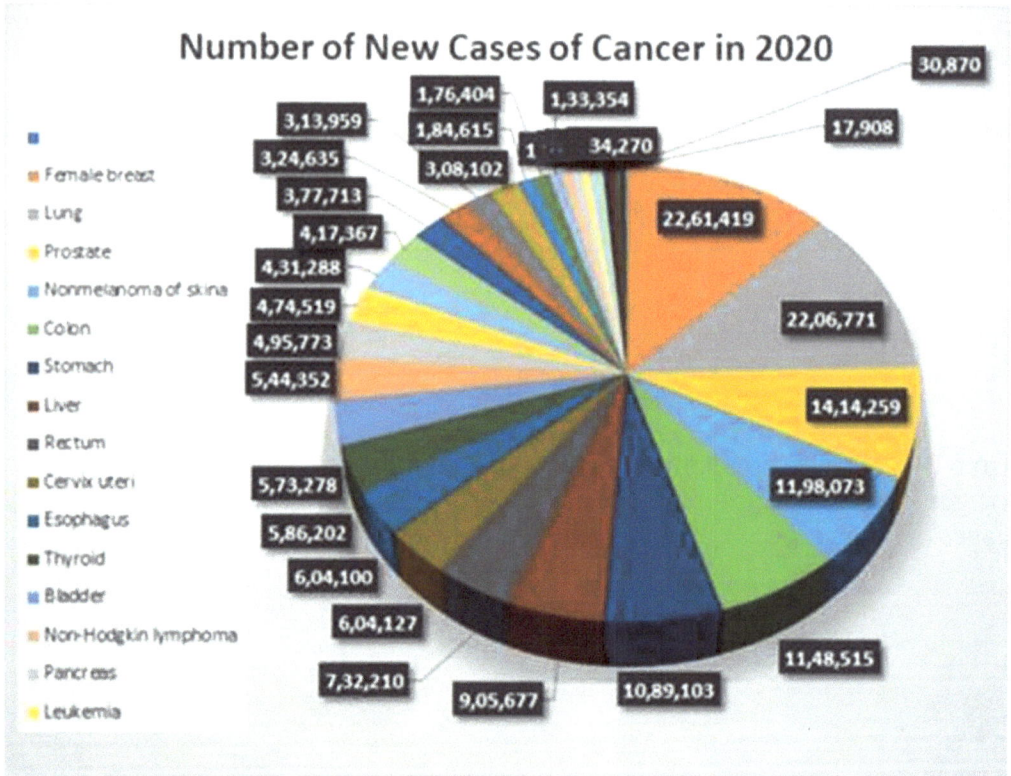

Fig. (2). Number of new cases of cancer in 2020 [4].

RELATED WORKS

QingZeng Song, Lei Zhao, XingKe Luo, and XueChen Dou, 2017 [1] used Lung Image Database Consortium (LIDC) - Image Database Resource Initiative (IDRI) dataset and compared three different categories of deep network models, namely CNN, DNN & SAE that are designed for lung calcification and passed the data to all the three networks, and leaky ReLU activation function is used. They concluded that the CNN network achieved the best performance with an accuracy of 84.15%, specificity of 84.15%, and sensitivity of 84.32%, which is the best among the three networks.

Siddharth Bhatia *et al.,* 2018 [5] have used an LIDC-IDRI dataset and deep residual learning. Features are extracted from CT scans using UNet and Resnet models. Then XGBoost and Random Forest are used for individual predictions. The highest accuracy of 84% is achieved. S. Sasikala *et al.,* 2018 [17] have used the LIDC-IDRI dataset and CNN architecture. The Median filter and ReLu activation function are used in the preprocessing stage. An accuracy of 96% is achieved. Ruchita Tekade *et al.,* 2018 [14] have conducted assessments using LIDC-IDRI, LUNA16, and Data Science Bowl 2017 datasets on CUDA-enabled GPU Tesla K20. They proposed two architectures, U-NET & VGG, for lung segmentation & prediction of malignancy level, respectively. Their approach gave an accuracy of 95.66% and a loss of 0.09, the dice coefficient is 90%, and for predicting log, the loss is 38%.

Sumita Mishra *et al.,* 2019 [6] used the LUNA16 data set and initiated a deep learning method that automatically withdraws and captures 3D features based on spatiotemporal statistics. An accuracy of 94.8% is obtained. Tulasi Krishna Sajja *et al.,* 20191 [18] used an LIDC-IDRI dataset and standard CNN pre-trained architecture (Alex Net, Google Net & ResNet50) on one side and the other and designed a proposed network. When 80% training samples are given to the following architectures Alex Net, Google Net, ResNet50 & Proposed Net, the validation accuracy is 100%,99.84%,100% & 100% respectively. Testing Accuracy is 89%,95.42%,97.42% & 99.03% respectively. Overall Proposed network has the highest accuracy, but among pre-trained networks, ResNet has the highest accuracy.

Weilun Wang *et al.,* 2019 [7] used the LIDC-IDRI dataset and 3D-CNN architecture to extract nodule features annotated by radiologists. By using their trained models, they computed features for nodules detection. A logistic regression model was trained to find the relation between nodule features and cancer labels. Overall, they achieved 82.39% accuracy. In 2019, Google underwent research in the early detection of lung cancer, and their dataset is a mixture of three significant datasets: NLST, LIDC-IDRI, and LUNA16. They achieved 94.4% accuracy by using AI.

Prasanta Das *et al.,* 2020 [8] used an unsharp masking filter for purifying the image. An adaptive canny edge detection algorithm was used to detect edges and cancer-affected regions. KNN (K-Nearest Neighbour) was used for segmentation. Finally, Bayesian Regularization Neural Network achieved an accuracy of 99.5%. Model performance was evaluated using Mean Square error (MSE). N. Kalaivani *et al.,* 2020 [9] used their dataset containing 201 lung images, and for classification purposes, they used Dense Net and an adaptive boosting algorithm. The accuracy obtained for the proposed network is 90.85%.

Diego Riquelme *et al.,* 2020 [10] have used different datasets like LIDC-IDRI, LUNA16, SPI E-AAPM-NCI lungs, NLST, ANODE09, D LCST, DSB and have explained different techniques used for nodule detection using U-Net, R-CNN, YOLO, VGG, ResNet, *etc.,* for initiating deep learning network models. Segmentation techniques like DeepLabv3+ and Gated-SCNN were also discussed.

Tafadzwa L. Chaunzwa *et al.,* 2021 [11] used Non-Invasive computed tomography data and CNN. They focused on detecting two common histological species: adenocarcinoma (AD C) and Squamous Cell Carcinoma (SCC). KNN and SVM on CNN derived quantitative radionics features and performance with an accuracy of 71%. Eali Stephen Neal Joshua *et al.,* 2021 [12] used the LUNA16 dataset and a 3D AlexNet architecture with the nature of the multiview network strategy. Through 10-fold cross-validation was achieved. The accuracy achieved is 97.17%.

METHODOLOGY

CT scan image: The mentioned work to detect lung cancer depends on CT scans of the patient's lung sections. An individual CT scan comprises a 3D data array with a single channel at each voxel. The components in the array (*i.e.,* voxels in the 3D image) consist of Hounsfield Units (HU) that evaluate the radio density at each position. Matter in the lung region has contrasting HU values, so the CT scans reveal the anatomy (such as the presence of tumors) inside the lung region. Fig. (**3**) shows sample images, and (Table **2**) includes the HU values of specific matters in the human body. Due to the different settings of the scanning devices, different CT scan images may have, unlike shapes and spacing. Thus we need to preprocess the CT scan image data. It needs to be converted into similar shapes and spacing before further processing.

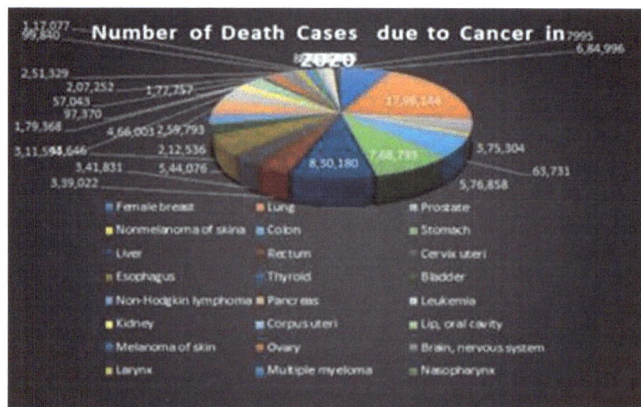

Fig. (3). Number of Death Cases due to cancer in 2020 [4].

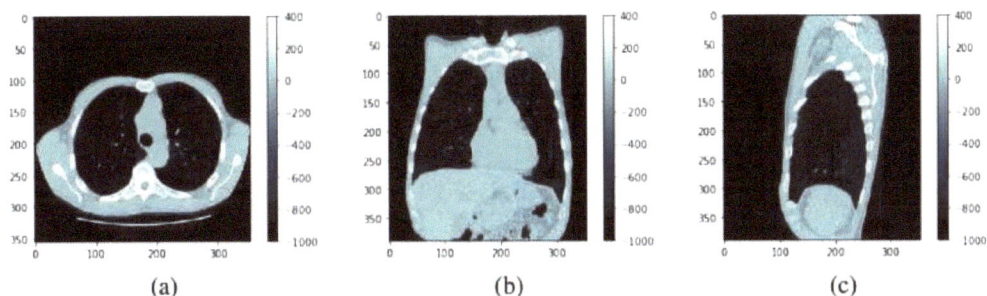

(a)   (b)   (c)

Fig. (4). Sample CT scan images from the Luna16 data set, presenting the slices of the 3D image and the HU values along the z-axis, y-axis, and x-axis for (a), (b), and (c) respectively.

Table 2. Hounsfield Unit (HU) values of matter/substances in the Human Body.

Substance	HU	Substance	HU	Substance	HU
Air	-1000	Lung	-500	Fat	-120 to -90
Water	0	Urine	-5 to +15	Bile	-5 to +15
CSF	+15	Kidney	+20 to +45	Lymph nodes	+10 to +20
Blood	+30 to +45	Muscle	+35 to +55	Grey matter	+37 to +45
White matter	+20 to +30	Liver	+40 to +60	Soft Tissue, Contrast	+100 to +300
Bone	+700 to +3000	Chyle	-30		

Data Pre-processing: The projected system uses a convolution neural network for the early detection of cancer using CT Scan pictures. In this system, we've used the Luna16 dataset. The Luna16 encompasses 754975 samples, and the nodules in each CT image are entitled with the X, Y, and Z coordinates and diameters. The primordial task on the LUNA-16 dataset is nodule segmentation, which means predicting the positions and sizes of all nodules in a given CT scan image. Fig. (5) shows a sample CT scan image and its nodule annotation in LUNA- 16.

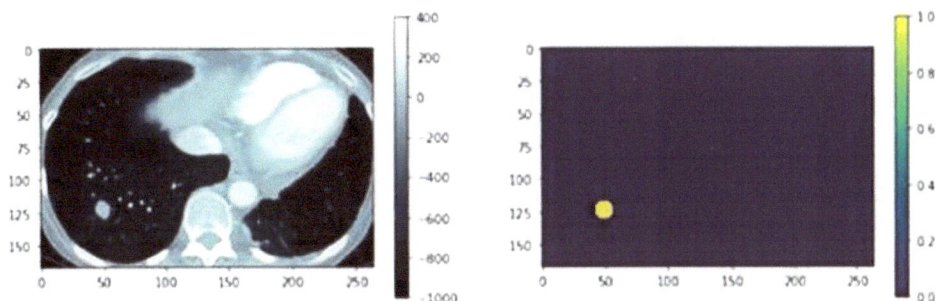

Fig. (5). Sample CT scan image in the LUNA-16 data set with corresponding annotated nodule mask (the yellow circular region) for a slice along the z-axis.

Before providing the CT scan images as input to our deep neural network model, we need to provide equal size and space for all CT scans and then segment the lung portion from these CT scans. Thus we resize all CT scans to amalgamate and provide spacing of 1mm with spline interpolation enacted by the function *scipy.ndimage.interpolation.zoom* in Python. Now the processed CT scan images have equal spacing: each voxel in the image is now proportional to the exact 1mm × 1mm × 1mm cubical region.

After providing equal size and space, we segment the lung portion from the CT scan images, and the lung region is segmented by detecting the most prominent interrelated elements. From Table 1, we observe that the lung tissues have HU values around -500, and the air in the lung has HU values around -1000. So the HU values of the entire lung portion should be more or less not higher than -500, while the bone regions are usually above 700. To partition the lung from the skeleton, we acquire a 3D binary mask by thresholding the 3D.

Computed Tomography scan images at -320: all the voxels with HU values under -320 are labelled as '1' (indicating lung portions) and '0' otherwise. Then, we find the most prominent connected element in the one voxel in the binary mask. A voxel is deemed connected to another voxel if they are adjacent and both have values '1' in the mask. This way, the CT scans can be partitioned into multiple connected elements per voxel connectivity. The most prominent connected element is the one with the maximum number of voxels, which can be achieved using the function *skimage.measure.label* in Python. This most significant connected component should cover most of the lung portion, and we treat it as the binary mask of the lung.

Tissues around the lung are also included as they might contain relevant information about cancer status. To do so, we dilate the most prominent connected element through binary erosion, expanding the lung mask by 5mm in all directions. Then we apply the dilated lung mask to the original CT scan image by maintaining the regions inside the mask and setting all voxels outside the mask to have -1000 HU. Fig. (**6**) shows a sample CT scan image and its segmented lung portions, from which it can be observed that the obtained segmentation mask corresponds precisely to the lung region.

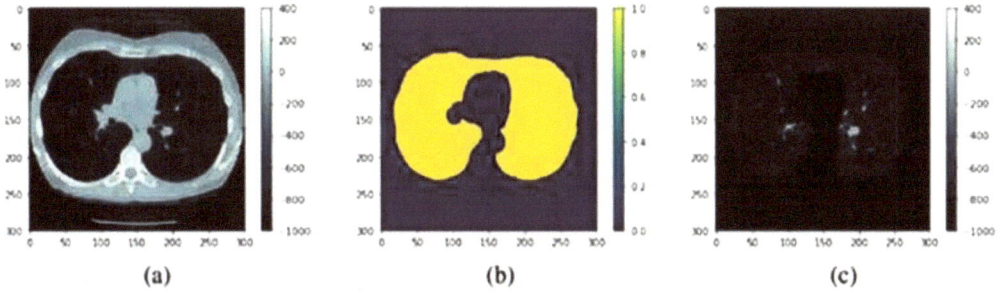

Fig. (6). Sample CT scan sliced along the z-axis, (a) shows the original CT scan image with HU values in the color bar. (b) shows a lung mask extracted from the largest connected elements. (c) shows a segmented lung portion after correlating the lung mask to the CT image.

The segmented image is finally subjected to ResNet-50 and VGG-16 feature extractor to extract the features such as area, perimeter, and length of the major and minor axis of the detected cancer nodule. Also, these features can be extracted for more than one cancer nodule.

VGG16 ARCHITECTURE

VGG is the standard architecture implemented using a convolutional neural network algorithm by Karen Simonyan and Andrew Zisserman in their paper "Very Deep Convolutional Networks for Large Scale Image Recognition" [13]. The motive was to develop a deep neural architecture with increasing depth and tiny filters to extract enormous features from the image.

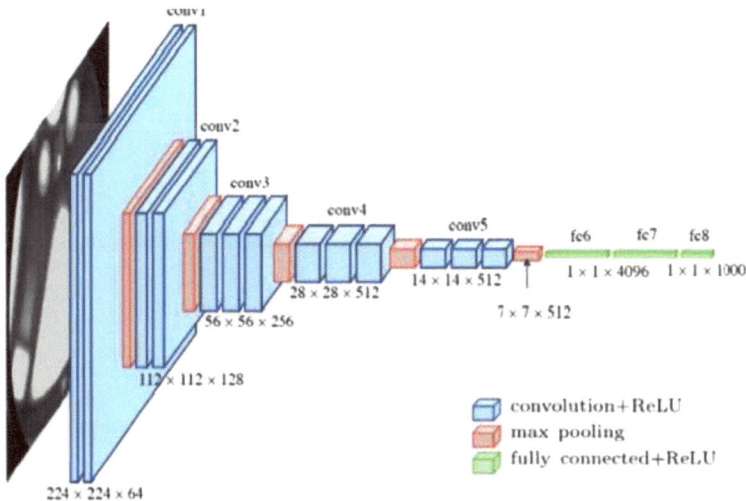

Fig. (7). VGG16 [19].

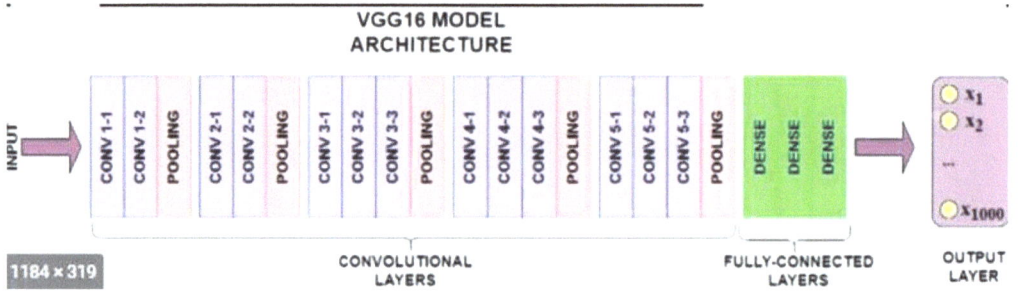

Fig. (8). VGG16 Architecture [15].

RESNET50 ARCHITECTURE

ResNet, also known as Residual Network, is a deep neural network architecture developed by Kaiming He, Xiangyu Zhang, Showing Ren, and Jain Sun in 2015. The authors reformulated the layers as learning residual functions concerning layer inputs instead of learning unreferenced functions [16]. ResNet provides excellent training efficiency compared to other deep network models.

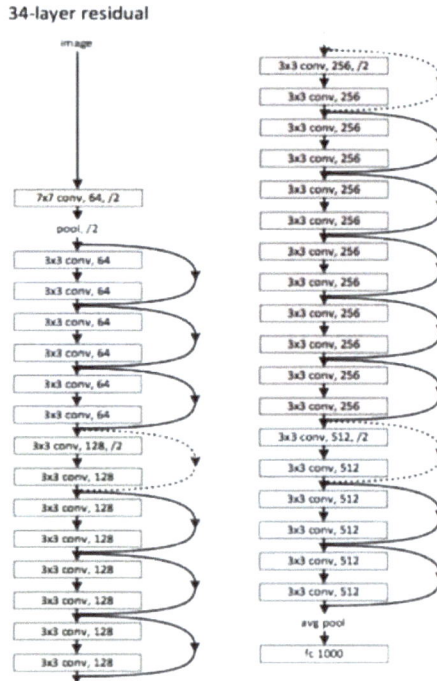

Fig. (9). ResNet 50 [16].

FLOWCHART OF THE METHODOLOGY

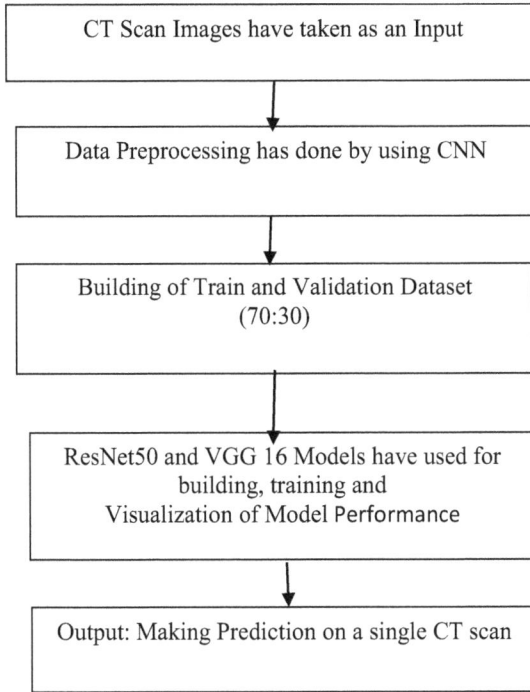

```
┌─────────────────────────────────────────────┐
│     CT Scan Images have taken as an Input     │
└─────────────────────────────────────────────┘
                      │
                      ▼
┌─────────────────────────────────────────────┐
│    Data Preprocessing has done by using CNN   │
└─────────────────────────────────────────────┘
                      │
                      ▼
┌─────────────────────────────────────────────┐
│      Building of Train and Validation Dataset │
│                    (70:30)                    │
└─────────────────────────────────────────────┘
                      │
                      ▼
┌─────────────────────────────────────────────┐
│   ResNet50 and VGG 16 Models have used for    │
│             building, training and            │
│      Visualization of Model Performance       │
└─────────────────────────────────────────────┘
                      │
                      ▼
┌─────────────────────────────────────────────┐
│  Output: Making Prediction on a single CT scan │
└─────────────────────────────────────────────┘
```

Fig. (10). Flowchart of Proposed Methodology.

EXPERIMENTAL RESULTS

Extracted features are applied to input layers of the network. A linear stack of layers was used to create the Convolutional Neural Network, ResNet-50, and VGG16 model for nodule detection. An exemplary tuned deep residual neural network with 50 layers is first implemented. A Residual Network is a deep neural network with a unique connection capability, *i.e.,* skip or short connection which results in improved accuracy and performance over other network layers. ResNet introduces an "identity shortcut connection" that skips one or more layers to avoid the vanishing gradient problem. This identity connection effectively avoids vanishing gradients in the neural network by utilizing the previous layer activation functions until the present layer learns its weights.

In ResNet-50, the network's (fc1000, fc1000_softmax, and Classification Layer_fc1000) layers are exchanged with newly defined layers, particularly a fully connected layer, softmax layer, and an output layer (classification layer). Afterward, the last remaining transferred layer on the network (avg_pool) is linked to the novel layer. A VGG network model can perform image processing deftly by rapidly approximating the target functions and extracting notable feature representations. VGG16 model may perform well in diagnosing CT scans, so we used it as a second deep network model. The final accuracy we got for both models is shown in terms of the graph below:

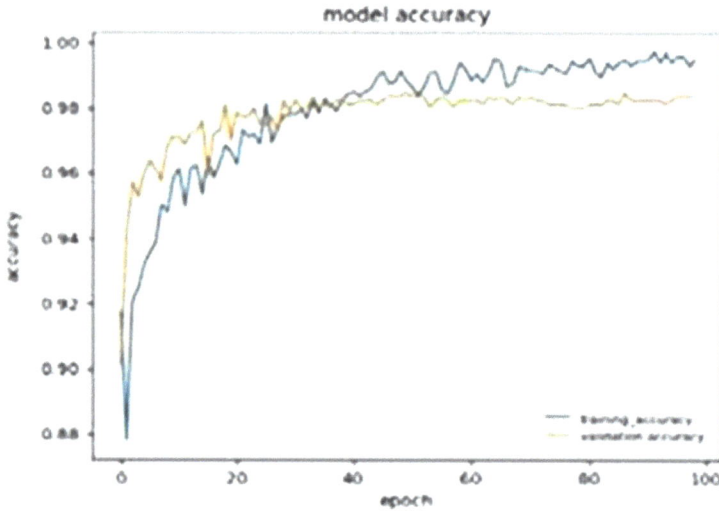

Fig. (11). Resnet-50 Accuracy Graph.

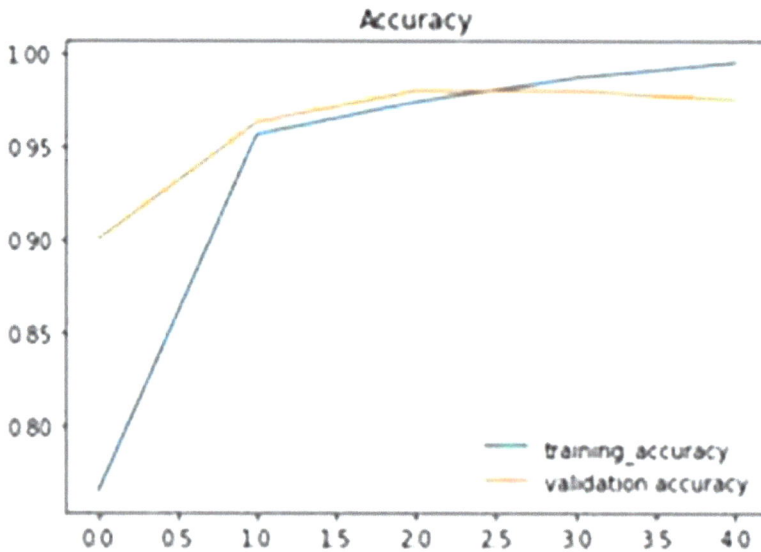

Fig. (12). VGG-16 Accuracy Graph.

CONCLUDING REMARKS

The preferred deep network models help to intensely examine variation between the normal and abnormal nodules in the lung CT scans. We first established a classification framework based on the ResNet50 model to provide sufficient space for lung cancer typing. We used the VGG16 model to make significant correct decisions, and later we compared both models. Both the models illustrated showed similar and statistically significant performance. A deep Residual Neural Network model with 50 layers exhibits an accuracy of 98%, whereas a VGG16 model (also known as OxfordNet) provides an accuracy of 96%. LUNA-16 was the data set used, which contained two classes of Lung infection; then we partitioned the data set into training, validation, and testing sets in the ratio of 70:20:10, respectively. Therefore, two pre-trained models, ResNet50 and VGG16, were trained using the theory of fine-tuning, which includes the exchange of the last three layers, where the output layer has to be well-matched with the required classes. Using a data set on fine-tuning models (Resnet50 and VGG16) could classify lung cancer data, *i.e.,* Classification of Benign and Malignant. By applying these techniques and obtaining a high performance of the model evaluation, we early confirmed lung cancer detection to protect patients from death.

In the future, we could focus more on the preliminary prediction of lung cancer built to discriminate between the four stages of lung cancer. The model should be trained according to stage 1 to stage 4 individually so that we can accurately diagnose patients according to the stages of lung cancer and save their precious lives.

ACKNOWLEDGEMENTS

I would like to thank Dr. Gyanendra Verma and Dr. Rajesh Doriya for their expert advice and for giving us this opportunity to write the book chapter.

REFERENCES

[1] Qing Zeng Song, Lei Zhao, Xing Ke Luo, and Xue Chen Dou, "Using Deep Learning for Classification of Lung Nodules on Computed Tomography Image". *Hindawi Journal of Healthcare Engineering Volume 2017*, Article ID 8314740.

[2] Ann Pietrangelo, Everything You Need To Know About Lung Cancer. https://www.healthline.com/health/lung-cancer#stages

[3] https://ebismedical.com/types-of-cancer/lung-cancer/stages-of-lung-cancer/

[4] Hyuna Sung Ph, acsjournals.onlinelibrary.wiley.com Feb 2021.

[5] S. Bhatia, Y. Sinha, and L. Goel, "Lung cancer detection: a deep learning approach." Soft Computing for Problem Solving: SocProS 2017, Volume 2. Springer Singapore, 2019.

[6] S. Mishra, N.K. Chaudhary, P. Asthana, and A. Kumar, "Deep 3D Convolutional Neural Network for

Automated Lung Cancer Diagnosis", arXiv:1906.0 1054v1 [eess.IV] 4 May 2019.
[http://dx.doi.org/10.1007/978-981-13-7150-9_16]

[7]   W. Wang, and G. Chakraborty, "Automatic prognosis of lung cancer using heterogeneous deep learning models for nodule detection and eliciting its morphological features", *ICAwST.,* vol. 8923147, p. 2019, 2019.

[8]   P. Das, B. Das, and H.S. Dutta, "Prediction of lungs cancer using machine learning",

[9]   N Kalaivani, N Manimaran, Dr. S Sophia, D Devi, "Deep Learning Based Lung Cancer Detection and Classification", *IOP Conf. Series Mater. Sci. Eng.,* 2020.

[10]   D. Riquelme, and M. A. Makhlouf, "Deep Learning for Lung Cancer Nodules Detection and Classification in CT Scan" by, *Mdpi journal AI* 1, 28–67, 2020.
[http://dx.doi.org/10.3390/ai1010003,2020]

[11]   Tafadzwa L. Chaunzwa, Ahmed Hosny, Yiwen Xu, Andrea Shafer, Nancy Diao, Michael Lanuti, David C. Christiani, Raymond H. Mak & Hugo J. W. L. Aerts, "Deep learning classification of lung cancer histology using CT images, Nature portfolio, Scientific reports 11, no. 1, pp.1-12, 2021. [http://dx.doi.org/10.1038/s41598-021-84630-x,2021]

[12]   E.S.N. Joshua, D. Bhattacharyya, M. Chakravarthy, and Y.C. Byun, "3D CNN with Visual Insights for Early Detection of Lung Cancer Using Gradient-Weighted Class Activation", *Hindawi Journal of Healthcare Engineering Volume 2021*, Article ID 6695518, 2021.

[13]   K. Simonyan and A. Zisserman, "Very Deep Convolutional Networks for Large-Scale Image Recognition", arXiv preprint arXiv:1409.1556.

[14]   Ruchita Tekade, prof. Dr. K. Rajeshwari, Detecting and classifying nodules in Lung CT scans, 978 - 1 - 53865 - 2572 / 18 / $31.00,2018 IEEE.

[15]   "Hands-on Transfer Learning with Keras and VGG16 Model" by author James McDermott: VGG16 Model Architecture.

[16]   K. He, X. Zhang, S. Ren, J. Sun, "Deep Residual Learning for Image Recognition". In Proceedings of the IEEE conference on computer vision and pattern recognition, pp. 770-778. 2016.

[17]   S. Sasikala, M. Bharathi, B. R. Sowmiya, "Lung Cancer Detection and Classification Using Deep CNN", *International Journal of Innovative Technology and Exploring Engineering (IJITEE)* ISSN: 2278-3075, Volume-8 Issue-2S December 2018.

[18]   T. K. Sajja, R. M. Devarapalli, H. K. Kalluri, "Lung Cancer Detection Based on CT Scan Images by Using Deep Transfer Learning", *Traitement du Signal* Vol. 36, No. 4, pp. 339-344, August 2019

[19]   Max Ferguson, Ronay ak, Yung-Tsun Tina Lee, and Kincho H. Law "Automatic localization of casting defects with convolutional neural networks", 2017.

## CHAPTER 5

Exploration of Medical Image Super-Resolution in terms of Features and Adaptive Optimization

Jayalakshmi Ramachandran Nair[1,*], **Sumathy Pichai Pillai**[2] and **Rajkumar Narayanan**[3]

[1] *Bharathidasan University, Department of Sciences, St. Claret College, Bengaluru, Karnataka, India*

[2] *Department of Computer Science & Applications, Bharathidasan University, Tiruchirappalli, Tamil Nadu India*

[3] *Department of Sciences, St. Claret College, Bengaluru, Karnataka India*

Abstract: Medical image processing takes many steps to capture, process, and convert the images for further analysis. The images are susceptible to distortions due to various factors related to the analysis tools, environment, system-generated faults, and so on. Image enhancement deals with enhancing the quality and resolution of images for accurately analyzing the original information from the images. The primary motivating aspect of research and reconstruction of such high-quality images and their challenges is image super-resolution for image upgrading. This chapter focuses on various image-enhancing strategies in implementing the super-resolution process. In this work, the methodologies of various image-enhancing strategies are explained clearly to provide the parameter selection points, feature comparisons, and performance evaluations that apply to high-resolution image processing. The drawbacks and challenges of each strategy are discussed to investigate the effectiveness of the methodologies. Further research is explored to find hybrid methods on various deep learning architectures to achieve higher accuracy in the field of medical image super-resolution.

Keywords: Image enhancement, Image feature mapping, Image processing, Image registration, Image resolution, Image segmentation, Medical imaging.

INTRODUCTION

Image enhancement improves the quality of pixel contents of the raw captured image data before sending it for further processing. Commonly used image enhancement techniques include contrast adjustment, spatial filtering, *etc*. The uniformity clears the uneven portion of pixel alignments and improves pixel qual-

---
* Corresponding author Jayalakshmi Ramachandran Nair: Bharathidasan University, Department of Sciences, St. Claret College, Bengaluru, Karnataka, India; E-mail: jayabinoy2020@gmail.com

Gyanendra Verma & Rajesh Doriya (Eds.)

ity. Spatial noise removal filters improve the naturally occurring lines, dead zones in the pixels, and shear zones.

On the other hand, density intervals are aligned by evenly spreading the grey tone to achieve high enhancement without breaking the pixels. Image contrast can be enhanced using linear transformation techniques that expand the original grey level [1].

In many medical applications, there has been a requirement to renovate low-resolution images into high-resolution ones to identify the faults correctly so that the issue can be recognized and evaluated excellently. In image super-resolution, the lower-resolution images (LR) are transformed into high-resolution images (HR) [2, 3]. The main applications of image super-resolution are in surveillance and healthcare. In the case of surveillance, detecting and identifying the face on low-quality camera images is one of the needs [4]. The adjustment and enhancement of pixels enable the process of finding the matching pattern [5, 12]. The adaptation of lower resolution to higher resolution can be processed by handling the pixels one by one or a patch of pixels together [6, 13]. When captured using MRI systems, medical images are high quality in nature [2, 3, 7, 8]. In this case, the time to complete the full scan, the spatial coverage, and signal-to-noise ratio (SNR) factors become tricky [9]. The super-resolution principle helps generate high-quality enhanced images from low-quality images [1, 10, 11]. This will highly reduce the processing time.

LITERATURE REVIEW

The interaction of clinical imaging, extraction, transformation, and capacity requires manual mediation [12, 13]. The images acquired by this interaction are, for the most part, degraded and crumbled because of the impact of different noticeable factors, for example, vulnerabilities present in the extreme climate, types of equipment utilized in the clinical imaging measure, and so on [14, 15]. Decay in the resolution of clinical images alludes to the deficiency of pertinent and noticeable data in clinical images. To upgrade the nature of these images, an image goal improvement method, for example, image super-resolution (SR) innovation, is utilized [16, 17]. This procedure will recreate the LR and change them into HR, which is broadly used in applications like clinical imaging, image and face acknowledgment, observation, satellite imaging, *etc* [18, 19]. Late headways in clinical image resolutions have recommended the execution of profound learning methods to work on the nature of images. Deep learning strategies have accomplished critical significance in image-preparing applications. Profound learning calculations have a hearty portrayal capacity contrasted with ordinary procedures [20, 21]. SR imaging strategies utilizing convolutional neural network (CNN) procedures have given agreeable outcomes in working on the goals of clinical images [22].

In recent years, innovative adaptations of CNN approaches like Fast Super-Resolution Convolutional Neural Networks (FSRCNN) and Super-Resolution Convolutional Neural Networks (SRCNN) have been proposed for clinical imaging [23, 24]. There have been various attempts to extricate resolution issues of a clinical image with the help of FSRCNN and SRCNN by quite a few researchers.

METHODOLOGIES

The low-quality pixels of the images are enhanced to high-resolution images based on the degradation function denoted by D. If the high-resolution image and low-resolution image are considered, the peak amount of noise present in the low-resolution image is represented by σ.

$$I_{High} = D(I_{Low}; \sigma) \tag{1}$$

The degradation parameter and σ are variables that deviate depending on the image quality, captured environment lighting, *etc.* Algorithms such as a neural network reveal the transfer function by inverting the degradation ratio using high-resolution and low-resolution data. Various super-resolution techniques are pre-up sampling super-resolution, post-up sampling super-resolution, residual networks, multi-stage residual networks, recursive networks, progressive reconstruction, multi-branch models, attention-based networks, and generative models. The efficiency of the super-resolution technique in producing the best outcome depends upon the provided image quality [25].

Pre-Upsampling Super Resolution

Image upsampling is the process of increasing the spatial resolution without changing the dimensional representation of the image. This principle safeguards the image during the zooming operation to avoid pixel breakage [26]. Examples of upsampling methods are traditional approaches such as bicubic interpolation, nearest-neighbour interpolation, bicubic spline interpolation, generalized bicubic interpolation, *etc.*

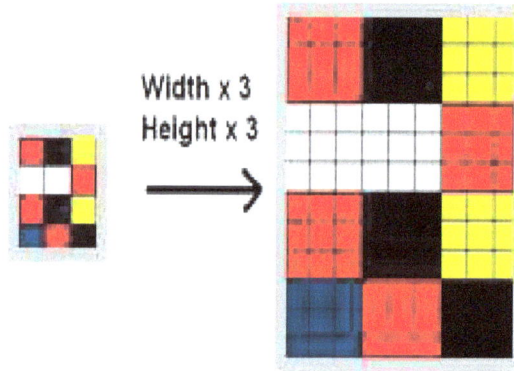

Fig. (1). Upsampling technique [27, 32].

Downscaling is the unique nature of image processing to preserve the quality of appearance of the image during the suppression of image size to save the storage area. It sometimes coincides with image compression, which is different from downscaling [28]. The traditional algorithms used for the downsampling process are Mip Map, Box sampling technique, Sinc, *etc.*

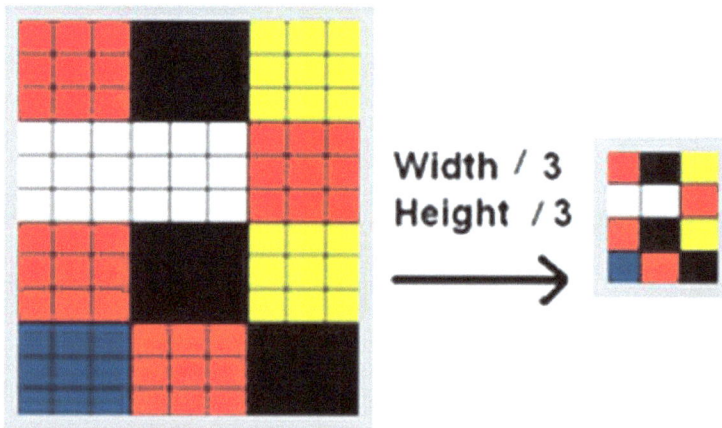

Fig. (2). Downsampling technique [29, 32].

The pre-up scaling Super-resolution technique (SRCNN) is one of the most vital CNN techniques. SRCNN is one of the simple CNN architectures framed with three layers. The first layer is used for patch extraction from the given image. The second one is used for non-linear mappings, and the final layer is used for image reconstruction [30]. The patch of the image is used to extract the dense region of the image and represent those using convolution filters. The non-linear mapping process enables the image patches to undergo several non-linear patches. The patches are variables that move up and down in the image slide depending on the selection [31]. The final output of the model gives the reconstructed high-resolution image.

Very Deep Super-Resolution Models

The improved version of SRCNN is the deep learning model that formulates the super-resolution with the addition of additional features. The model executes deep CNN convolution filters that are larger. The convolution filters are used to work out the patch process [32]. The residuals of the VDSR network are processed back to learn the network. Gradient suppressions are enabled to make the low-resolution input image into high-resolution output.

Post Upsampling Super Resolution

Learned upsampling or deconvolution is used instead of simple bicubic interpolation for upsampling [33]. The processes of enhancing the LR into HR conclude with the analysis of the post-process evaluation results. Hence the HR features are highlighted in the post-upsampling only.

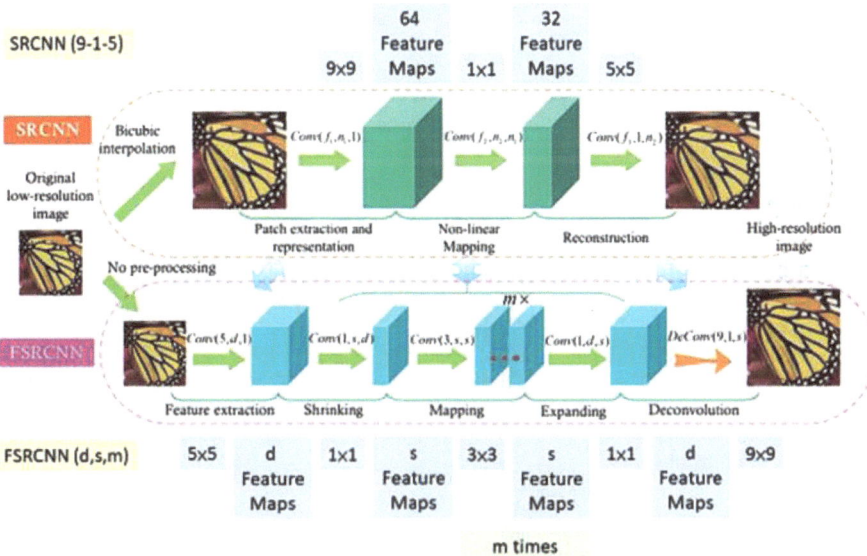

Fig. (3). FSRCNN Fast Super-Resolution Convolution neural network [33].

The feature inputs are extracted at the LR phase itself. Instead of more extensive convolution filters, smaller filter channels are expanded with multiples of n layers. The improved levels of convolution filters in the FSRCNN effectively contribute to the resolution of images. FSRCNN is also called a relatively shallow network, which clearly understands each component [29, 34].

Residual Networks

A residual Network (Res-Net) is the recurrently occurring neural network model that works with the paramedical cells of layers that jump and connect with the required layers, utilising shortcuts but with the number of complex layers of residual filters that keep working with the channel-assigned filters. The SR-Re--Nets use many high-resolution residual blocks. Depending on the system memory available, the layers can be tuned in connectivity. Customizable network layers enable the efficient utilization of memory space. The complete super-resolution residual network block consists of smaller stacks of Residual Network blocks. In terms of accelerating the speed, the depth of the network with fewer extra parameters reduces the fading problems. The weights of the residual networks can also be adjusted during the training process [29].

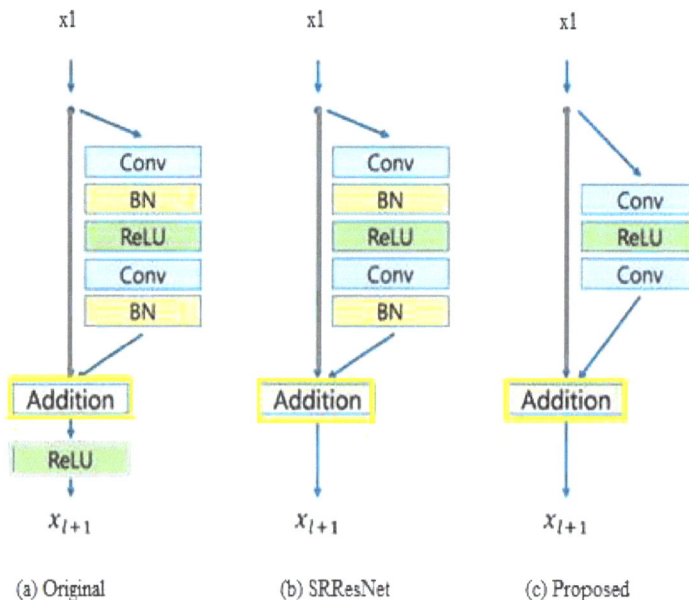

(a) Original   (b) SRResNet   (c) Proposed

Fig. (4). Residual Network (Res-Net) [29].

Multi-stage Residual Networks (MDSR)

MDSR is an alternative for residual networks, incorporated with multiple input and output modules that provide equal tenacity. At the initial condition, the preprocessing elements for range-specific inputs currently consist of two residual blocks with small kernels. An extensive set of kernels is utilized for the pre-processing layers to follow the network resilience while still reaching the high accessible ground. At the end of the initial processing, modules are the mutual residual blocks, a communal block for low and high-resolution data. The number of parameters utilized for the MDSR models is half that used in the EDSR since the shared parameters reduce it.

Balanced Two-Stage Residual Networks

Balanced networks are required for both low-resolution and high-resolution stages. In the low-resolution image processing stage, the filter size of features is small; whether these feature maps are large in high-resolution image processing. The bicubic sampling process consists of different low-resolution and high-resolution stages [34]. The author [34] defined a tunable novel structure *Pconv*, as the block achieves high-performance accuracy. Batch normalization is not used in the balanced Two-Stage Res-Nets.

Recursive Networks

Recursive networks are similar to deep neural networks formulated by repeatedly applying the same weights over the same structure to obtain a scalar prediction. It is used as a general method to conduct logic analysis to derive the maximum adaptable value. These networks are formally called adaptive models, capable of getting in-depth features. Recursive networks consist of several neurons incorporating the reinforcement mapping features.

Many layers of non-linear processing units are utilized for these tasks. The process includes accumulated feature points, features extraction, weighted bias units, *etc*. Recursive networks are commonly used artificial neural network models used for pattern matching compared with other applications. The most impacted drawbacks of the recursive grid are the gradient vanishing and exploding problems. It cannot be used for a long process because of the Tanh and ReLu transfer functions.

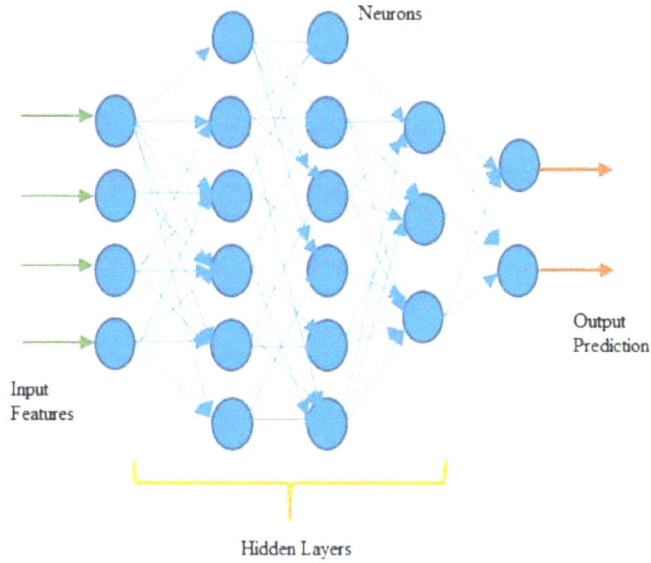

Fig. (5). Recursive Neural Network.

Deep Recursive Convolution Network (DRCN)

Deep Recursive Convolution Network (DRCN) comprises of convolution layer to be applied for N number multiple times. The fixed convolution layers are considered the residual network blocks. The outputs from each residual convolution block are accumulated together at the reconstruction network to generate the output. These kinds of deep networks are also called ensemble networks. Image resolution enhancement using DRCN is probably used in cases where only part of the image area is required to get altered. Patch-making or inpainting are the techniques that act as the outcome of such a model.

Progressive Reconstruction Networks

The high-resolution image with a high scaling factor is difficult to process with neural networks. The number of neurons involved in the network architecture increases the resolution of steps. This progressive model is also called the Laplacian Pyramid super-resolution network. The ensemble of two categories, namely features embedding block and image reconstruction block, *etc.* In input, a low-quality image is fetched into the feature extraction block, which is further transformed into stacked transposed convolution layers. The output of one feature extraction block is passed into the next stage of the feature extraction block and processed again. The result of each block is the fine-tuned pixel data that is refined to reach a high resolution. The network can review each stage's outcome, which helps learn a model network that continuously adapts to the weightage of the process reconstruction. The N features used in each step can be altered based on the memory allocation. Hence the shared resource is applicable in such cases. The loss function of each stage gradually reduces when the stage increases. In deep learning models, cascaded architecture is always helpful in improving learning capability.

Attention-Based Network

ABN(Attention-based network) works with image super-resolution to capture a particular region, select the area and work out the specific locations alone to attain high resolution. The selection of areas is tunable to evaluate the model according to the complexity of the image input. The low-resolution images are treated with the traditional bicubic interpolation method, whereas the selected area alone is treated with highly efficient CNN or recursive models. The transfer function is determined by the complexity of the image [33]; as per the author, the network is called as selNet since the network model is based on the selective process. In this attention-based network, various loss functions are discussed, such as pixel loss, perceptual loss, and adversarial loss.

Pixel Loss

Since most pixel loss changes cannot be visible to the human eye, the original image and the processed image look similar. In the training of super-resolution networks, the most straightforward and standard function analyzed is pixel loss. The minute pixel losses are statistically evaluated through the Pixel Loss function. The optimized PSNR value can determine pixel loss.

Perceptual Loss

Perceptual loss is the systematic method of matching the obtained outcome of the image with the trained image to evaluate the difference between both. Feature differences and outputs between the predicted and output images act as the loss function.

Adversarial Loss

In most generalized adversarial networks, the output processed image resembles the exact outcome of the original image. To fake, some regions present with the patches are compared and in-painted with the reference image. To evaluate the affected areas that affect the originality, Adversarial loss functions are determined.

SYSTEM TOOLS

Image resolution enhancement is a complex process requiring highly efficient processing tools to adapt to the steps involved in each stage. Image processing tools contain dedicated image libraries, image segmentation, and enhancement commands to help attain that standard. MATLAB is one of the vital computing tools with incorporated toolboxes for image processing and convolutional networks. To evaluate a novel architecture for the super-resolution process, standard platforms are needed with behavioural functionality. The tool selection is determined based on the industrial standard, expected outcome, and flexible availability.

FINDINGS

The study on the super-resolution image enhancement process indicates the availability of multiple methods of image enhancement techniques that can provide the basic idea of implementing super-resolution image process principles. The study helped to find the impact of the accurate prediction model. It is clear from the above work that tuning hybrid deep learning networks are today's preferred prediction model, and adaptive networks are highly helpful in understanding region-based enhancement. The study also helped to understand the significance of optimized residual networks in generating efficient prediction models of super-resolution.

CONCLUSION

Medical image resolution is one of the long-lasting research areas that could stand out over the years. Scholarly articles and contributions are beneficial in extending the study of the image enhancement process, specifically image super-resolution techniques. This work narrates the advantages of various deep learning architectures. With the aid of features, parameters, evaluation results, and error factors, the chapter discusses the methodologies in medical image super-resolution. The findings and solutions are limited to the present form since more computational methods must be practically implemented, tested, and evaluated through standard image processing tools. In the extended study, the research is motivated to develop such deep learning-based optimized residual networks with the help of publicly available medical image datasets.

ACKNOWLEDGEMENTS

This paper and the research in the wake of it would not have been promising without the exceptional support of my guide, Dr. Sumathy Pichai Pillai Her keenness, expertise, and thorough attention to various aspects have been an encouragement to keep the work on a track with relevant findings. Dr. Rajkumar Narayanan my co-guide, has also dealt with the transcriptions and supported dealing with various concepts discussed as part of the paper. We would like to extend sincere thanks to the anonymous referees for their constructive suggestions.

REFERENCES

[1]   X. Zhu, H. Cao, Y. Zhang, K. Tan, and X. Ling, "Fine Registration for VHR Images Based on Superpixel Registration-Noise Estimation", *IEEE Geosci. Remote Sens. Lett.,* vol. 15, no. 10, pp. 1-5, 2018.
[http://dx.doi.org/10.1109/LGRS.2018.2849696]

[2]   L. Gong, L. Duan, Y. Dai, Q. He, S. Zuo, T. Fu, X. Yang, and J. Zheng, "Locally Adaptive Total p-Variation Regularization for Non-Rigid Image Registration With Sliding Motion", *IEEE Trans. Biomed. Eng.,* vol. 67, no. 9, pp. 2560-2571, 2020.
[http://dx.doi.org/10.1109/TBME.2020.2964695] [PMID: 31940514]

[3]   J. Zhang, W. Ma, Y. Wu, and L. Jiao, "Multimodal Remote Sensing Image Registration Based on Image Transfer and Local Features", *IEEE Geosci. Remote Sens. Lett.,* vol. 16, no. 8, pp. 1210-1214, 2019.
[http://dx.doi.org/10.1109/LGRS.2019.2896341]

[4]   Y. Zhang, Q. Fan, F. Bao, Y. Liu, and C. Zhang, "Single-Image Super-Resolution Based on Rational Fractal Interpolation", *IEEE Trans. Image Process.,* vol. 27, no. 8, pp. 3782-3797, 2018.
[http://dx.doi.org/10.1109/TIP.2018.2826139] [PMID: 29698209]

[5]   J. Huang, L. Wang, J. Qin, Y. Chen, X. Cheng, and Y. Zhu, "Super-Resolution of Intravoxel Incoherent Motion Imaging Based on Multisimilarity", *in IEEE Sensors Journal,* vol. 20, no. 18, pp. 10963-10973, 2020. 15 Sept.15.
[http://dx.doi.org/10.1109/JSEN.2020.2993873]

[6]   Z.W. Pan, and H.L. Shen, "Multispectral Image Super-Resolution *via* RGB Image Fusion and Radiometric Calibration", *IEEE Trans. Image Process.,* vol. 28, no. 4, pp. 1783-1797, 2019.
[http://dx.doi.org/10.1109/TIP.2018.2881911] [PMID: 30489268]

[7]   H. Zhao, N. Chen, T. Li, J. Zhang, R. Lin, X. Gong, L. Song, Z. Liu, and C. Liu, "Motion Correction in Optical Resolution Photoacoustic Microscopy", *IEEE Trans. Med. Imaging,* vol. 38, no. 9, pp. 2139-2150, 2019.
[http://dx.doi.org/10.1109/TMI.2019.2893021] [PMID: 30668495]

[8]   Y. Li, D. Liu, H. Li, L. Li, Z. Li, and F. Wu, "Learning a Convolutional Neural Network for Image Compact-Resolution", *IEEE Trans. Image Process.,* vol. 28, no. 3, pp. 1092-1107, 2019.
[http://dx.doi.org/10.1109/TIP.2018.2872876] [PMID: 30281453]

[9]   W. Wei, J. Nie, Y. Li, L. Zhang, and Y. Zhang, "Deep Recursive Network for Hyperspectral Image Super-Resolution", *IEEE Trans. Comput. Imaging,* vol. 6, pp. 1233-1244, 2020.
[http://dx.doi.org/10.1109/TCI.2020.3014451]

[10]   F. Fang, J. Li, and T. Zeng, "Soft-Edge Assisted Network for Single Image Super-Resolution", *IEEE Trans. Image Process.,* vol. 29, pp. 4656-4668, 2020.
[http://dx.doi.org/10.1109/TIP.2020.2973769] [PMID: 32092001]

[11]   Q. Liu, A. Liu, Y. Wang, and H. Li, "A Super-Resolution Sparse Aperture ISAR Sensors Imaging Algorithm *via* the MUSIC Technique", *IEEE Trans. Geosci. Remote Sens.,* vol. 57, no. 9, pp. 7119-7134, 2019.
[http://dx.doi.org/10.1109/TGRS.2019.2911686]

[12]   H. Irmak, G.B. Akar, and S.E. Yuksel, "A MAP-Based Approach for Hyperspectral Imagery Super-

Resolution", *IEEE Trans. Image Process.,* vol. 27, no. 6, pp. 2942-2951, 2018.
[http://dx.doi.org/10.1109/TIP.2018.2814210] [PMID: 29994066]

[13] G. Zurakhov, Z. Friedman, D.S. Blondheim, and D. Adam, "High-Resolution Fast Ultrasound Imaging With Adaptive-Lag Filtered Delay-Multiply-and-Sum Beamforming and Multiline Acquisition", *IEEE Trans. Ultrason. Ferroelectr. Freq. Control,* vol. 66, no. 2, pp. 348-358, 2019.
[http://dx.doi.org/10.1109/TUFFC.2018.2886182] [PMID: 30571619]

[14] Y. Tao, M. Xu, F. Zhang, B. Du, and L. Zhang, "Unsupervised-Restricted Deconvolutional Neural Network for Very High Resolution Remote-Sensing Image Classification", *IEEE Trans. Geosci. Remote Sens.,* vol. 55, no. 12, pp. 6805-6823, 2017.
[http://dx.doi.org/10.1109/TGRS.2017.2734697]

[15] R.A. Farrugia, C. Galea, and C. Guillemot, "Super Resolution of Light Field Images Using Linear Subspace Projection of Patch-Volumes", *IEEE J. Sel. Top. Signal Process.,* vol. 11, no. 7, pp. 1058-1071, 2017.
[http://dx.doi.org/10.1109/JSTSP.2017.2747127]

[16] Y. Xu, L. Peng, and G.Y. Li, "Multi Modal Registration of Structural Features and Mutual Information of Medical Image", *Future Gener. Comput. Syst.,* vol. 93, pp. 499-505, 2019.
[http://dx.doi.org/10.1016/j.future.2018.09.059]

[17] K. de Haan, Z.S. Ballard, Y. Rivenson, Y. Wu, and A. Ozcan, "Resolution Enhancement in Scanning Electron Microscopy using Deep Learning", *Sci. Rep.,* vol. 9, no. 1, p. 12050, 2019.
[http://dx.doi.org/10.1038/s41598-019-48444-2] [PMID: 31427691]

[18] X. Xu, W. Liu, and L. Li, "Low-resolution face recognition in surveillance systems", *Journal of Computer and Communications,* vol. 2, no. 2, pp. 70-77, 2014.
[http://dx.doi.org/10.4236/jcc.2014.22013]

[19] W. Witwit, Y. Zhao, K. Jenkins, and Y. Zhao, "Satellite image resolution enhancement using discrete wavelet transform and new edge-directed interpolation", *J. Electron. Imaging,* vol. 26, no. 2, p. 023014, 2017.
[http://dx.doi.org/10.1117/1.JEI.26.2.023014]

[20] A. Bashar, "Survey on evolving deep learning neural network architectures", *Journal of Artificial Intelligence,* vol. 1, no. 02, pp. 73-82, 2019.

[21] M. Tan, and Q.V Le, "Efficient net: Rethinking model scaling for convolutional neural networks", arXiv preprint arXiv:1905.11946.

[22] E. Ahn, A. Kumar, D. Feng, M. Fulham, and J Kim, "Unsupervised feature learning with K-means and an ensemble of deep convolutional neural networks for medical image classification", arXiv preprint arXiv:1906.03359.

[23] C. Dong, C.C. Loy, K. He, and X. Tang, "Learning a deep convolutional network for image super-resolution", *European conference on computer vision,* 2014pp. 184-199
[http://dx.doi.org/10.1007/978-3-319-10593-2_13]

[24] C. Dong, C.C. Loy, and X. Tang, "Accelerating the super-resolution convolutional neural network", *European conference on computer vision,* 2016pp. 391-407

[25] C.H. Pham, C. Tor-Díez, H. Meunier, N. Bednarek, R. Fablet, N. Passat, and F. Rousseau, "Multiscale brain MRI super-resolution using deep 3D convolutional networks", *Comput. Med. Imaging Graph.,* vol. 77, p. 101647, 2019.
[http://dx.doi.org/10.1016/j.compmedimag.2019.101647] [PMID: 31493703]

[26] X. Bing, W. Zhang, L. Zheng, and Y. Zhang, "Medical image super-resolution using improved generative adversarial networks", *IEEE Access,* vol. 7, pp. 145030-145038, 2019.
[http://dx.doi.org/10.1109/ACCESS.2019.2944862]

[27] D. Mahapatra, B. Bozorgtabar, and R. Garnavi, "Image super-resolution using progressive generative adversarial networks for medical image analysis", *Comput. Med. Imaging Graph.,* vol. 71, pp. 30-39,

2019.
[http://dx.doi.org/10.1016/j.compmedimag.2018.10.005] [PMID: 30472408]

[28]   D. Qiu, L. Zheng, J. Zhu, and D. Huang, "Multiple improved residual networks for medical image super-resolution", *Future Gener. Comput. Syst.,* vol. 116, pp. 200-208, 2021.
[http://dx.doi.org/10.1016/j.future.2020.11.001]

[29]   C. Wang, Z. Wang, W. Xi, Z. Yang, G. Bai, R. Wang, and M. Duan, "MufiNet: Multiscale Fusion Residual Networks for Medical Image Segmentation", *2020 International Joint Conference on Neural Networks (IJCNN),* 2020pp. 1-7
[http://dx.doi.org/10.1109/IJCNN48605.2020.9207314]

[30]   D. Mahapatra, and B Bozorgtabar, "Progressive generative adversarial networks for medical image super-resolution", arXiv preprint arXiv:1902.02144.

[31]   T.K. Lai, A.F. Abbas, A.M. Abdu, U.U. Sheikh, M. Mokji, and K. Khalil, "Super-resolution of car plate images using generative adversarial networks. In 2019 IEEE 15th International Colloquium on Signal Processing & Its Applications (CSPA) (pp. 80-85). ", IEEE.
[http://dx.doi.org/10.1109/CSPA.2019.8696010]

[32]   Matthew Giassa, https://www.giassa.net/

[33]   C. Dong, C.C. Loy, and X. Tang, Accelerating the Super-Resolution Convolutional Neural Network.*Computer Vision – ECCV 2016. ECCV 2016.,* B. Leibe, J. Matas, N. Sebe, M. Welling, Eds., vol. 9906. Springer: Cham, 2016.Lecture Notes in Computer Science
[http://dx.doi.org/10.1007/978-3-319-46475-6_25]

[34]   Y. Fan, "Balanced Two-Stage Residual Networks for Image Super-Resolution", *2017 IEEE Conference on Computer Vision and Pattern Recognition Workshops (CVPRW),* 2017pp. 1157-1164
[http://dx.doi.org/10.1109/CVPRW.2017.154]

## CHAPTER 6

Analyzing the Performances of Different ML Algorithms on the WBCD Dataset

Trupthi Muralidharr[1,*], Prajwal Sethu Madhav[1], Priyanka Prashanth Kumar[1] and Harshawardhan Tiwari[1]

[1] Jyothy Institute of Technology, Pipeline Rd, near Ravi Shankar Guruji Ashram, Thathaguni, Karnataka India

Abstract: Breast cancer is a disease with a high fatality rate each year. It is the most frequent cancer in women and the leading cause of death in women worldwide. The method of machine learning (ML) is an excellent way to categorize data, particularly in the medical industry. It is widely used for decision-making, categorization, and analysis. The main objective of this study is to analyze the performances of different ML algorithms on the WBCD dataset. In this paper, we analysed the performances of different ML algorithms, i.e., XGboost Classifier, KNN, Random Forest, and SVM (Support Vector Machine). Accuracy was used in the study to determine the performance. Experimental result shows that SVMs perform better and are more accurate than KNNs as the amount of training data increases. The SVM produces better results when the main component (PC) value grows and the accuracy rating exceeds the kNN.

Keywords: Breast Cancer, Decision Tree, Exploratory Data Analysis, Histograms, KNN, Random Forest, SVM, UCI Machine Learning Repository, WBCD, XgBoost.

INTRODUCTION

Breast Cancer is a critical illness seen mainly in women and has been one of the leading causes of their death. Breast cancer can mainly be detected by physical examination or techniques like Fine Needle Aspiration (FNA) and Mammography. These cancers start with a lump in the chest. Lumps formed in the chest can be benign or can be malignant. Benign tumors are the ones that are non-cancerous and malignant tumors are the cancerous tumors.

In 2020, there were 2.3 million women diagnosed with breast cancer and 685 000 deaths globally. As of the end of 2020, breast cancer was the world's most preval-

* **Corresponding author Trupthi Muralidharr:** Jyothy Institute Of Technology Pipeline Rd, near Ravi Shankar Guruji Ashram, Thathaguni, Karnataka India; E-mail: trupthimuralidharr@gmail.com

ent cancer [1]. Many women with breast cancer have no symptoms, so early detection helps the treatment process and increases survival rates. Machine Learning plays an important role in the early detection of breast cancer. Many algorithms are used in both supervised and unsupervised learning. The data set that is being implemented is the Wisconsin Breast Cancer Diagnosis (WBCD), and the methods being used are Decision Tree Classification using the Algorithms Regression tree, XG Boosting, Random Forest, and Ada-Boost [2].

LITERATURE REVIEW

Machine learning classifiers have long been used in medical research, particularly in breast cancer diagnosis. Classification is one of the most prevalent sorts of machine learning jobs. ML classifiers have been employed in various medical research initiatives, including the WBCD. According to previous research, the classifiers used in this study have a high level of classification accuracy [3]. Shokoufeh Alaei and Hadi Shahraki use the wrapper strategy. The study used three different breast cancer datasets and three different classifiers on Wisconsin breast cancer datasets: artificial neural network (ANN), PS-classifier, and genetic algorithm-based classifier (GA-classifier) (WBC). According to the findings, feature selection can aid classifiers in improving their accuracy, specificity, and sensitivity.

Jian Ping Li and his colleagues employed a recursive feature selection technique [4]. This method is used to train and test the classifier for the best prediction model. Additionally, performance evaluation criteria such as classification, specificity, sensitivity, Matthews' correlation coefficient, F1-score, and execution time have been used to assess the classifier's performance. The dataset "Wisconsin Diagnostic Breast Cancer" was used in this investigation. On this best subset of features, SVM achieved the best classification performance. Matthews' correlation coefficient is 99 percent, and the SVM kernel linear obtained high classification accuracy (99 percent), specificity (99 percent), and sensitivity (98 percent).

Li Chen and his colleagues suggest a combination of K-means and Boosted C5 (K-Boosted C5.0) based on undersampling to overcome the two-class unbalanced problem in breast cancer detection. To evaluate the new hybrid classifier's performance, it is applied to 12 small-scale and two large-scale datasets (Protein homology prediction and Breast Cancer) used in class unbalanced learning [5].

Their proposed hybrid approach outperforms most competing algorithms in terms of Matthews' correlation coefficient (MCC) and accuracy indices according to extensive experimental data.

The Quality Control Charts and Logistic Regression were used to diagnose breast cancer by Omar Graja, Muhammad Azam, and Nizar Bouguila. Data pre-processing, which involves removing outliers and reducing dimensionality to visualize the data, is a contribution of this study. Following the presentation of the data, the best machine learning algorithm for this diagnostic can be proposed. They employed the UCI machine learning breast cancer Wisconsin (original) dataset (WBCD) for the evaluation of our suggested approach [6].

The effect of dimensionality decreases utilization of free part examination (ICA) on bosom malignant growth choice emotionally supportive networks utilizing an assortment of classifiers, including fake neural organizations (ANN), k-closest neighbor (k-NN), spiral premise work neural organization (RBFNN), and backing vector machine (SVM) [7] were researched by Erdem Bilgili and Ahmet Mert. Thus, the characterization precision rates for thirty unique elements, except for RBFNN, have diminished hardly from 97.53 percent to 90.5 percent. Be that as it may, the RBFNN classifier is recognized with higher precision from 87.17 percent to 90.49 percent when utilizing the one-layered element vector.

Sulyman Age Abdulkareema and Zainab Olorunbukademi Abdulkareemb used the WBCD dataset to test the performance of two ensemble ML classifiers: Random Forest (RF) and eXtreme Gradient Boosting (XGBoost) [8]. The study's main goal was to assess the accuracy of the classifiers in terms of their efficiency and effectiveness in categorizing the dataset. This was accomplished by selecting all and reducing features from the dataset using the Recursive Feature Elimination (RFE) feature selection approach. According to the findings, XGBoost with five reduced features, and the RFE feature selection approach have the highest accuracy (99.02%) and the lowest error rate.

Liu et al. proposed a decision tree-based breast cancer prediction algorithm that balanced the training data using a sampling method. According to the experimental data, the proposed method generated good accuracy [9].

Krzysztof and Duch used the Separability of Split Value (SSV) criteria to create a heterogeneous forest of decision trees. The majority of their work involved extracting logical rules from diverse decision trees [10].

Stephan and Lucila contrasted logistic regression versus artificial neural networks in a range of medical categorization tasks. They proved the benefits of using logistic regression in the medical field from a technical aspect, as it is a white box model with interpretable results [11].

Salama and his colleagues [10] used the WEKA data mining technology to conduct a study titled "Breast Cancer Diagnosis on Three Different Datasets

Using MultiClassifiers." WBCD was one of the three breast cancer datasets used in the research. The datasets were binary classified using five distinct ML classifiers (NB, MLP, J48, SMO, and IBK). The SMO classifier achieved the best classification accuracy (96.9957 percent) in the WBCD experiment, whereas the IBK classifier had the worst (94.5637 percent). Furthermore, a fusion of J48 and MLP with PCA was able to reach a higher level of accuracy (97.568%), but J48 and NB with PCA had the lowest level of accuracy (95.8512 percent) [12].

DATASET DESCRIPTION

The Wisconsin Breast Cancer Database (WBCD) from the UCI Machine Learning Repository is our dataset in this study [13].

This is a 569-instance multivariate database. This dataset contains 32 attributes. These characteristics are derived from a digital breast mass fine needle aspiration (FNA) image. They describe the properties of the nuclei that can be seen in the imaging

The following is the attribute information:

ID number

Diagnosis (M = malignant, B = benign)

For each cell nucleus, ten real-valued characteristics are computed:

Fractal dimension, Radius, Texture, Perimeter, area, smoothness, Compactness, Concavity, Cona-ve points, Symmetry.

PRE-PROCESSING OF DATA

Exploratory Data Analysis(EDA)

Two ways are used to analyze the data:

1. Descriptive statistics reduces a data set's primary properties to basic numerical measurements. Mean, standard deviation, and correlation are examples of common metrics.

2. The transformation of data into a Cartesian space or an abstract image is the process of viewing it. Many aspects of data mining, including preprocessing, modeling, and interpretation of results, rely on data exploration.

Descriptive statistics:

	radius_mean	texture_mean	perimeter_mean	area_mean	smoothness_mean	compactness_mean	concavity_mean	concave points_mean	symmetry_mean	fractal_dimension_mean	...
count	569.000000	569.000000	569.000000	569.000000	569.000000	569.000000	569.000000	569.000000	569.000000	569.000000	
mean	14.127292	19.289649	91.969033	654.889104	0.096360	0.104341	0.088799	0.048919	0.181162	0.062798	
std	3.524049	4.301036	24.298981	351.914129	0.014064	0.052813	0.079720	0.038803	0.027414	0.007060	
min	6.981000	9.710000	43.790000	143.500000	0.052630	0.019380	0.000000	0.000000	0.106000	0.049960	
25%	11.700000	16.170000	75.170000	420.300000	0.086370	0.064920	0.029560	0.020310	0.161900	0.057700	
50%	13.370000	18.840000	86.240000	551.100000	0.095870	0.092630	0.061540	0.033500	0.179200	0.061540	
75%	15.780000	21.800000	104.100000	782.700000	0.105300	0.130400	0.130700	0.074000	0.195700	0.066120	
max	28.110000	39.280000	188.500000	2501.000000	0.163400	0.345400	0.426800	0.201200	0.304000	0.097440	

	mean	...	radius_worst	texture_worst	perimeter_worst	area_worst	smoothness_worst	compactness_worst	concavity_worst	concave points_worst	symmetry_worst	fractal_dimension_worst
	0.000		569.000000	569.000000	569.000000	569.000000	569.000000	569.000000	569.000000	569.000000	569.000000	569.000000
	62798		16.269190	25.677223	107.261213	880.583128	0.132369	0.254265	0.272188	0.114606	0.290076	0.083946
	07060		4.833742	6.146258	33.602542	569.356993	0.022832	0.157336	0.208624	0.065732	0.061867	0.018061
	49960		7.930000	12.020000	50.410000	185.200000	0.071170	0.027290	0.000000	0.000000	0.156500	0.055040
	57700		13.010000	21.080000	84.110000	515.300000	0.116600	0.147200	0.114500	0.064930	0.250400	0.071460
	61540		14.970000	25.410000	97.660000	686.500000	0.131300	0.211900	0.226700	0.099930	0.282200	0.080040
	66120		18.790000	29.720000	125.400000	1084.000000	0.146000	0.339100	0.382900	0.161400	0.317900	0.092080
	97440		36.040000	49.540000	251.200000	4254.000000	0.222600	1.058000	1.252000	0.291000	0.663800	0.207500

Fig. (1). Descriptive statistics.

The purpose of visualizing the data here is to see which features are most effective for predicting malignant or benign cancer and see if any general trends can help us with model and hyper-parameter selection.

Apply three strategies to understand each attribute of your dataset individually.

- Histograms.
- Box and Whisker Plots.
- Density Plots

of observations

diagnosis

B   357

M   212

Fig. (2). Observations and count.

The conversion of the diagnosis category data into numeric data is validated using binary encoding, with

- Malignant = 1. (indicates the presence of cancer cells)
- 0 (Benign) = 0 (Benign) = 0 (Benign) (indicates absence)

Three hundred fifty-seven observations show the lack of cancer cells and 212 observations that reveal the presence of cancer cells.

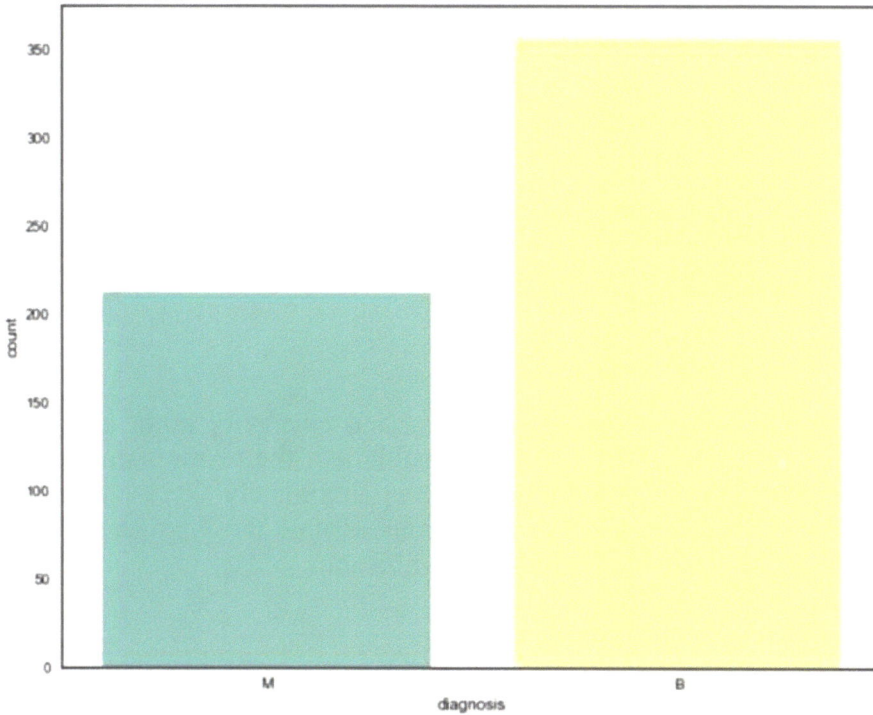

Fig. (3). The Graph Of Benign and Malignant Tumors.

Histograms:

Histograms are a popular way to depict numerical data. After the variable values are grouped (binned) into a finite number of intervals, a histogram is similar to a bar chart (bins).

Histograms divide data into bins and count how many observations are in each bin. It can be seen whether a property is Gaussian, skewed, or has an exponential distribution by looking at the shape of the bins. It can also help spot potential outliers.

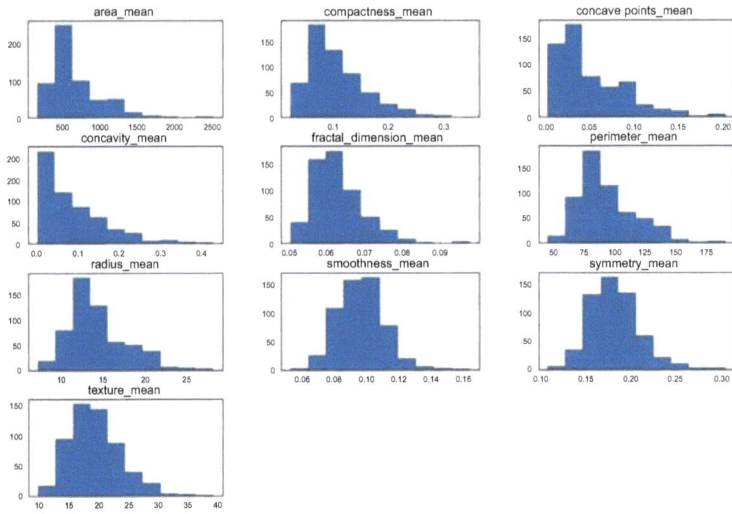

Fig. (4). Histograms.

We can see that the attributes concavity and concavity point could have an exponential distribution (). It is also possible that the texture, smoothness, and symmetry attributes have a Gaussian or approximately Gaussian distribution. Because many machine learning algorithms assume the input variables have a Gaussian univariate distribution, this is significant.

Density Plots:

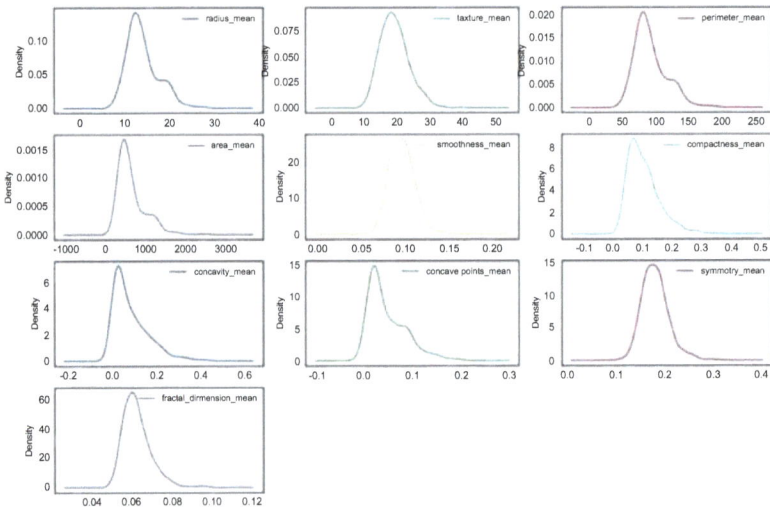

Fig. (5). Density Plots Deception.

We can see that the perimeter, radius, area, concavity, and attribute parameters may have an exponential distribution (). It is also feasible that roughness, smoothness, and symmetry distributions are Gaussian or nearly Gaussian. This is important because many machine learning algorithms assume the input variables have a Gaussian univariate distribution.

Box Plots

The parameters perimeter, radius, area, concavity, and impactness all have a conceivable exponential distribution, as can be seen (). We can also see that roughness, smoothness, and symmetry have a Gaussian or roughly Gaussian distribution. This is important because many machine learning algorithms assume that the input variables have a Gaussian univariate distribution.

Multimodal Data Visualizations

- Scatter plots
- Correlation matrix

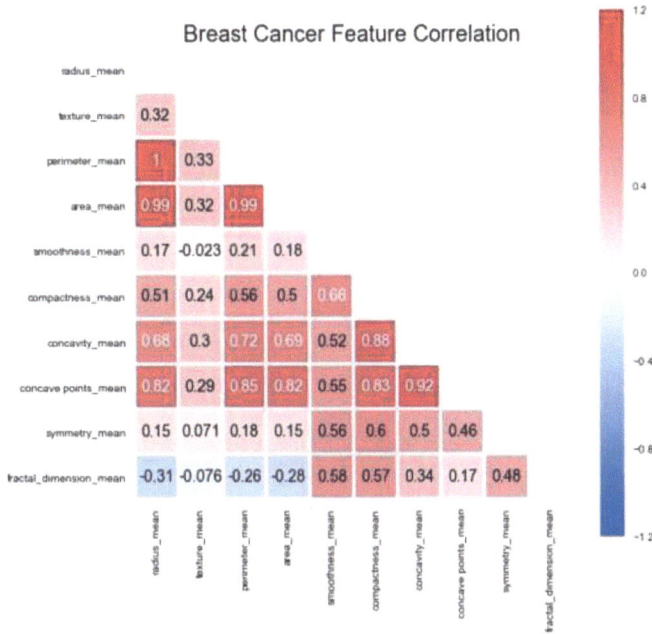

Fig. (6). Correlation Matrix.

We can observe that the mean values parameter has a substantial positive relationship between 1-and 0.75.

The mean area of the tissue nucleus has a relatively favorable relationship (r between 0.5-0.75) with concavity and area, concavity and perimeter, and other characteristics.

Similar to radius, texture, and parameter mean values, the fractal dimension has a strong negative correlation.

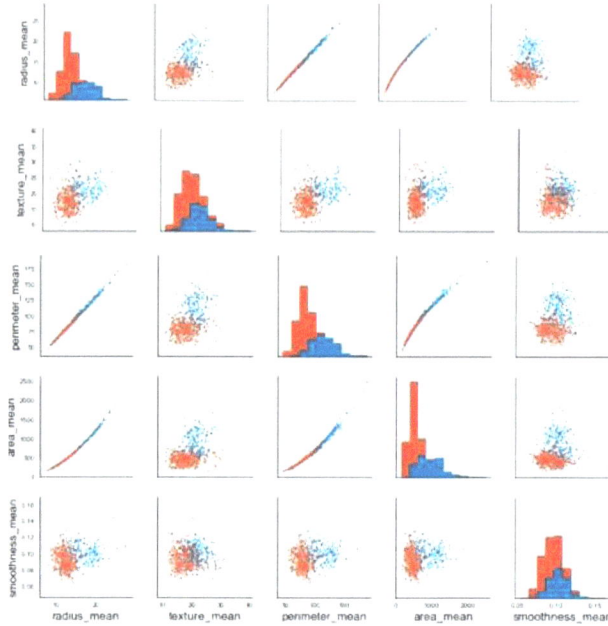

Fig. (7). Scatter Plot Deception.

Perimeter, Mean values of cell radius, area, compactness, concavity, and concave regions can be used to categorize cancer. Higher values of these indicators are linked to the existence of malignant tumors. There are no clear significant outliers that need to be cleaned up in any histograms.

Methodology:

These are the following methods and algorithms discussed in this paper, for the classification of Breast cancer using the WBCD data set.

XGboost Classifier: XGBoost (eXtreme Gradient Boosting) is a set of gradient boosting techniques targeted to contemporary data science issues and technology. The key benefits of XGBoost are that it is highly scalable/parallelizable, quick to run, and frequently outperforms other methods. It also controls over-fitting with a more regularised model formalization, resulting in increased performance [14].

KNN:

A non-parametric classification method is a k-NN approach. Class membership is the result of this categorization. The object is assigned to the most frequent class among its k nearest neighbors after a majority of its neighbors vote to classify it (k is a positive integer, typically small). If k = 1, the item is assigned to the item's closest neighbor class. It is the most basic of all the machine learning algorithms [15].

This model has a 98 percent accuracy rate and a 96 percent three-fold cross-validation accuracy rate.

```
[[107    0]
 [ 10   54]]
                 precision    recall   f1-score    support

             0       0.91      1.00       0.96        107
             1       1.00      0.84       0.92         64

      accuracy                            0.94        171
     macro avg       0.96      0.92       0.94        171
  weighted avg       0.95      0.94       0.94        171
```

Fig. (8). KNN Output.

Random Forest: A random forest is a classifier made up of a group of random-based regression trees that are independently identically distributed outputs of a randomization variable and are used to classify data. These random trees are then concatenated to give aggregate regression estimates.

The training set does not include any resampling or bootstrapping steps, and the model is independent of the training sample. Random forest, in general, takes an existing input parameter, crosses it with each tree in the forest, and then averages the replies of all trees. Each tree must take into consideration a unique set of random factors. Calculate the error if the parameter value appears in every out-o--bag (OOB) observation while selecting the most informative parameter. The prediction error increases when the parameter value reported in all OOB observations is computed for each tree, then the entire ensemble is averaged and divided by the ensemble's standard deviation [16].

Ada-Boost (Adaptive Boosting): Ada-Boost is an iterative ensemble boosting classifier. Combine all of the low-performing classifiers to create a robust classifier with high accuracy. The idea behind Adaboost is to train the data using various weights for the classifier at each iteration. This enables you to forecast abnormal observations with pinpoint accuracy. AdaBoost is a method for training an upgraded classifier.

Decisions Tree:

The Decision Tree is a supervised learning technique for solving classification and regression issues. It is, nevertheless, most typically used to tackle categorization problems. In this tree-structured classifier, internal nodes hold dataset properties, branches provide decision rules, and each leaf node concludes.

A Decision tree's two nodes are the Decision Node and the Leaf Node. Choice nodes are used to make any decision and have numerous branches, whereas Leaf nodes result from such decisions and do not have any more branches.

The evaluations or tests are based on the qualities of the dataset that has been presented.

On the test set of the WBCD dataset, the accuracy was 93 percent, with a 3-fold cross-validation accuracy score of 90 percent.

```
Accuracy on training set: 1.000
Accuracy on test set: 0.930
[[102    5]
 [  7   57]]
               precision    recall  f1-score   support

           0       0.94      0.95      0.94       107
           1       0.92      0.89      0.90        64


    accuracy                           0.93       171
   macro avg       0.93      0.92      0.92       171
weighted avg       0.93      0.93      0.93       171
```

Fig. (9). Decision Tree Output.

SVM:

Support Vector Machine is a classification and regression technique.

It is, however, most typically linked to categorization issues. This method is typically used to solve classification issues.

- Even if the data includes just a few characteristics, SVMs allow for complicated decision boundaries.
- They operate well with both low-dimensional and high-dimensional data (i.e., few and many features), but they do not scale well with sample size.
- SVMs need rigorous data preparation and parameter optimization. This is why, in many situations, people nowadays choose to employ tree-based models such as random forests or gradient boosting (which need little or no preprocessing).
- SVM models are tough to inspect; it might be challenging to comprehend why a specific prediction was produced, and explaining the model to a nonexpert can be challenging.

Each data point is plotted in n-dimensional space (where n is the number of features), with the feature value representing the value of a specific coordinate. The two classes can then be distinguished by determining the hyper-plane that effectively divides them.

Kernel SVMs have a lot of crucial parameters that must be considered.

Regularization parameter C, kernel choice (linear, radial basis function (RBF), or polynomial) Kernel-specific parameters.

The model's complexity is controlled by the values of gamma and C, with large values of either resulting in a more sophisticated model. As a result, the two parameters' optimal values are frequently linked, and C and gamma values should be tweaked together.

Algorithm used:

```
%matplotlib inline
import matplotlib.pyplot as plt

#Load libraries for data processing
import pandas as pd #data processing, CSV file I/O (e.g. pd.read_csv)
import numpy as np
from scipy.stats import norm
```

```python
## Supervised learning.
from sklearn.preprocessing import StandardScaler
from sklearn.preprocessing import LabelEncoder
from sklearn.model_selection import train_test_split
from sklearn.svm import SVC
from sklearn.model_selection import cross_val_score
from sklearn.pipeline import make_pipeline
from sklearn.metrics import confusion_matrix
from sklearn import metrics, preprocessing
from sklearn.metrics import classification_report

# visualization
import seaborn as sns
plt.style.use('fivethirtyeight')
sns.set_style("white")

plt.rcParams['figure.figsize'] = (8,4)
#plt.rcParams['axes.titlesize'] = 'large'


data = pd.read_csv('data/clean-data.csv', index_col=False)
data.drop('Unnamed: 0',axis=1, inplace=True)
#data.head()



#Assign predictors to a variable of ndarray (matrix) type
array = data.values
X = array[:,1:31] # features
y = array[:,0]

#transform the class labels from their original string representation (M and B) into integers
le = LabelEncoder()
y = le.fit_transform(y)

# Normalize the  data (center around 0 and scale to remove the variance).
scaler =StandardScaler()
Xs = scaler.fit_transform(X)
# 5. Divide records in training and testing sets.
X_train, X_test, y_train, y_test = train_test_split(Xs, y, test_size=0.3, random_state=2, stratify=y)

# 6. Create an SVM classifier and train it on 70% of the data set.
clf = SVC(probability=True)
clf.fit(X_train, y_train)

 #7. Analyze accuracy of predictions on 30% of the holdout test sample.
classifier_score = clf.score(X_test, y_test)
print '\nThe classifier accuracy score is {:03.2f}\n'.format(classifier_score)
```

```
# Get average of 3-fold cross-validation score using an SVC estimator.
n_folds = 3
cv_error = np.average(cross_val_score(SVC(), Xs, y, cv=n_folds))
print '\nThe {}-fold cross-validation accuracy score for this classifier is {:.2f}\n'.format(n_folds, cv_error)


from sklearn.feature_selection import SelectKBest, f_regression
clf2 = make_pipeline(SelectKBest(f_regression, k=3),SVC(probability=True))

scores = cross_val_score(clf2, Xs, y, cv=3)

# Get average of 3-fold cross-validation score using an SVC estimator.
n_folds = 3
cv_error = np.average(cross_val_score(SVC(), Xs, y, cv=n_folds))
print '\nThe {}-fold cross-validation accuracy score for this classifier is {:.2f}\n'.format(n_folds, cv_error)


print scores
avg = (100*np.mean(scores), 100*np.std(scores)/np.sqrt(scores.shape[0]))
print "Average score and uncertainty: (%.2f +- %.3f)%%"%avg
```

Model Accuracy: Receiver Operating Characteristic (ROC) curve:

Consider the confusion matrix, which is a two-dimensional table with the classifier model on the vertical axis and ground truth on the horizontal, as shown below. There are two potential values for each of these axes (as depicted).

Model says "+"	Model says "-"	
True positive	False negative	**Actual: "+"**
False positive	True negative	Actual: "-"

Fig. (10). Confusion Matrix.

As mentioned above, the values "true positive," "false negative," "false positive," and "true negative" are events (or their probabilities). In a ROC curve, "True Positive Rate" is plotted on the Y-axis, and "False Positive Rate" is plotted on the X-axis.

The true positive rate (tpr) is the chance that the model will output "+" when the true value is "+." (i.e., a conditional probability). This, however, does not indicate the chance of accurately calling "+" (i.e., the likelihood of a real positive if the test result is "+").

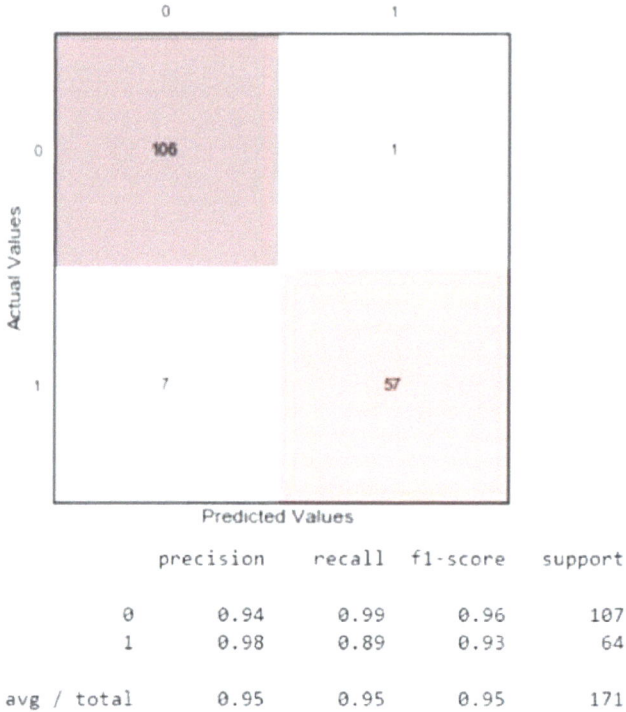

	precision	recall	f1-score	support
0	0.94	0.99	0.96	107
1	0.98	0.89	0.93	64
avg / total	0.95	0.95	0.95	171

Fig. (11). SVM Results.

A total of 174 predictions were produced by the classifier.

The classifier correctly predicted "yes" 58 times and "no" 113 times out of 174 instances.

In actuality, 64 of the 107 people in the sample have the condition, whereas the remaining 107 do not.

Rates as computed from the confusion matrix

1. Accuracy: (57+106)/171 = 0.95

2. Misclassification Rate: (1+7)/171 = 0.05

3. True Positive Rate Yes = 57/64 = 0.89, also known as "Sensitivity" or "Recall"

4. False Positive Rate: 1/107 = 0.01 FP/actual no

5. .Specificity: TN/actual no = 106/107 = 0.99.

6. Precision: Yes = 57/58 = 0.98

7. Prevalence: 64/171 = 0.34;

RESULTS

We find that SVMs perform better and are more accurate than CNN as the training data grows. The performance of the kNN classifier is dependent on the value of k. The worse the result, the lower the value of k, and the better the result, the higher the value of k.

In comparison to kNN, PCA is more sensitive to SVM. The SVM results better when the main component (PC) value grows, and the accuracy rating exceeds the kNN. For PC = 1 and K = 9, the maximum accuracy rating (97.95) is obtained.

It can be deduced that the SVM has the maximum accuracy of 99 percent, compared to 98 percent for KNN and 93 percent for Random forest. The SVM has a three-fold cross-validation accuracy score of 97 percent, the KNN has 96 percent, and the Random Forest has 90 percent. In comparison to the other methods presented, these results indicate that SVM is the best choice for the classification of Breast cancer in this dataset.

CONCLUSION

In conclusion, the paper presents a view on the analysis of different algorithms both structured and unstructured. The dataset used is the WBCD, the missing values were eliminated and preprocessing was done using EDA (Exploratory Data Analysis), the algorithms employed showed varied results. With SVM being the most accurate. Other algorithms also showed promising results but SVM was the most efficient.

ACKNOWLEDGEMENTS

Acknowledgment to Principal, Jyothy Institute of technology to support in conducting research work.

REFERENCES

[1]   https://www.cancer.org/cancer/breast-cancer/screening-tests-and-early-detection.html

[2]   Aalaei, Shokoufeh, Hadi Shahraki, Alireza Rowhanimanesh, and Saeid Eslami. "Feature selection using genetic algorithm for breast cancer diagnosis: experiment on three different datasets." Iranian journal of basic medical sciences 19, no. 5, pp. 476, 2016.

[3]   Memon, Muhammad Hammad, Jian Ping Li, Amin Ul Haq, Muhammad Hunain Memon, and Wang Zhou. "Breast cancer detection in the IOT health environment using modified recursive feature selection." wireless communications and mobile computing pp. 1-19, 2019.

[4]   W. Zhou, *Hindawi Wireless Communications and Mobile Computing Volume*, 2019.

[5]   Jue Zhang, Li Chen, and Fazeel Abid. "Prediction of Breast Cancer from Imbalance Respect Using Cluster-Based Undersampling Method". *Hindawi Journal of Healthcare Engineering Volume 2019*, Article ID 7294582, 10 pages.

[6]   Graja, M. Azam, N. Bouguila. "Breast Cancer Diagnosis using Quality Control Charts and Logistic Regression-Omar". In 2018 9th International Symposium on Signal, Image, Video and Communications (ISIVC), pp. 215-220. IEEE, 2018.

[7]   Mert, Ahmet, Niyazi Kılıç, Erdem Bilgili, and Aydin Akan. "Breast cancer detection with reduced feature set." Computational and mathematical methods in medicine Volume 2015, Article ID 265138, pp. 11, 2015.

[8]   Abdulkareem, Sulyman Age, and Zainab Olorunbukademi Abdulkareem. "An evaluation of the Wisconsin breast cancer dataset using ensemble classifiers and RFE feature selection." Int. J. Sci., Basic Appl. Res. 55, no. 2, pp. 67-80, 2012.,

[9]   Y-Q. Liu, C. Wang, and L. Zhang, "Decision tree-based predictive models for breast cancer survivability on imbalanced data", *Proceedings of the 2009 3rd International Conference on Bioinformatics and Biomedical Engineering,* pp. 1-4, 2009. [http://dx.doi.org/10.1109/ICBBE.2009.5162571]

[10]   K. Gr ̦abczewski, and W. Duch, "Heterogeneous forests of decision trees", *International Conference on Artificial Neural Networks,* pp. 504-509, 2002.

[11]   S. Dreiseitl, and L. Ohno-Machado, "Logistic regression and artificial neural network classification models: a methodology review", *J. Biomed. Inform.,* vol. 35, no. 5-6, pp. 352-359, 2002. [http://dx.doi.org/10.1016/S1532-0464(03)00034-0] [PMID: 12968784]

[12]   G.I. Salama, M. Abdelhalim, and M.A-e. Zeid, "Breast cancer diagnosis on three different datasets using multi-classifiers", *Breast Cancer,* vol. 32, no. 569, p. 2, 2012. [WDBC].

[13]   https://archive.ics.uci.edu/ml/datasets/Breast+Cancer+Wisconsin+(Diagnostic)

[14]   G. gayakwad, C. kumari. "Breast Cancer Detection Using Machine Learning Classifier". *International Journal of Multidisciplinary and Current Educational Research (IJMCER)* ISSN: 2581- 7027 Vol 3, no 4, pp. 115-121, 2021.

[15]   J. Salvador–Meneses, Z. Ruiz–Chavez and J. Garcia–Rodriguez. "Compressed kNN: K-Nearest Neighbors with Data Compression". *Facultad de Ingeniería, Ciencias Físicas y Matemática, Universidad Central del Ecuador*, Quito 170129, Ecuador.

[16]   T. L. Octaviani and Z. Rustam. "Random forest for breast cancer prediction". In AIO AIP Conference Proceedings. Vol. 2168, pp. 020050; Published Online: 04 November 2019. [http://dx.doi.org/10.1063/1.5132477]

## CHAPTER 7

Application and Evaluation of Machine Learning Algorithms in Classifying Cardiotocography (CTG) Signals

Srishti Sakshi Sinha[1] and **Uma Vijayasundaram**[1,*]

[1] *M.Tech CSE, Pondicherry University, Puducherry, India*

Abstract: Cardiotocography (CTG) is a clinical procedure performed to monitor fetal health by recording uterine contractions and the fetal heart rate continuously. This procedure is carried out mainly in the third trimester of pregnancy. This work aims at proving the significance of upsampling the data using SMOTE (Synthetic Minority Oversampling Technique) in classifying the CTG traces. The project includes the comparison of different Machine Learning approaches, namely, Logistic Regression, Support Vector Machine (SVM), Naïve Bayes, Decision Tree, Random Forest, and K-nearest Neighbor (KNN) classifiers on the CTG dataset to classify the records into three classes: normal, suspicious and pathological. The results prove that applying SMOTE increases the performance of the classifiers.

Keywords: Classification algorithms, CTG, Decision Tree, Fetal Heart Rate, K-nearest Neighbors, Logistic Regression, Naïve Bayes, Random Forest, Support Vector Machine.

INTRODUCTION

Doctor Alan Bradfield, Orvan Hess, and Edward Hon invented Fetal Monitoring and Cardiotocography (CTG), a technical method of fetal monitoring by continuously recording the fetal heart rate (FHR) and the Uterine Contractions (UC) during pregnancy. The machine used to perform CTG is called Cardiotocograph, aka Electronic Fetal Monitoring (EFM). Later, Konrad Hammacher developed CTG for Hewlett-Packard.

CTG monitoring is used to assess fetal well-being and is performed in the third trimester of pregnancy. There are two methods for carrying out CTG: External and Internal. The external CTG can be used for continuous or intermittent monito-

---

* **Corresponding author Uma Vijayasundaram:** Assistant Professor, Department of Computer Science, Pondicherry University, Puducherry, India; Email: umabskr@gmail.com

Gyanendra Verma & Rajesh Doriya (Eds.)

ring. The FHR and UC are detected using the transducers attached to the mother's body.

The internal CTG is mainly used for more accurate tracking since it is detected by attaching electronic transducers to the fetal scalp. CTG is practiced because it assesses fetal health and well-being and identifies any changes that may or may not be associated with any complications or issues that may arise during pregnancy or labor. It is conducive to high-risk pregnancy conditions.

Different classification approaches have been applied for CTG analysis to date. Machine learning approaches like Support Vector Machine (SVM), Random Forest classifier (RF Classifier), K-nearest Neighbor (K-NN) [1, 2], decision tree, and Deep learning approaches like Artificial Neural Network (ANN), Deep Neural Network (DeepNN) [3], Convolutional Neural Network (CNN), Long Short-Term Memory Neural Network (LSTM-NN), *etc.* have been used till now. An advanced Deep Learning enhanced technology might be used to analyze the CTG traces in real-time with better accuracy than clinicians. This is why experiments and studies are going on in this field. This experiment studies different classification models in Machine learning (ML) and Deep Learning (DL) and their behavior on CTG datasets. Classification algorithms are used for predictive modeling where a class for a set of inputs is predicted. In simple terms, in machine learning, the data is used to train the algorithms, models are built based on the training, and decisions are made by the models based on what they have been taught. While deep learning algorithms learn and make intelligent decisions on their own. They have the capacity to execute feature engineering on their own. Deep Learning, a subset of Machine learning, is performed using advanced machine learning approaches. The features used in implementations make an important impact on how the algorithm will behave. Thus, feature engineering is a necessary procedure to be carried out while implementing any classification approach. Feature engineering mainly has two goals: to prepare an input dataset that is compatible with the learning models' requirements and improve the models' performance. Few of the techniques for feature engineering techniques are outlier detection, log transform, scaling, one-hot encoding, *etc*. The machine models used for classification in this study are Logistic Regression, the probabilistic classifier viz. Naïve Bayes classifier, Instance based classifier viz. K-nearest Neighbor, SVM, Decision Tree, and the ensemble classifier viz. Random Forest Classifier.

The following section provides a survey of the works related to CTG analysis. The architectural details follow this. The basic ML models are explained in the section Models and Methods. The experimentation details and result analysis are provided in further sections, along with performance measures and experimental analysis and results.

LITERATURE REVIEW

Since the invention of CTG, or continuous fetal heart record in 1957, many types of research have been carried out on and off since the mid-1980s. Different researchers have tried different approaches for the classification of CTG recordings. Czabanski *et al.* classified the fetal state using a hybrid model, viz. ANN-based on Logical Interpretation of Fuzzy rules [4]. Hakan Sakin *et al.* used a hybrid model comprising ANN and Simple Logistic for the same purpose [5]. Zafer Comert *et al.* published several papers in this field. They have done studies and experiments on different models like ANN and variations of Neural Network such as Deep CNN and other ML classifiers for CTG classification [6, 7], hypoxia detection [8], prediction, and assessment of the fetal distress during the trimester of pregnancy [9, 10]. Along with these, they have developed a useful software for CTG Analysis called CTG-OAS, which is an open-access software. The input can be a CTG recording in MATLAB file format. It offers several features like preprocessing of the CTG record and extraction of morphological, time domain, nonlinear and IBTF features, as well as application of SVM, ANN, and K-nearest Neighbor classifiers. Satish Chandra *et al.* published a paper on classification and feature selection approaches for CTG using ML techniques. They applied the same techniques that we have used but on a different dataset [1]. Noora Jamal *et al.* applied the Firefly algorithm and Naïve Bayesian classifier to the CTG dataset and achieved better prediction accuracy [11]. C. Ricciardi *et al.* have implemented SMOTE and various ML algorithms on the CTG dataset for the classification of the type of delivery from CTG signals [2]. Haijing Tang *et al.* and MS Iraji *et al.* have experimented on neural networks with different variations for the classification [12, 13].

Adulaziz Alsayyari experimented with Legendre Neural Network for CTG monitoring as well [14]. Bursa *et al.* have experimented with the use of CNN in biomedical data processing [15]. PA Warrik *et al.* classified intrapartum fetal state using an LSTM [16]. Paul Fergus *et al.* published a paper about their most recent work, which included the application of Multilayer Feedforward NN, one dimensional-CNN, and other ML classifiers for modeling segmented CTG time-series signals [17]. Zhidong Zhao *et al.* performed several experiments as well. Their recent investigation implemented 8- layer deep CNN and CWT on CTG signals for intelligent prediction of fetal academia [3]. This model achieved higher sensitivity (True Positive Rate) and specificity (True Negative Rate) when compared with other modern methods.

Before presenting the proposed work, we would like to highlight the contribution and merit of the proposed system.

1. SMOTE (Synthetic Minority Oversampling Technique) is applied to the dataset to overcome the class imbalance problem.

2. Upsampling performed using SMOTE improves the performance of the ML algorithms.

ARCHITECTURE AND DATASET DETAILS

The project is about studying and implementing several classification models of Machine Learning in python on a text-based CTG dataset. The multivariate dataset is the CTG recordings from UCI Machine Learning Repository. This dataset has 2126 CTG traces. The dataset is the textual records of the recordings donated by the Biomedical Engineering Institute, Porto, and the University of Porto, Porto, Portugal, in the year 2010. The dataset has 21 attributes as input characteristics, and the output is predicted according to the final output attribute, NSP, which stands for normal, suspicious, and pathological. The architecture and flow of this project are described in Fig. (**1**).

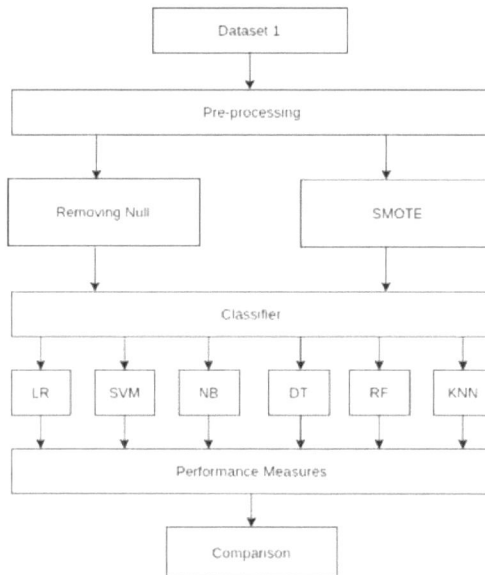

Fig. (1). Architecture of the Proposed System.

MODELS AND METHODS

Following are the models that have been implemented in python on the CTG datasets:

Logistic Regression

Logistic Regression is used when the target variable (variable to be predicted) is categorical. A classic example of logistic regression is the spam filter in which the email is spam or is not predicted. In classification problems, the prediction is made in discrete values. Classifications can be binary or multiclass. The logistic function is also called the sigmoid function. Logistic regression is widely used in many ML applications.

```python
Python code block:
from sklearn.linear_model import LogisiticRegression
lrmodel = LogisticRegression(max_iter=2200)
lrmodel.fit(X_train,y_train)
prediction1 = lrmodel.predict(X_test)
```

Support Vector Machine

The objective of the SVM algorithm is to maximize the margin of the hyperplane that classifies the points in the N-dimensional input space. It is widely used for classification but can also be used for regression too. SVM produces significant accuracy with less computation power. Separating two classes of data points can be done with many possible hyperplanes. But, SVM finds an optimal plane using the concept of the Lagrange multiplier.

```python
Python code block:
from sklearn.svm import SVC
SVMmodel = SVC()
SVMmodel.fit(X_train,y_train)
prediction2 = SVMmodel.predict(X_test)
```

Naïve Bayes

Naïve Bayes is a machine learning model based on the concept of the Bayes Theorem. Bayes theorem finds the probability that a hypothesis A will happen, given that the evidence B that has occurred can be calculated. The model assumes that features are independent, which means the presence of one feature doesn't bother the other. That's why it is called Naïve. The types of Naïve Bayes are – Multinomial, Bernoulli and Gaussian Naïve Bayes. This algorithm is fast and easy to implement. But in real-life datasets, the features can be co-dependent, which may hinder the classifier's performance. In this study, we have used Gaussian Naïve Bayes.

```python
Python code block:
from sklearn.naive_bayes import GaussianNB
nb = GaussianNB()
nb.fit(X_train, y_train)
prediction3 = nb.predict(X_test)
```

Decision Tree

A decision tree is a powerful tool for real-world datasets. It is also used in the construction of a Random Forest classifier. A decision tree is constructed by finding the splitting criteria (feature) using the information present in the training dataset. The best splitting feature is identified using any of the three approaches, viz., Information Gain, Gain ratio, and Gini index. The decision tree is constructed based on the best splitting criteria identified using the abovementioned algorithms. A decision tree is a hierarchical structure having nodes and directed edges. A decision tree with more depth results in overfitting. So, an optimal decision tree is to be constructed to achieve better classification accuracy.

```python
Python code block:
from sklearn.tree import DecisionTreeClassifier()
dtree = DecisionTreeClassifier()
dtree.fit(X_train, y_train)
prediction4 = dtree.predict(X_test)
```

Random Forest

Random Forest is an ensemble-based classification technique used in machine learning. It trains several decision trees in parallel, and the training is followed by the aggregation of their outputs. That is, each decision tree makes its own prediction, and then the class with the most number of predictions becomes the classifier's prediction. It also maintains that each decision tree is not too correlated with the other. Bagging (Bootstrap Aggregation) and Feature Randomness are two techniques for the same, i.e., to ensure that every tree is different from the other. The training set can significantly affect the working of a decision tree. Random forest works on the principle of random sampling with replacement. Since the decision trees in Random Forest are constructed using a random subset of features, the resultant classification is more accurate. This results in more variation, less correlation, and more diversification in the trees. This is called feature randomness.

```python
Python code block:
from sklearn.ensemble import RandomForestClassifier
rfc = RandomForestClassifier()
rfc.fit(X_train, y_train)
prediction5 = rfc.predict(X_test)
```

K-nearest Neighbor

K-nearest Neighbor algorithm is an instance-based parameterized machine learning algorithm used for performing regression and classification. The algorithm works on the principle that objects with similar features exist together in the feature space. K represents the number of neighbors to be considered in performing classification or regression. For each test sample in the dataset, the distance between the various data points in the feature space and the test sample is calculated using either Euclidean distance or Manhattan distance. Euclidean distance is widely used. The classification of the test sample is done by performing majority voting. The distances of the samples to the test sample are arranged, and the closest K neighbors are identified. Then, majority voting is performed in the case of classification. For regression, the mean of the K labels and for classification, the mode of the K labels is considered. The advantage of the K-nearest Neighbor is that it is easy to implement and is simple. There's no need to build an entire model or tune several parameters, *etc*. And the disadvantage of this algorithm is that the algorithm gets significantly slower with the increase in data or features. It is otherwise called a lazy learner.

```
Python code block:
from sklearn.neighbors import KNeighborsClassifier
knn = KNeighborsClassifier(n_neighbors = 2)
knn.fit(X_train, y_train)
prediction6 = knn.predict(X_test)
```

SMOTE (Synthetic Minority Oversampling Technique)

Imbalanced datasets reduce the performance of the classification algorithms. To overcome this drawback, SMOTE approach is used in our proposed system. Using this approach, duplicates of minority classes are created, and the dataset is balanced. When ML algorithms are applied to this balanced dataset, better results are obtained.

Method

This is an experimental study of the application and analysis of different Machine Learning classification algorithms on the CTG dataset. The experimentation is performed using the libraries in Python. Python libraries that are used in this experiment are NumPy, pandas, matplotlib, scipy, imb-learn, and sci-kit-learn. Using these libraries, we have preprocessed the data, performed SMOTE – Synthetic Minority Oversampling Technique, and applied the models mentioned above to the dataset. SMOTE is the method to upsample the dataset. Since the original dataset had 2126 records, we applied smote and upsampled the dataset so that we could achieve better accuracy. The resultant dataset was found to be balanced, and hence the ML algorithms performed better. Table 1 presents the details regarding the various parameters used in implementing the model.

Table 1. Models used in ML algorithms

S.No.	ML Algorithms	Models Used
1	Logistic Regression	sklearn.linear_model
2	Decision Tree	sklearn.tree
3	Naïve Bayes	sklearn.naive_bayes
4	SVM	sklearn.svm

S.No.	ML Algorithms	Models Used
5	KNN	sklearn.neighbors
6	Random Forest	sklearn.ensemble

PERFORMANCE MEASURES

The measures used in evaluating the proposed system are precision, recall, f1-score, and accuracy. These values are calculated using the confusion matrix. The confusion matrix shows the True Positive (TP), True Negative (TN), False Positive (FP), and False Negative (FN) based on the actual and predicted labels in the dataset. The confusion matrix function available in python is used for this purpose.

Precision: Precision helps us in knowing the prediction accuracy. It is found by dividing the correctly predicted positive samples by the total samples predicted as positive in the dataset. It is a measure of the accuracy of predicted positive samples.

Recall: It is the measure that finds the ratio of the number of correctly predicted positive samples to the total positive samples in the dataset. It is also called Sensitivity or True Positive Rate.

F1-Score: F1-Score can be said as the trade-off between Precision and Recall. Precision and recall are generally expected to be high, and maintaining a balance between them can become another task. So, a good F1 score can be aimed as an indication of good precision and a good recall value.

EXPERIMENTAL ANALYSIS AND RESULTS

As mentioned earlier, there are three output classes - Normal, Suspicious, and Pathological. In the preprocessing part, the null values were removed, and the upsampling of the dataset was done by SMOTE technique. The precision, recall, and f1-score values for each output class produced by the implementation of the machine learning models were recorded. The models implemented are

 i. Logistic Regression (LR)
 ii. Decision Tree (DT)
iii. Naive Bayes (NB)
 iv. Support Vector Machine (SVM)
  v. K-Nearest Neighbor (KNN)
 vi. Random Forest (RF)

The results shown in Table 2 prove that all the ML models perform better when SMOTE is applied.

Table 2. Performance analysis of ML Models

Algorithm	Classes	Precision		Recall		F1-score	
		with SMOTE	w/o SMOTE	with SMOTE	w/o SMOTE	with SMOTE	w/o SMOTE
LR	1	0.95	0.93	0.85	0.97	0.90	0.95
	2	0.81	0.67	0.85	0.90	0.83	0.57
	3	0.88	0.81	0.92	0.82	0.90	0.82
SVM	1	0.90	0.89	0.83	0.98	0.87	0.93
	2	0.78	0.64	0.84	0.45	0.81	0.53
	3	0.88	0.91	0.89	0.41	0.89	0.57
DT	1	0.92	0.94	0.94	0.96	0.93	0.95
	2	0.94	0.82	0.72	0.72	0.73	0.77
	3	0.98	0.85	0.88	0.88	0.88	0.87
RF	1	0.97	0.96	0.95	0.90	0.96	0.98
	2	0.96	0.96	0.97	0.78	0.96	0.86
	3	0.88	0.96	0.92	0.94	0.99	0.95
NB	1	0.91	0.99	0.80	0.80	0.89	0.89
	2	0.67	0.45	0.89	0.94	0.76	0.60
	3	0.85	0.63	0.67	0.63	0.75	0.63
KNN	1	0.98	0.93	0.91	0.96	0.95	0.94
	2	0.92	0.70	0.78	0.62	0.95	0.65
	3	0.98	0.93	0.99	0.82	0.99	0.87

This shows that there is a class imbalance issue in the dataset, and this can be overcome by SMOTE. ML algorithms applied to the balanced dataset provide better results. The improvement in accuracy achieved using various ML approaches when integrated with SMOTE is shown graphically in Fig. (**2**).

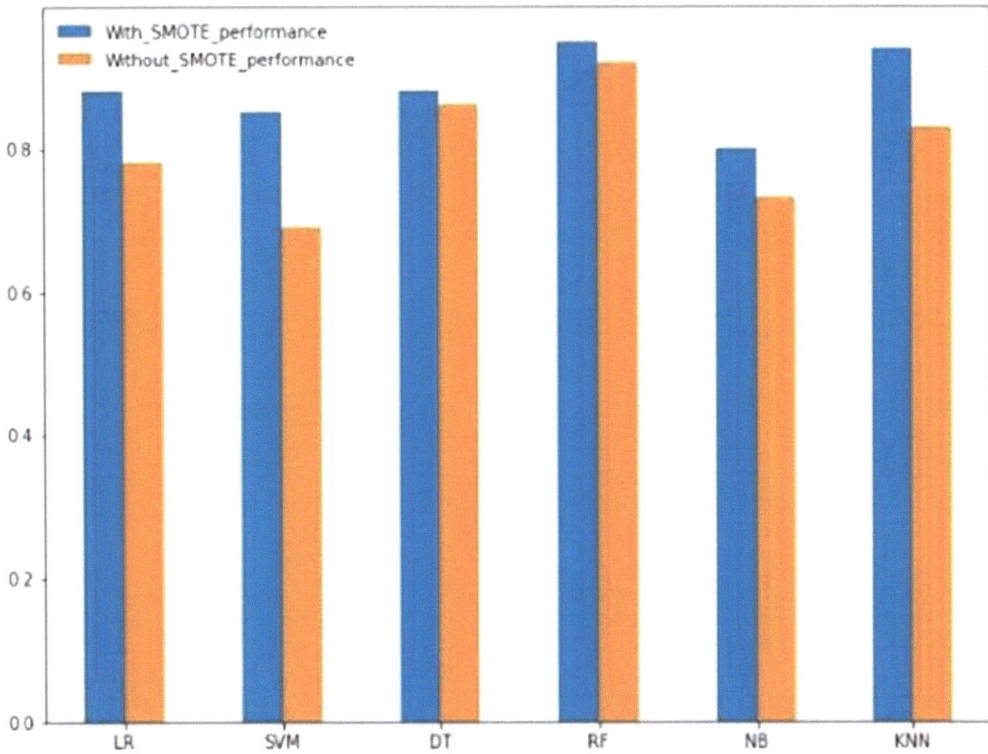

Fig. (2). Accuracy Analysis of ML Models.

CONCLUSION

The performance of various machine learning models on CTG datasets is analyzed. It was found that when the class imbalance issue was removed from the dataset, the models performed pretty well, which is represented through a comparison graph in Fig. (**2**). Since this is an experimental study about the behavior of these machine learning algorithms only, the future work for this project requires the study of Deep learning approaches and their performances on these datasets. For this entire field of research, the most recent work is the 8-layer CNN. In interpreting the CTG signals, DL algorithms can be utilized, and accuracy comparable to the clinician interpretation can be achieved. This could result in better neonatal outcomes. Thus, the future scope of this project is to implement the Deep CNN model so that it yields, even more, higher accuracy.

CONSENT FOR PUBLICATION

Not applicable.

CONFLICT OF INTEREST

The authors declare no conflict of interest, financial or otherwise.

ACKNOWLEDGEMENT

Declared none.

REFERENCES

[1]   S.C.R. Nandipati and C. XinYing, "Classification and Feature Selection Approaches for Cardiotocography by Machine Learning Techniques". ISSN: 2180 – 1843 e- ISSN: 2289-8131, 2020.

[2]   G. Ricciardi, Improta, F. Amato, G. Cesarelli, M. Romano, "Classifying the type of delivery from cardiotocographic signals: A machine learning approach". ISSN 0169-2607, 2020. [http://dx.doi.org/10.1016/j.cmpb.2020.105712]

[3]   Z. Zhao, Y. Deng, Y. Zhang, Y. Zhang, X. Zhang, and L. Shao, "DeepFHR: intelligent prediction of fetal Acidemia using fetal heart rate signals based on convolutional neural network", *BMC Med. Inform. Decis. Mak.,* vol. 19, no. 1, p. 286, 2019. [http://dx.doi.org/10.1186/s12911-019-1007-5] [PMID: 31888592]

[4]   R. Czabanski, M. Jezewski, J. Wrobel, K. Horoba, and J. Jezewski, "A Neuro-Fuzzy Approach to the Classification of Fetal Cardiotocograms". In: Katashev A., Dekhtyar Y., Spigulis J. (eds) 14th Nordic-Baltic Con-ference on Biomedical Engineering and Medical Physics. IFMBE Proceedings, vol 20. Springer, Berlin, Heidelberg [http://dx.doi.org/10.1007/978-3-540-69367-3_120]

[5]   H. Sahin and A. Subasi. "Classification of Fetal State from the Cardiotocogram Recordings using ANN and Simple Logistic." In: ISSD Conference, Bosnia & Herzegovina.

[6]   Cömert, Z. Kocamaz, A. Gungor, Sami. "Cardiotocography signals with artificial neural network and extreme learning machine". In: 2016 24th Signal Processing and Communication Application Conference (SIU) 1493-1496. 10.1109/SIU.2016.7496034. Turkey

[7]   Z. Cömert, and A. Kocamaz, "A Study of Artificial Neural Network Training Algorithms for Classification of Cardiotocography Signals", *Bitlis Eren University Journal of Science and Technology,* vol. 7, no. 2, pp. 93-103, 2017. [Turkey.]. [http://dx.doi.org/10.17678/beuscitech.338085]

[8]   Cömert, Zafer & KOCAMAZ, Adnan. "A Study Based on Gray Level Co- Occurrence Matrix and Neural Network Community for Determination of Hypoxic Fetuses". In: International Artificial Intelligence and Data Processing Symposium'16, Malatya.,

[9]   Z. Cömert, and A. Fatih, "Evaluation of Fetal Distress Diagnosis during Delivery Stages based on Linear and Nonlinear Features of Fetal Heart Rate for Neural Network Community", *Int. J. Comput. Appl.,* vol. 156, no. 4, pp. 26-31, 2016. [Turkey.]. [http://dx.doi.org/10.5120/ijca2016912417]

[10]   Z. Cömert, and A.F. Kocamaz, "Fetal Hypoxia Detection Based on Deep Convolutional Neural Network with Transfer Learning Approach", In: *Software Engineering and Algorithms in Intelligent Systems. CSOC2018 2018. Advances in Intelligent Systems and Computing.,* R. Silhavy, Ed., vol. Vol. 763. Springer: Cham, 2019. [http://dx.doi.org/10.1007/978-3-319-91186-1_25]

[11]   N.J.A. Kadhim and J.K. Abed "Enhancing the Prediction Accuracy for Cardiotocography (CTG) using Firefly Algorithm and Naive Bayesian Classifier". In 2020 IOP Conf. Ser.: Mater. Sci. Eng 745012101

[12]   H. Tang, T. Wang, M. Li, and X. Yang, *The Design and Implementation of Cardiotocography Signals Classification Algorithm Based on Neural Network,* 2018.

[http://dx.doi.org/10.1155/2018/8568617]

[13]   M.S. Iraji, "Prediction of fetal state from the cardiotocogram recordings using neural network models", *Artif. Intell. Med.,* vol. 96, pp. 33-44, 2019.
[http://dx.doi.org/10.1016/j.artmed.2019.03.005] [PMID: 31164209]

[14]   A. Alsayyari, "Fetal cardiotocography monitoring using Legendre neural networks", *Biomedical Engineering / Biomedizinische Technik,* vol. 64, no. 6, pp. 669-675, 2019.
[http://dx.doi.org/10.1515/bmt-2018-0074] [PMID: 31199757]

[15]   Bursa, Miroslav & Lhotska, Lenka. (2017). "The Use of Convolutional Neural Networks in Biomedical Data Processing". In: International Conference on Information Technology in Bio- and Medical Informatics, Czech Republic
[http://dx.doi.org/10.1007/978-3-319-64265-9_9]

[16]   P.A. Warrick, and E.F. Hamilton, "Intrapartum fetal-state classification using long short- term memory neural networks," 2017.*Computing in Cardiology.* CinC: Rennes, 2017, pp. 1-4.
[http://dx.doi.org/10.22489/CinC.2017.262-444]

[17]   P. Fergus, C. Chalmers, C.C. Montanez, D. Reilly, P. Lisboa, and B. Pineles, "Modelling Segmented Cardiotocography Time-Series Signals Using One Dimensional Convolutional Neural Networks for the Early Detection of Abnormal Birth Outcomes",
[http://dx.doi.org/10.1109/TETCI.2020.3020061]

## CHAPTER 8

Deep SLRT: The Development of Deep Learning based Multilingual and Multimodal Sign Language Recognition and Translation Framework

Natarajan Balasubramanian[1] and **Elakkiya Rajasekar**[1,*]

[1] *Research Scholar, Assistant Professor, School of Computing, SASTRA Deemed to be University, Thanjavur, Tamilnadu, India*

Abstract: Developing deep neural models for continuous recognition of sign gestures and generation of sign videos from spoken sentences is still challenging and requires much investigation in earlier studies. Although the recent approaches provide plausible solutions for these tasks, they still fail to perform well in handling continuous sentences and visual quality aspects. The recent advancements in deep learning techniques envisioned new milestones in handling such complex tasks and producing impressive results. This paper proposes novel approaches to develop a deep neural framework for recognizing multilingual sign datasets and multimodal sign gestures. In addition to that, the proposed model generates sign gesture videos from spoken sentences. In the first fold, it deals with the sign gesture recognition tasks using a hybrid CNN-LSTM algorithm. The second fold uses the hybrid NMT-GAN techniques to produce high-quality sign gesture videos. The proposed model has been evaluated using different quality metrics. We also compared the proposed model performance qualitatively using different benchmark sign language datasets. The proposed model achieves 98% classification accuracy and improved video quality in sign language recognition and video generation tasks.

Keywords: Convolutional Neural Network, Feature extraction, Generative Adversarial Networks, Long short-term Memory, Machine Translation, Recognition, Sign Language, Subunit modeling, Translation, Video generation.

INTRODUCTION

The World Health Organization (WHO) has reported five percent of the world's population, or approximately 466 million people globally, who have hearing problems. Sign Language (SL) plays a vital role in deaf and dumb communication. Sign languages are gesture-based and follow their own grammatical rules.

---

* **Corresponding author Elakkiya Rajasekar:** Research Scholar, Assistant Professor, School of Computing, SASTRA Deemed to be University, Thanjavur, Tamilnadu, India; E-mail: elakkiyaceg@gmail.com

Sign Languages are communicated through hand expressions and involve the eye, head, and mouth movements [1]. Ordinary people's recognition of sign gestures still poses enormous difficulties in understanding and replying. Due to these issues, communication between ordinary people and deaf-mute society is lacking. Although substantial research works are carried out in this area, the problems persist in handling continuous sentences. We investigate the recent advancements in deep learning techniques and propose a novel approach to construct a robust framework to address this issue. In addition to that, the different variants of sign languages added another difficulty in handling multilingual sign gestures and multimodal features. The proposed model is developed to address all these challenges as mentioned above. The proposed model follows the bidirectional approaches to recognition and video generation tasks. The recognition of sign gestures and translating them into text involves subunit modeling [2] and manual and non-manual feature extraction methods [3, 4]. The recognition accuracy of the model will be evaluated using generated text output and cost functions. On the other hand, the sign video generation from given spoken sentences is implemented using advancements in Generative Adversarial Network (GAN) models, Recurrent Neural Network (RNN) and its variants, and neural machine translation techniques [5].

The sign video generation approach involves the translation of spoken sentences into sign glosses and mapping them with sign gesture images. The frame sequences will be arranged properly and produce a plausible video output. In general sign language, hand gestures are divided into four categories: manipulative, conversational, controlling, and communicative. Sign Language is based on the communicative type of gestures considered testbed for computer vision techniques [6]. Two main approaches are sensor-based and vision-based approaches. Sensor-based techniques use electronic devices such as surface Electromyography (sEMG)] [7], ECG [8], Data gloves [9], colored gloves [10], depth cameras [11], Kinect Sensors [12] and Leap Motion Sensors [13]. Wearing these devices creates discomfort for normal people and lacks a user-friendly approach. Vision-based techniques employ deep artificial models to recognize images or videos directly, explore deep insights about gesticulation information and benefit the users. Image segmentation, classification, and feature extraction techniques are employed for continuous DSL recognition. The classifiers such as Hidden Markov Models (HMM) [14 - 17], K-Nearest Neighbour (KNN) [18], SVM - Support Vector Machine [18], Convolutional Neural Network (CNN) [19 - 24], RNN [25], LSTM - Long short term memory [26], Recurrent CNN [27], and Gated Recurrent Unit (GRU) [28] Techniques attained wider attention in Sign Language recognition and Translation (SLRT) research. Many research works have been carried out in past decades to improve Sign Language communication using smart devices. SL entails the human body's various segments, specifically fingers, hands, mouth, arm, head, body movements, facial postures, and gaze movements to deliver information.

The recognition of continuous gestures of signers is challenging because of the occlusion, articulation, and epenthesis movements of sign language. The proposed model aims to recognize the signs accurately in a real-time, continuous, and automated way. The various dimensions of research in sign language communication are elaborated (Fig. **1**).

Fig. (1). Various dimensions of Sign Language based Deep learning Research.

The objectives of this work are listed below:

- Development of continuous sign corpus for Indian Sign Language (ISL) using multi-signers and various background conditions and lighting. This corpus mainly aimed to cover 100 common English words used daily.
- Development of SLRT Model for ISL recognition, translation, and sign video

generation by employing advancements in deep learning techniques and targeted for above 95% classification accuracy.

- Automating the SLRT process in real-time using mobile devices provides solutions to the various challenges in SLRT research areas.
- Developing an end-to-end framework for SLRT explores the real-time solution for normal people to communicate with deaf-mute and aims to provide photo-realistic high-quality sign video output.

Continuous SL recognition, translation, and video generation involve various steps of development, which are discussed in the proceeding sections. Section 2 discusses the related works of deep learning-based sign language research and developments. We also discuss the subunit modeling and manual and non-manual feature extraction techniques. Section 3 provides details about the proposed model development, and the experimental results are discussed in section 4 followed by a conclusion.

RELATED WORKS

The research studies on sign language recognition and video generation attained a broader focus among researchers to develop the framework for handling multilingual sign corpus and multimodal features of sign gestures. This section discusses the development of our own sign corpus for ISL-related research and the existing developments in SLRT research. It provides a clear understanding and pitfalls of traditional approaches. However, the development of such deep neural models should address the common challenges present in recognizing and translating sign languages. The recognition of sign gestures poses self-occlusion, epenthesis movements, co-articulation, and grammatical inflection issues, and translation involves alignment risks between sentence structure and sign sequences. Due to these challenges, the model development accolades higher complexity and grasps a broader focus in the research area. In this paper, we investigate subunit modeling, feature extraction techniques, and various deep learning algorithms to provide solutions to the challenges mentioned above that persist in the SLRT process. These approaches are identified based on complexities present in different taxonomies proposed by researchers. This work investigates the successful implementation of SLRT with above 95% accuracy and addresses the common challenges faced by the researchers. Finally, it explores valuable insights into the field of real-time automated SLRT research and points to future research directions.

Sign language gestures vary based on country and region, resulting in the development of various datasets for research purposes. The American Sign Language (ASL) word-level datasets comprise 2000 words performed by 100 signers [29]. In many educational institutes in the USA, courses for ASL have been taught to the deaf-mute community. The University of Science and Technology of China (USTC) created a video dataset for Chinese Sign Language (sentence level) using 50 signers [30]. The fingerspelling dataset for Japanese Sign Language [31] is also present. Arabic Sign Language (ArSL) annotated video data set [32] is developed. The development of continuous sign corpus for ISL is an intelligent tool that connects hearing loss and dumb people with others.

Most of the country's researchers have developed their SL datasets. The sign Language dataset constitutes sign images for alphabet and numerical numbers, words, sentences, and videos. ASL datasets [7], namely CUNY ASL, Boston ASL LVD, and MSR Gesture 3D, are present in video format for SLRT research purposes. The DEVISIGN series of CSL deals only with word-level of signs. German country Sign Language dataset named RWTH PHOENIX Weather 2014 dataset [33] and DGS Kinect 40 is developed for word and sentence level. Table **1** discusses various country-based SL datasets and elaborates on the various details. These datasets are created using different native signers and follow the cultures of other countries.

The dataset for sentence-level recognition of sign languages is limited. It shows the need for developing a sign corpus for ISL. Although various SL datasets are present globally, a standard dataset for ISL is still not available. Available resources consist of only a limited number of gesture images, isolated images for alphabets, numerical numbers, and words. The existing ISL dataset is created for a limited number of sign gestures [34]. To develop a novel heterogeneous database for ISL, it is planned to capture multiple signer sign videos for common and frequently used English words without considering background environments, illumination, and sensor devices. We created the ISL-CSLTR dataset using seven different signers. This corpus contains sentence information, class-based isolated images, and frame sequences for sentences and videos. This corpus was published in Mendeley Data and made publically available [35].

Table 1. Overview of various countries' Sign language dataset.

Reference	Sign language	Country	Dataset	Type	Level	Number of Signers	Isolated / Continuous	Sensor- Based / Vision-Based	Component Used	Annotation
Lu *et al.* [7]	ASL	USA	CUNY ASL Motion-Capture Corpus	Videos	Sentence	3	I	S	Motion Capture Camera	gloss level
Wilbur *et al.* [29]	ASL	USA	Purdue RVL-SLLL ASL Database	Images, videos	Word	14	I	V	controlled lighting condition	linguistic
Latif *et al.* [32]	ArSL	Saudi Arabia	ArASL	alphabets, images	word	40	I	V	Smart Camera	Fully labeled
Forster *et al.* [33]	GSL	Germany	RWTH-PHOENIX-Weather	Videos	Sentence	7	I	V	Color camera, dark clothes, right-dominant signers	gloss level

(Table 1) cont.....

Nandy *et al.* [34]	ISL	IIITA - ROBITA	India	Videos	word	5	I	V	Camera	gloss level
Hosoe *et al.* [35]	JSL	Japan	Japanese Finger spelling Dataset	Images	alphabets	10	I	V	RGB Camera	gloss level
Neidle *et al.* [36]	ASL	USA	Boston ASLLVD	Videos	Tokens	6	I	V	4 Synchronized Cameras	linguistic
Schembri *et al.* [37]	BSL	UK	BSLCP	Videos	Word	76	I	V	Unique color back ground	gloss level
Camgoz *et al.* [39]	TSL	Turkey	Bosphorus Sign Corpus	Videos	Word, phrases	10	C	S	Microsoft Kinect v2	Border
Fang *et al.* and Yang *et al.* [40, 41]	CSL	China	DEVISIGN- G	videos	word	8	I	V	RGB features	gloss level
			DEVISIGN- D							
			DEVISIGN-L							
Ronchetti *et al.* [42]	LSA	Argentina	LSA64	videos	word	10	I	V	RGB Camera	gloss level
Von *et al.* [43]	GSL	SIGNUM	Germany	videos	Sentence	25	C	V	Color Video Camera	gloss level annotations

* S - Sensor- Based, V - Vision-Based.

The developments of the ISL corpus help the research community with sufficient dataset availability for SLRT research. Although it was created for limited vocabularies, it can be further extended for large vocabularies in the future. The model performance using ISL corpus is analyzed in different dimensions using a wide range of deep learning techniques, and the results are shown in the experimental results section. This analysis aids the development of the SLRT model in an advanced way. The training and testing performance are compared with benchmark sign corpora. These research works encourage the researchers to focus on developing SLRT models to automate hard-of-hearing people's learning and communication processes. The sign video generation part specifically investigated using GAN models and their variants for providing high-quality videos without blurring and noisy results. The embedding of GAN with LSTM networks automatically translates the word sequences order into sign sequences order. Image interpolation techniques create the intermediate frames between two sign gesture classes and provide continuous human-based real sign gesture movements in the video output. The produced results are clear and consistent. In the last decades, many approaches have been proposed using alphabet images, numerical number images, and sign glosses images for words, sentences, and videos. Besides all the studies, the system to recognize continuous signs is still a challenging task. The conversion of speech to text and video frames are employed but still face difficulties recognizing continuous SL.

Subunit Modelling and Extraction of Manual Features and Non-manual Features

Subunit modeling deals with classifying the sign gestures into the related group of subunits [2] by reviewing the current research works. Subunit modeling is broadly divided into two ways known as linguistic-based approach and visual-based approach. Block of sign words can be explored as isolated signs to train the system. Subunit modeling handles large lexicons and tolerates sign variations [3]. Han *et al.* define that subunits are sequences of frames for sign glosses, which comprise spatial and temporal details of gestures [44]. Elakkiya R *et al.* [4] designed a 3-subunit sign modeling framework that contributes the aspects of continuous and parallel blocks of signs into subunits. Although the HMM, SVM methods used to classify the signs still lack recognition, the Continuous SL [45]. The cross signer validation strategy enhances the model performance in the signer independent environment-based performance evaluation. The numerous research works on Subunit modeling Techniques are tabulated for understanding the various parameters. Real-time efficiency, scalability, and robustness are enhanced. The estimation of subunits focuses on the spatial cues (hand) and temporal cues such as head and hand positions and the velocity of hand poses. The Bayesian model-based probability computations are performed using the eq. (1).

$$P\left(\omega_{Ma|Nm}^{ss}\right) = \frac{P\left(\omega_{Ma|Nm}^{ss}\right)h(Ma)}{P\left(\omega_{Nm|Ma}^{ss}\right)h(Ma)+P\left(\omega_{Ma|\ Nm}^{ss}\right)h(\neg Ma)} \tag{1}$$

The sign sequence is represented as ss; Ma denotes manual cues, and Nm denotes non-manual cues. The estimations of subunits use binominal condition-based opinions. Further, it extracts the various body components as features to identify the extract sign gesture word. The existing works of subunit modeling are discussed in Table **2**. It compares the multiple levels of subunit modeling in signer independent and dependant environments and also compares the various datasets used and recognition accuracy. We can optimize the model performance based on a comparison to produce more outstanding classification and recognition accuracy. We achieved above 95% accuracy in the classification of the ISL-CSLTR dataset.

Table 2. Summary of the various subunit modeling framework

Reference	Isolated/ Continuous	Signer Independent/ Dependent	Vision/Sensor	Sign level / Sub unit level	Dataset	Recognition Accuracy	Modelling frame work
Elakkiya *et al.* [4]	Isolated, Continuous	I	V	Subunit	ASLLVD, RWTH-PHOENIX-Weather dataset	97.3%	SMP-H1%IM, MEC+DTW
Bauer *et al.* [15]	Continuous	I	V	Self-organizing sub-units	own	91.80%	HMM Classifier
Han *et al.* [44]	Isolated, continuous	I	V	Subunit (Boundary detection)	ECHO²	85%	Temporal clustering

(Table 2) cont.....

Refer ence	Isolated/ Continuous	Signer Independent/ Dependent	Vision/Sensor	Sign level / Sub unit level	Dataset	Recognition Accuracy	Modelling frame work
Vogler *et al.* [46]	Isolated	D	V	Phoneme	53 Sign Vocabulary	87.71% (context Independent) 89.91% (context dependent)	HMM
Kadir *et al.* [47]	Isolated	I	V	sign	164 common lexicon words	92% (lexicon)	Sequential Boosting
Yuan *et al.* [48]	Continuous	D	V	Sub-word	40 continuous sign	70%	HMM
Fang *et al.* [49]	Isolated	D	V	Sign	CSL database	90.5%	K-means
Yang *et al.* [50]	Continuous	D	V	Sign	CSL database	NA	CRF + Epentheses THM:M
Kelly *et al.* [51]	Isolated, Continuous	D	V	Sign	Marcel Interact Play Database	NA	GTHMM
Kong *et al.* [52]	Continuous	D	V	Sub- segments	74 distinct sentences	86.6% (recall) 89.8% (precision rates)	SVM and Semi-Markov CRF
Yang *et al.* [53]	Continuous	I	V	Sign	KINECT dataset	NA	Enhanced Level Building method
Pitsikalis *et al.* [54]	Isolated	D	V	Phoneme	GSL database	NA	HamNoSys
Li *et al.* [55]	Isolated, Continuous	I	V	Sign	1,024 testing sentences	87.4%	HMM

SL communication encompasses a seamless transition signs by engaging disparate parts human body to human body to deliberate the information associated with it, resulting in a Multimodal Approach [56]. Sign Language is made up of manual, non-manual, and multimodal features. The recognition of continuous gesture sequences is a challenging task because of the multimodal nature of SL. The manual parts are hand movements, shapes, and positions. While the non-manual feature is facial expression, mouth, head position, gaze expressions, and arm and body postures. The extraction of these features determines the movement ambiguity, which needs to be addressed in SLRT research. The CNN and its variants produced more remarkable results in object detection techniques. The CNN networks handle the images directly and learn the numerous features of an image to yield the desired results. The various research works related to subunit modeling are discussed in Table **3**.

Table 3. Various taxonomies of Manual feature and non-manual Feature Extraction in Sign Frames.

Reference	Isolated / Continuous Sign	Dataset used	Feature Extraction Method	Features used	Segmentation Method	Classification Method	Recognition Accuracy	Focus
Elakkiya *et al.* [4]	I & C	ASL + GSL	M & N	All	3-SU	BPaHMM	91% (5356 Sentences) and 98.64% (3300 signs)	Subunit modelling
Koller *et al.* [17]	C	PHOENIXWeather 2014	M & N	All	Temporal Segmentation	HMM+CNN+ LSTM	NA	1000 classes, 60 different hand shapes
Tharwat *et al.* [18]	I	ArSL	SIFT	Hand	LDA	SVM, KNN(K=5)	99%	2D images Robustness, scalability
Masood *et al.* [19]	I	Argentinean Sign Language (LSA) gestures Dataset	M	Hand	NA	CNN (spatial)+ RNN (temporal)	95.2%	Real-time SLR
Köpüklü *et al.* [20]	C	EgoGesture and NVIDIA Dynamic Hand Gesture Datasets	M	Hand	Video segmentation	deep 3D CNN	94.04%	Object detection
Pradeep Kumar *et al.* [22]	I	7500 (ISL) gestures consist of 50 different sign-words	M	Hand	Hand Segmentation	HMM + BLSTM-NN	97.85% (single-handed)	single hand and two-handed dynamic gestures
Ma *et al.* [23]	C	8,280 gestures	M & N	Hand, arm and face	Manual	CNN	86.66%	Multi singer
AnanthaRao *et al.* [24]	C	selfie sign language dataset	Manual	One Hand	NA	Deep CNN	92.88%	Different CNN architectures were designed
Cui *et al.* [27]	C	RWTH-PHOENIX-Weather multi-signer 2014	M	Hand	Segmented video glosses	CTC + RCNN	NA	effectively avoid overfitting problem
Starner *et al.* [57]	C	ASL	M & N	all	NA	HMM	92%	One-color camera, 40-word lexicon Sentence Level, Single Camera Singer Independent
Necati *et al.* [58]	C	RWTH-PHOENIX-Weather-2014T (PHOENIX14T) dataset	M & N	All	Automatic Segmentation Methods	CNN	NA	Sign Language Translation Sign2Text
Yanqiu Liao *et al.* [59]	C	DEVISIGN_D dataset	M	Hand	Temporal Segmentation	B3D ResNet	89.8%	Video sequence
		SLR_Dataset					86.9%	
Cui *et al.* [60]	C	RWTH-PHOENIX-Weather 2014	Spatial and temporal	Hand	Gesture segmentation	R-CNN (Softmax Classifier)	NA	Images
		SIGNUM benchmark						

(Table 3) cont.....

Reference	Isolated / Continuous Sign	Dataset used	Feature Extraction Method	Features used	Segmentation Method	Classification Method	Recognition Accuracy	Focus
Mittal *et al.* [61]	I & C	942 ISL Sentences	2D CNN	Hand	NA	Modified LSTM	The average accuracy of 72.3% and 89.5%	35 different sign words, Leap Motion Sensor, Two-handed
Cooper *et al.* [62]	I	20 GSL signs	M	Hand	Subunit Segmentation	HMM+ Sequential Pattern Boosting	NA	linguistic sub-units
Jiang *et al.* [63]	I	Chinese Finger sign language dataset	M	Hand	NA	Eight layers of CNN	89.32%	Fingerspelling
Xiao *et al.* [64]	C	Kinect RGB-D database	M & N	All	fuzzy C-means (FCM)	LSTM	82.55%	Skeleton based approach

*C- Continuous, I- Isolated

Challenges and Deep Learning Methods for SLRT Research

The challenges of SLRT development are analyzed and reviewed on a grander scale. The manual and non-manual features extraction, recognition of sign gestures, signer's speed, hand and head orientation, torso movements, eyes actions, lips, teeth and gaze moments, a facial expression of emotions (angry, happy, sad), and singer expertise create additional overhead to the model performance. On the other hand, recognition of new user sign gestures, classifying the wrong gestures, and accurate prediction of class labels add new challenges to SLRT development. The mindset and styles of signers need to be recognized intelligently. The brain-inspired cognitive systems create a machine model similar to the human brain using artificial intelligence techniques. The development of SLRT identical to the human brain requires a lot of research efforts in this area.

The SLRT development needs to incorporate the continuum of the language spoken (phonology) and the linguistic structure of languages. The SLRT model addresses all these challenges in a single unified framework using CNN, LSTM, Neural machine translation, and GAN methods. This hybrid model is trained and tested for handling different sign corpus. The results are plausible and visually appealing, shown in Fig. (2). The comparison results show the model performance using a diverse benchmark sign corpus.

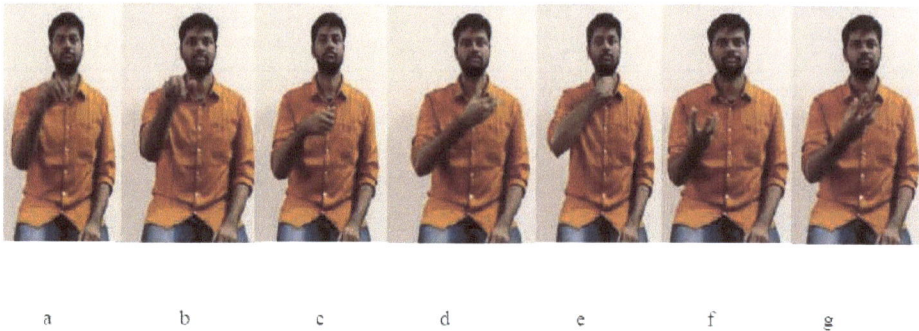

Fig. (2). Sign frames for the ISL English word "How old are you".

In Fig. (**2**), the sign gesture sequences are depicted for the complete sentence - "HOW OLD ARE YOU," but a direct translation of this approach is prone to errors. Analyzing the sequence of frames from the generated one demands efficient alignment approaches. This approach drastically changes for each gesture by moving the hand actions from one pose to another, resulting in the problem of recognizing the epenthesis movements. In a two-handed sign, the system may fail to recognize the occlusion due to hidden objects in the frames. The recognition of multiple country languages accords a multilingual approach, and translating it requires high computing devices for training and testing. Augmentative communication resembles various input methods to assist people in understanding SL communication more easily. A digital input device, talk assistants, auto speech to word converters, and speech recognizers must be compatible with this model, which benefits the user's comfort. Converting speaking language into sign language and the reverse process is still challenging in the research area due to inflections in recognizing signs.

The sample video frame sequences are depicted in Fig. (**2**) for the sentence "How old are you." The signer performing sign different sign gestures to cover the sentences, mainly the (Figs. **2a**) denote the word 'you,' 2(**e**) denotes old, and 2(**g**) denotes 'how. We can conclude that the sentence order and execution of sign gestures order are different. The proposed model adopts these changes using image alignment techniques using LSTM and produces accurate translation. Deep Learning is an emerging approach for computer vision tasks, especially the recognition and processing of large input volumes. SLRT can be implemented either using vision-based approaches or sensor-based approaches. Due to the high cost of hardware devices and recognition accuracy, sensor-based approaches are not highly recommended. To handle vision-based approaches efficiently, we used deep learning techniques to produce significant improvements in results. To advance the field of SLRT, deep learning techniques will be used to generate SL videos from the given text or spoken language sentence. Image generation is a well-known problem in the research area, and there is a need for progress in video generation.

Text/spoken sentence to video generation requires a stronger conditional generator than what is necessary for text/spoken to image generation due to the increased dimensionality of the videos. The GAN architecture [65] based on 3D convolutions is proposed to generate video sequences, but it can only generate fixed-length videos. While this model is not designed to handle conditional video generation, text-conditioned video synthesis [66, 67] is performed by using sentence embedding as a conditional input. However, these conditional generative models are based on 3D convolutions, and they can only produce fixed-length low-resolution videos. The Recurrent Neural Network-based encoder-decoder model has been used to generate sequences for body postures of human actions from words and connect them to a Baxter robot. However, their results are purely qualitative and rely on human interpretation. Subhashini *et al.* [68] discuss that that the translation of video into text will be implemented by converting video into a sequence of frames and then generating a sequence of words using LSTM-RNN-based methods. The authors Ibrahim *et al.* [69] propose the ArSLRS method using hand, head tracking, segmentation, and classification features to convert Arabic sign language into text or voice.

The CNN and variants of RNN called LSTM and GRU are the widely used deep learning techniques for SLRT. The conditional GAN techniques are used for translation to produce high-resolution videos of varying lengths. The translation of the spoken text into sign words (glosses) is obtained using NMT techniques. Then, a mapping between glosses and video sequences is implemented using the open pose library. On the other hand, using CNN, LSTM and media pose will recognize multilingual datasets that comprise isolated signs and continuous sign sentences by considering multimodal features. Homonyms words related to the position in a text/sentence generation need to comply with grammatical procedures for language construction because of expertise knowledge, which is very important because the same word could be used as a noun, verb, pronoun, and phrase, and idioms, singular plural context. The translation of sign gestures into appropriate words is not an easy task, as it demands more training to understand the different signer gesticulation styles and variations in hand positions. Sign video generation is possible when it learns from images present in the fashion of spatial and temporal features. The synthesis of sign videos using GAN networks follows video prediction and video generation strategy. The recent advancements of GAN and its variants are tabulated in Table **4**.

Table 4. Overview of various Video Generation Taxonomies

Reference	Methodology	Dataset
Carl *et al.* [65]	VideoGAN	YFCC100M (Flickr)
Cho *et al.* [70]	GAN	MNIST
Yan *et al.* [71]	conditional GAN	KTH and Human3.6M
Yamamoto *et al.* [72]	3D CNN + tempCAE	Own created video dataset
Hao *et al.* [73]	sparse-to-dense flow completion and pixel hallucination	Robot Pushing, KITTI, UCF-101
Denton *et al.* [74]	SVG-FP and SVG-LP	Stochastic Moving MNIST, KTH Action, BAIR robot pushing
Wang *et al.* [75]	VAE	Stochastic Moving MNIST, Weizmann Action, BAIR Robot Pushing, Hu-man3.6M
Pan *et al.* [76]	cVAE	Cityscapes UCF101 KTH Action dataset KITTI
Saito *et al.* [77]	TGAN	moving MNIST
Tulyakov *et al.* [78]	MoCoGAN	Tai-Chi dataset
Kanaa *et al.* [79]	Neural ODEs	Moving MNIST dataset
Clark *et al.* [80]	DVD-GAN	Kinetics-600 dataset UCF-101
He *et al.* [81]	VAE	Chair CAD, Weizmann Human Action, and YFCC – MIT Flickr

THE PROPOSED MODEL

The proposed model is developed as an end-to-end framework for performing both recognition and video generation tasks, as shown in Fig. (**3**). In the forward phases, it takes the input from the webcam and passes it to the CNN pre-trained Model VGG-19 to predict the sign gesture-related classes. The VGG_19 model uses 19 layers, in which 16 layers are allocated for convolution operation, 3 fully connected layers. A Pooling and softmax operation is performed and produces a probability of classes. Based on the class prediction, the LSTM layers compute the sentence structures. The recurrent nature of networks effectively hands the sequences of sign words. LSTM networks effectively reconstruct the original sentences using attention mechanisms. The use of forget gates, input gate, and output gates handles these tasks effectively and produces accurate results. The backward part reverses this approach by generating sign gesture videos from spoken sentences. The spoken sentences are pre-processed and <start>, <end> tokens are added. These translated texts are fed into the NMT layer to predict the sign words related to the sentences. The text vector values are normalized using an attention mechanism to produce improved results. Based on the predictions, the GAN networks generate the Sign gesture Videos. The generator network generates the sign gesture images similar to the real ones from latent vectors. The discriminator network distinguishes the generated results by comparing them with real data. The real and fake samples are identified, and iteratively, models improve the fine-tuning performance for high-quality video generation. Algorithm 1 explains the SL recognition steps, and Algorithm 2 explores the steps for video generation.

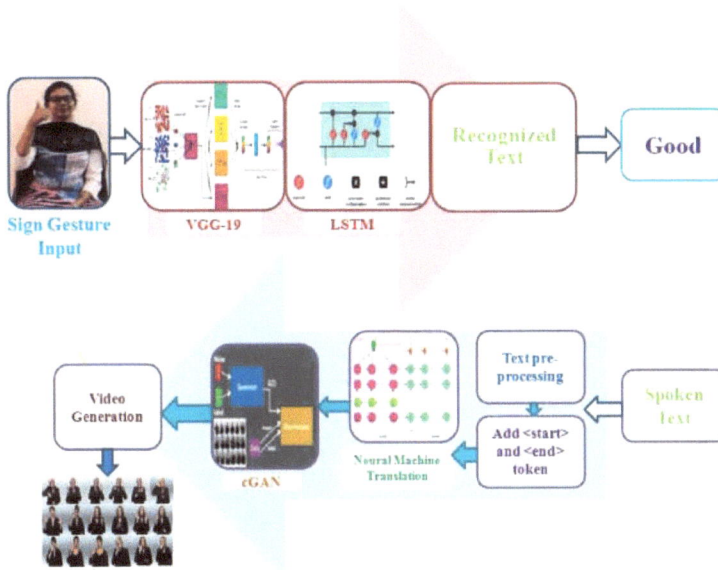

Fig. (3). The proposed Deep SLRT system architecture.

Algorithm: 1 CNN-LSTM based Deep SLRT Recognition (Forward)

Step 1: Read the sign gesture input from the web camera device

Step 2: Pass the frame sequences to VGG-19

Step 3: Compute the classification results

Step 4: Collect the predicted class label details

Step 5: Forward the input to LSTM Layer

Step 6: Predict the matching sentences

Step 7: Compare the generated results with real data

Step 8: Analyse the Accuracy of performance

Step 9: Evaluate Loss functions

Step 10: Print the results

Step 11: End the process

Algorithm: 2 NMT-GAN based Deep SLRT Video Generation (Backward)

Step 1: Read the spoken text input from the user

Step 2: Perform Text pre-processing steps

Step 3: Convert the Text into sign words (glosses) using NMT Technique

Step 4: Generate the matching sign frames from latent space using Generator Network

Step 5: Generate the intermediary frames between sign gestures using video Completion techniques

Step 6: Compare the generated results with real data distribution using Discriminator Network

Step 7: Fine-tune the model performance

Step 8: Optimize the hyperparameters to produce improved video quality results

Step 9: Evaluate the video quality using various metrics

Step 10: End the process

Training Details

We trained our model using the NVIDIA Quadro P4000-based GPU computing device. It takes 6 hours to complete the full training for 200 epochs with 100 samples. We use three LSTM layers of size 64, 128, 64, and three dense layers of size 32, 64 with activation function relu. The final dense layer uses a softmax activation function, and the dropout is 0.1. The video generation performance of conditional GAN performance is fine-tuned using Adam optimizer and batch Normalization Techniques. The initial drop value is set as 0.5, and the learning rate is 0.01. The model performances are evaluated using classification accuracy and video quality metrics. The classification accuracy results are shown in Fig. (**4**).

```
Epoch 190/200
100/100 - 0s - loss: 0.0042 - accuracy: 1.0000 - val_loss: 0.1321 - val_accuracy: 0.9643
Epoch 191/200
100/100 - 0s - loss: 0.0032 - accuracy: 1.0000 - val_loss: 0.0998 - val_accuracy: 0.9643
Epoch 192/200
100/100 - 0s - loss: 0.0018 - accuracy: 1.0000 - val_loss: 0.0701 - val_accuracy: 0.9643
Epoch 193/200
100/100 - 0s - loss: 0.0020 - accuracy: 1.0000 - val_loss: 0.0526 - val_accuracy: 0.9643
Epoch 194/200
100/100 - 0s - loss: 0.0030 - accuracy: 1.0000 - val_loss: 0.0489 - val_accuracy: 0.9643
Epoch 195/200
100/100 - 0s - loss: 0.0027 - accuracy: 1.0000 - val_loss: 0.0730 - val_accuracy: 0.9643
Epoch 196/200
100/100 - 0s - loss: 0.0016 - accuracy: 1.0000 - val_loss: 0.1022 - val_accuracy: 0.9643
Epoch 197/200
100/100 - 0s - loss: 0.0018 - accuracy: 1.0000 - val_loss: 0.0976 - val_accuracy: 0.9643
Epoch 198/200
100/100 - 0s - loss: 0.0017 - accuracy: 1.0000 - val_loss: 0.0511 - val_accuracy: 0.9643
Epoch 199/200
100/100 - 0s - loss: 0.0029 - accuracy: 1.0000 - val_loss: 0.0432 - val_accuracy: 0.9643
Epoch 200/200
100/100 - 0s - loss: 0.0028 - accuracy: 1.0000 - val_loss: 0.0679 - val_accuracy: 0.9643
```

Fig. (4). Classification Accuracy of Deep SLRT Model.

EXPERIMENTAL RESULTS

This section showcases the model performance over the different sign language datasets. The analysis of the model's performance helps identify the recognition rate, the available quantity of data, the quality of videos, and word or sentence level details. Using different metrics, the model performances are evaluated for isolated images and continuous frames. The computation of cost functions shows the loss values of the existing corpus to adopt the proposed SLRT model. Fig. (**5**) and (Fig. **6**) show the proposed model's results for recognition and video generation tasks. This section also compares the proposed model performance with different deep models and various sign corpora. The results are depicted in Fig. (**7**). (a),7. (b),8.(a),8.(b),9.(a),9.(b),10.(a),10.(b),and 11.

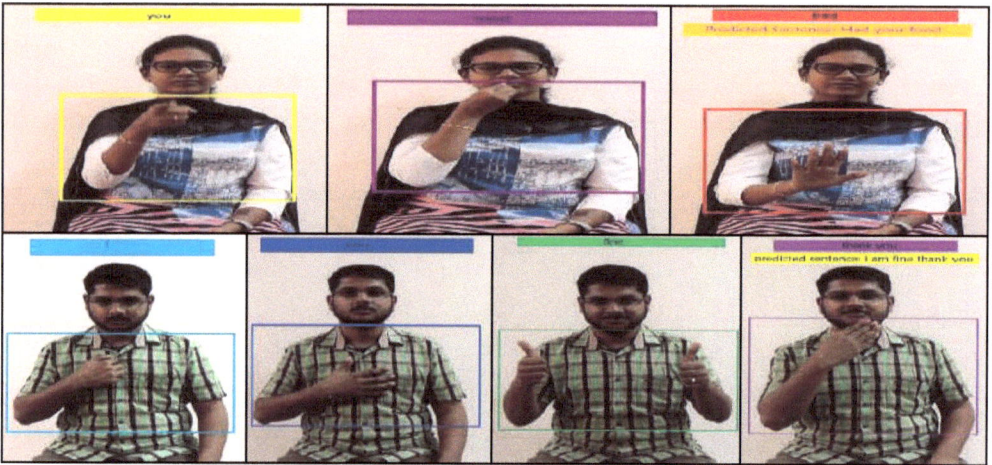

Fig. (5). Results of Deep SLRT Recognition.

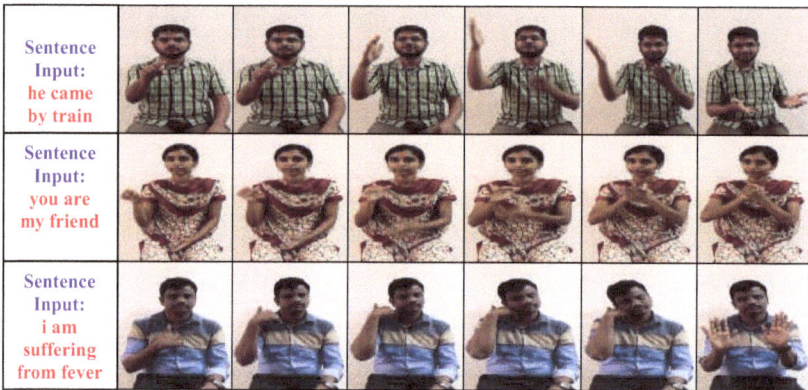

Fig. (6). Results of Deep SLRT Video Generation.

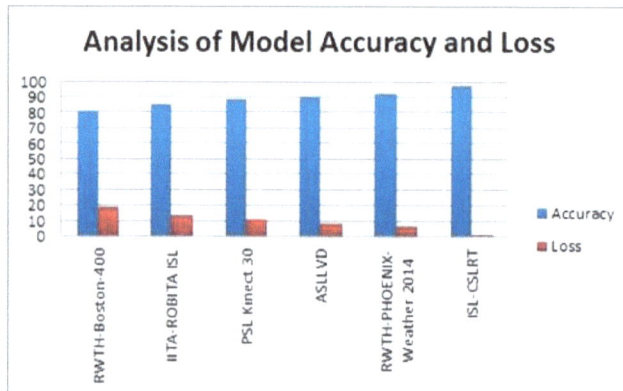

Fig. (7a). Comparison of model performance

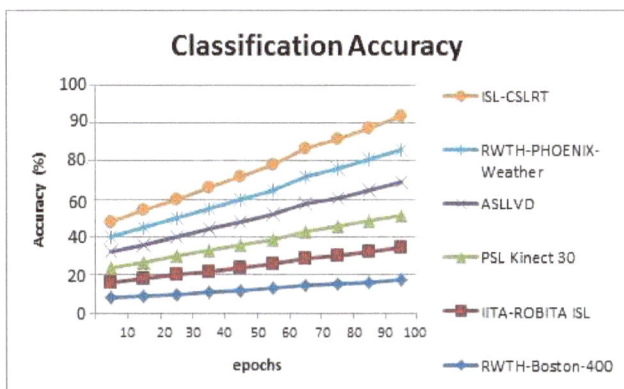

Fig. (7b). Comparison of classification performance.

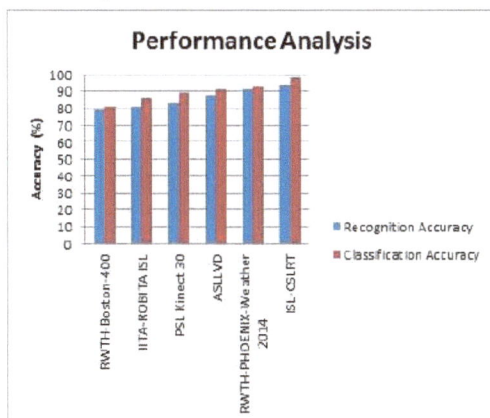

Fig. (8a). Comparison of model accuracy for various sign language datasets.

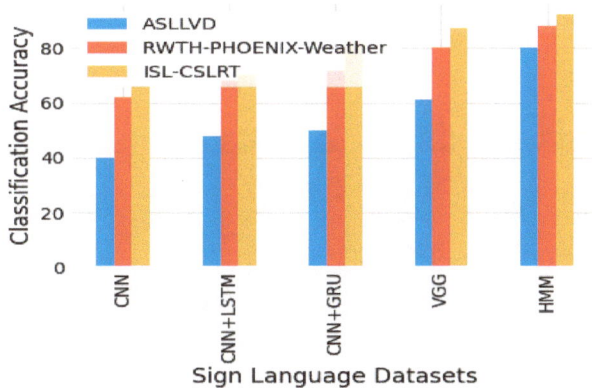

Fig. (8b). Comparison of classification performance of different models.

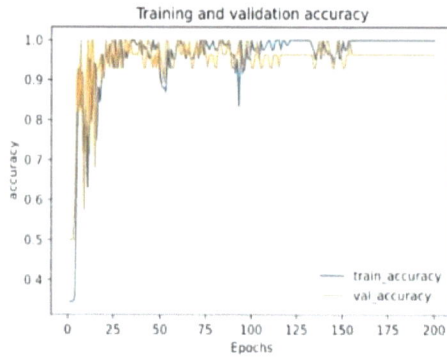

Fig. (9a). Training and validation accuracy of Deep SLRT Model

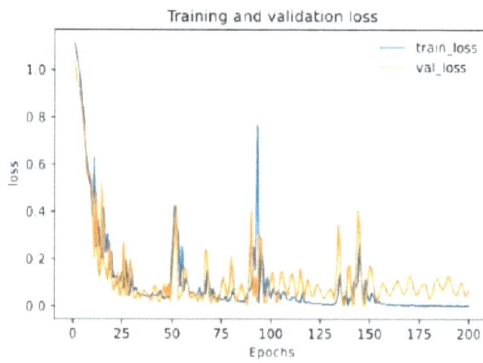

Fig. (9b). Loss computation of Deep SLRT Model.

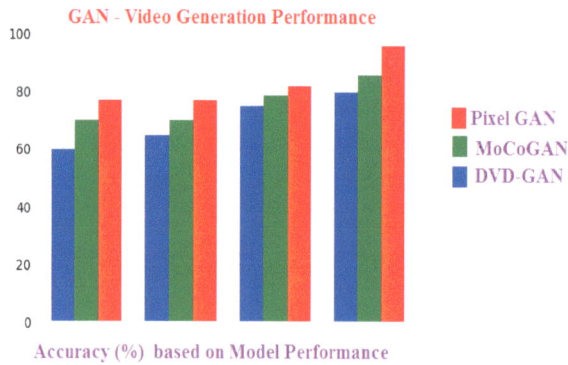

Fig. (10a). The analysis of various GAN model performances over video generation

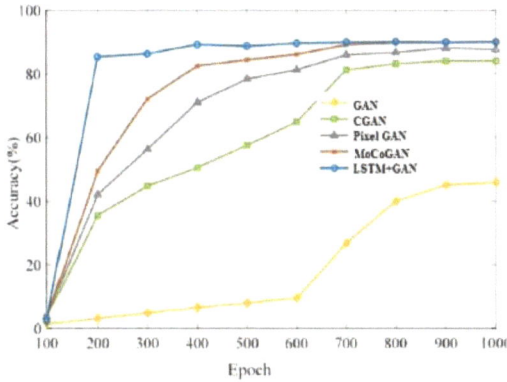

Fig. (10b). Loss computation of Deep SLRT Model.

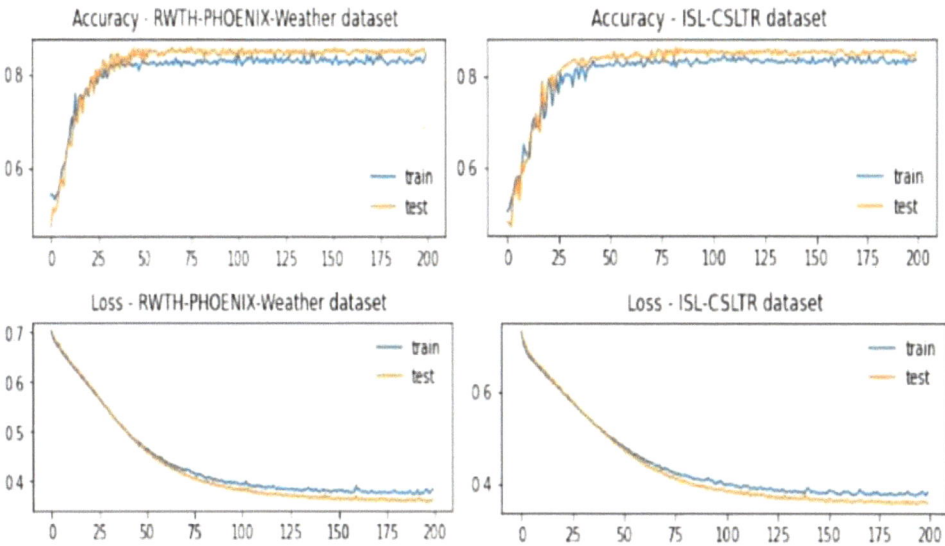

Fig. (11). Analysis of accuracy and loss of the proposed model on benchmark datasets.

CONCLUSION

The development of deep learning techniques based on SLRT models provides impressive results in Sign language recognition, translation, and sign video generation. The end-to-end framework offers an incredible support to ordinary people to communicate with deaf-mute society. Incorporating NMT, CNN, LSTM, and GAN techniques improved the model performance to new heights. The proposed model achieves above 95% recognition accuracy and 98% classification accuracy. The generated sign gesture videos' quality is compared with various quality metrics, showing the proposed model's improved performance. Developing our self-created ISL-CSLTR corpus greatly supports the research community in developing efficient sign language recognition, translation, and video generation models. The classification performance of the SLRT model is analyzed and shows comparatively better results. In the future, we plan to extend the vocabulary size of the corpus to produce a considerable size of the dataset for ISL research and development.

ACKNOWLEDGEMENTS

I wish to express my gratitude to the Science & Engineering Research Board, Department of Science & Technology, Government of India, for sanctioning the project under the Start-up Research Grant program SRG/2019/001338 and supporting the project ostensibly.

REFERENCES

[1]   S.C.W. Ong, and S. Ranganath, "Automatic sign language analysis: a survey and the future beyond lexical meaning", *IEEE Trans. Pattern Anal. Mach. Intell.,* vol. 27, no. 6, pp. 873-891, 2005.
[http://dx.doi.org/10.1109/TPAMI.2005.112] [PMID: 15943420]

[2]   E. R, and S. K, "Subunit sign modeling framework for continuous sign language recognition", *Comput. Electr. Eng.,* vol. 74, pp. 379-390, 2019.
[http://dx.doi.org/10.1016/j.compeleceng.2019.02.012]

[3]   E. R, and S. K, "Extricating manual and non-manual features for subunit level medical sign modelling in automatic sign language classification and recognition", *J. Med. Syst.,* vol. 41, no. 11, p. 175, 2017.
[http://dx.doi.org/10.1007/s10916-017-0819-z] [PMID: 28940043]

[4]   E. R, and S. K, "Enhanced dynamic programming approach for subunit modelling to handle segmentation and recognition ambiguities in sign language", *J. Parallel Distrib. Comput.,* vol. 117, pp. 246-255, 2018.
[http://dx.doi.org/10.1016/j.jpdc.2017.07.001]

[5]   L. Zhou, J. Zhang, and C. Zong, "Look-ahead attention for generation in neural machine translation", *National CCF Conference on Natural Language Processing and Chinese Computing,* Springer: Cham, pp. 211-223, 2017.

[6]   Y. Wu, and T.S. Huang, "Human hand modeling, analysis and animation in the context of HCI", In: *Image processing", ICIP 99. Proceedings. 1999 international conference.* IEEE, 1999, pp. 6-10.

[7]   P. Lu, and M. Huenerfauth, "Cuny american sign language motion capture corpus: first release. In: Proceedings of the 5th Workshop on the Representation and Processing of Sign Languages: Interactions between Corpus and Lexicon", The 8th International Conference on Language Resources and Evaluation (LREC 2012), Istanbul, Turkey, 2012.

[8]   T. Allevard, and E. Benoit, and Laurent Foulloy, "Hand posture recognition with the fuzzy glove", Modern Information Processing, Elsevier Science, 2006 pp. 417-427.

[9]   J-H. Kim, "Nguyen DucThang, and Tae-Seong Kim, 3-d hand motion tracking and gesture recognition using a data glove", *IEEE International Symposium on Industrial Electronics,* IEEE, 2009.

[10]   M. Mustafa, "RETRACTED ARTICLE: A study on Arabic sign language recognition for differently abled using advanced machine learning classifiers", *J. Ambient Intell. Humaniz. Comput.,* vol. 12, no. 3, pp. 4101-4115, 2021.
[http://dx.doi.org/10.1007/s12652-020-01790-w]

[11]   T. Kapuscinski, M. Oszust, M. Wysocki, and D. Warchol, "Recognition of hand gestures observed by

depth cameras", *Int. J. Adv. Robot. Syst.,* vol. 12, no. 4, p. 36, 2015.
[http://dx.doi.org/10.5772/60091]

[12]   H.D. Yang, "Sign language recognition with the Kinect sensor based on conditional random fields", *Sensors (Basel),* vol. 15, no. 1, pp. 135-147, 2014.
[http://dx.doi.org/10.3390/s150100135] [PMID: 25609039]

[13]   C-H. Chuan, E. Regina, and C. Guardino, "American sign language recognition using leap motion sensor", *13th International Conference on Machine Learning and Applications,* IEEE, pp. 541-544, 2014.
[http://dx.doi.org/10.1109/ICMLA.2014.110]

[14]   J. Pu, W. Zhou, J. Zhang, and H. Li, "Sign language recognition based on trajectory modeling with hmms", *International Conference on Multimedia Modeling,* Springer: Cham, pp. 686-697, 2016.
[http://dx.doi.org/10.1007/978-3-319-27671-7_58]

[15]   B. Bauer, and K. Karl-Friedrich, "Towards an Automatic Sign Language Recognition System Using Subunits", *International Gesture Workshop,* Springer: Berlin, Heidelberg, pp. 64-75, 2001.

[16]   W. Yang, J. Tao, and Z. Ye, "Continuous sign language recognition using level building based on fast hidden markov model", *Pattern Recognit. Lett.,* vol. 78, no. 78, pp. 28-35, 2016.
[http://dx.doi.org/10.1016/j.patrec.2016.03.030]

[17]   T. Starner, J. Weaver, and A. Pentland, "Real-time american sign language recognition using desk and wearable computer based video", *IEEE Trans. Pattern Anal. Mach. Intell.,* vol. 20, no. 12, pp. 1371-1375, 1998.
[http://dx.doi.org/10.1109/34.735811]

[18]   A. Tharwat, T. Gaber, A.E. Hassanien, M. Shahin, and B. Refaat, "Sift-based arabic sign language recognition system", In: *Afro-European conference for industrial advancement.* Springer, 2015, pp. 359-370.
[http://dx.doi.org/10.1007/978-3-319-13572-4_30]

[19]   S. Masood, A. Srivastava, H.C. Thuwal, and M. Ahmad, "Real-time sign language gesture (word) recognition from video sequences using CNN and RNN", In: *Intelligent Engineering Informatics.* Springer: Singapore, 2018, pp. 623-632.
[http://dx.doi.org/10.1007/978-981-10-7566-7_63]

[20]   O. Köpüklü, A. Gunduz, N. Kose, and G. Rigoll, "Real-time hand gesture detection and classification using convolutional neural networks", *14th IEEE International Conference on Automatic Face & Gesture Recognition,* IEEE, pp. 1-8, 2019.
[http://dx.doi.org/10.1109/FG.2019.8756576]

[21]   O. Koller, "Weakly supervised learning with multi-stream CNN-LSTM-HMMs to discover sequential parallelism in sign language videos", *IEEE Trans. Pattern Anal. Mach. Intell.,* 2019.
[PMID: 30990421]

[22]   O. Koller, N.C. Camgoz, H. Ney, and R. Bowden, "Weakly supervised learning with multi-stream CNN-LSTM-HMMs to discover sequential parallelism in sign language videos", *IEEE Trans. Pattern Anal. Mach. Intell.,* vol. 42, no. 9, pp. 2306-2320, 2020.
[http://dx.doi.org/10.1109/TPAMI.2019.2911077] [PMID: 30990421]

[23]   Y. Ma, G. Zhou, Wang S. Zhao, H. and W. Jung, "Signfi: Sign language recognition using wifi", Proceedings of the ACM on Interactive, Mobile, Wearable and Ubiquitous Technologies, 2018, no. 2, pp. 1-21.

[24]   G.A. Rao, K. Syamala, P.V.V. Kishore, and A.S.C.S. Sastry, "Deep convolutional neural networks for sign language recognition", *2018 Conference on Signal Processing and Communication Engineering Systems (SPACES),* IEEE, pp. 194-197, 2018.
[http://dx.doi.org/10.1109/SPACES.2018.8316344]

[25]   M. Borg, and K.P. Camilleri, "Sign language detection in the wild with recurrent neural networks", In

ICASSP 2019-2019 IEEE International Conference on Acoustics, Speech and Signal Processing (ICASSP), pp. 1637-1641. IEEE, 2019.
[http://dx.doi.org/10.1109/ICASSP.2019.8683257]

[26]   T. Liu, W. Zhou, and H. Li, "Sign language recognition with long short-term memory", In: *In 2016 IEEE international conference on image processing (ICIP)* IEEE, 2016, pp. 2871-2875.

[27]   R. Cui, H. Liu, and C. Zhang, "Recurrent convolutional neural networks for continuous sign language recognition by staged optimization", *Proceedings of the IEEE conference on computer vision and pattern recognition,* pp. 7361-7369, 2017.
[http://dx.doi.org/10.1109/CVPR.2017.175]

[28]   R. Rastgoo, K. Kiani, and S. Escalera, "Hand pose aware multimodal isolated sign language recognition", *Multimedia Tools Appl.,* vol. 80, no. 1, pp. 127-163, 2021.
[http://dx.doi.org/10.1007/s11042-020-09700-0]

[29]   R. Wilbur, and A. C. Kak, "Purdue rvl-slll american sign language database". 2006.

[30]   H. Wang, X. Chai, X. Hong, G. Zhao, and X. Chen, "Isolated sign language recognition with grassmann covariance matrices", *ACM Trans. Access. Comput.,* vol. 8, no. 4, pp. 1-21, 2016. [TACCESS].
[http://dx.doi.org/10.1145/2897735]

[31]   B. Kwolek, W. Baczynski, and S. Sako, "Recognition of JSL fingerspelling using Deep Convolutional Neural Networks", *Neurocomputing,* vol. 456, pp. 586-598, 2021.
[http://dx.doi.org/10.1016/j.neucom.2021.03.133]

[32]   G. Latif, N. Mohammad, J. Alghazo, R. AlKhalaf, and R. AlKhalaf, "ArASL: Arabic Alphabets Sign Language Dataset", *Data Brief,* vol. 23, p. 103777, 2019.
[http://dx.doi.org/10.1016/j.dib.2019.103777] [PMID: 31372425]

[33]   J. Forster, *RWTH-PHOENIX-Weather: A Large Vocabulary Sign Language Recognition and Translation Corpus.* vol. Vol. 9. LREC, 2012.

[34]   A. Nandy, S. Mondal, J.S. Prasad, P. Chakraborty, and G.C. Nandi, "Recognizing &interpreting Indian Sign Language gesture for Human-Robot Interaction", *International Conference on Computer and Communication Technology (ICCCT),* pp. 712-717, 2010.Allahabad, Uttar Pradesh
[http://dx.doi.org/10.1109/ICCCT.2010.5640434]

[35]   R. Elakkiya, B, NATARAJAN, "ISL-CSLTR: Indian Sign Language Dataset for Continuous Sign Language Translation and Recognition"*Mendeley Data,* .
[http://dx.doi.org/10.17632/kcmpdxky7p.1]

[36]   C. Neidle, A. Thangali, and S. Sclaroff, "Challenges in development of the american sign language lexicon video dataset (asllvd) corpus", In 5th workshop on the representation and processing of sign languages: interactions between corpus and Lexicon, LREC, 2012.

[37]   A. Schembri, J. Fenlon, R. Rentelis, S. Reynolds, and K. Cormier, "Building the British sign language corpus", *Lang. Doc. Conserv.,* no. 7, pp. 136-154, 2013.

[38]   H. Hana, S. Sako, and B. Kwolek. "Recognition of JSL finger spelling using convolutional neural networks." 2017 Fifteenth IAPR International Conference on Machine Vision Applications (MVA). IEEE, 2017.

[39]   Camgöz, Necati Cihan, Ahmet Alp Kındıroğlu, Serpil Karabüklü, Meltem Kelepir, Ayşe Sumru Özsoy, and Lale Akarun, "Bosphorus Sign: a Turkish sign language recognition corpus in health and finance domains." *Proceedings of the Tenth International Conference on Language Resources and Evaluation (LREC'16)* pp. 1383-1388. 2016.

[40]   G. Fang, X. Gao, W. Gao, and Y. Chen, "A novel approach to automatically extracting basic units from chinese sign language", *Proceedings of the 17th International Conference on Pattern Recognition,* vol. vol. 4, pp. 454-457, 2004.
[http://dx.doi.org/10.1109/ICPR.2004.1333800]

[41]   HD Yang, S Sclaroff, and SW Lee, 2009, "Sign language spotting with a threshold model based on conditional random fields", IEEE Transactions on Pattern Analysis and Machine Intelligence, vol .31, no. 7, pp. 1264- 1277.
[http://dx.doi.org/10.1109/TPAMI.2008.172]

[42]   Ronchetti, Franco, *et al.* "LSA64: an Argentinian sign language dataset." XXII CongresoArgentino de Ciencias de la Computación (CACIC 2016). 2016.

[43]   A. Von, "Recent developments in visual sign language recognition," Univ. Access in the Info", *Society,* vol. 6, no. 4, pp. 323-362, 2008.

[44]   J. Han, G. Awad, and A. Sutherland, "Modelling and segmenting subunits for sign language recognition based on hand motion analysis", *Pattern Recognit. Lett.,* vol. 30, no. 6, pp. 623-633, 2009.
[http://dx.doi.org/10.1016/j.patrec.2008.12.010]

[45]   S. Tornay, O. Aran, and M.M. Doss, "An HMM Approach with Inherent Model Selection for Sign Language and Gesture Recognition", *Proceedings of The 12th Language Resources and Evaluation Conference,* 2020.

[46]   C. Vogler, and D. Metaxas, "Adapting hidden Markov models for ASL recognition byusing three-dimensional computer vision methods", *IEEE International Conference on Systems, Man, and Cybernetics,* vol. vol. 1, pp. 156-161, 1997.

[47]   T. Kadir, R. Bowden, E.J. Ong, and A. Zisserman, "Minimal Training, Large Lexicon, Unconstrained Sign Language Recognition", *British Machine Vision Conference,* pp. 1-10, 2004.
[http://dx.doi.org/10.5244/C.18.96]

[48]   Q. Yuan, W. Geo, H. Yao, and C. Wang, "Recognition of strong and weak connection models in continuous sign language", In: *Object recognition supported by user interaction for service robots.* vol. Vol. 1. IEEE, 2002, pp. 75-78.
[http://dx.doi.org/10.1109/ICPR.2002.1044616]

[49]   G. Fang, X. Gao, W. Gao, and Y. Chen, "A novel approach to automatically extracting basic units from chinese sign language", *Proceedings of the 17th International Conference on Pattern Recognition,* vol. vol. 4, pp. 454-457, 2004.
[http://dx.doi.org/10.1109/ICPR.2004.1333800]

[50]   HD Yang, S Sclaroff, and SW Lee, "Sign language spotting with a threshold model based on conditional random fields", IEEE Transactions on Pattern Analysis and Machine Intelligence, vol .31, no. 7, pp. 1264- 1277.
[http://dx.doi.org/10.1109/TPAMI.2008.172]

[51]   D. Kelly, J. McDonald, and C. Markham, "Recognition of spatiotemporal gestures in sign language using gesture threshold hmms",
[http://dx.doi.org/10.1007/978-0-85729-057-1_12]

[52]   W.W. Kong, and S. Ranganath, "Towards subject independent continuous sign language recognition: A segment and merge approach", *Pattern Recognit.,* vol. 47, no. 3, pp. 1294-1308, 2014.
[http://dx.doi.org/10.1016/j.patcog.2013.09.014]

[53]   W. Yang, J. Tao, and Z. Ye, "Continuous sign language recognition using level building based on fast hidden Markov model", *Pattern Recognit. Lett.,* vol. 78, pp. 28-35, 2016.
[http://dx.doi.org/10.1016/j.patrec.2016.03.030]

[54]   V. Pitsikalis, S. Theodorakis, C. Vogler, and P. Maragos, "Advances in phonetics-based sub-unit modeling for transcription alignment and sign language recognition", IEEE Computer Society Conference on Computer Vision and Pattern Recognition Workshops(CVPRW), pp. 1- 6.
[http://dx.doi.org/10.1109/CVPRW.2011.5981681]

[55]   K. Li, Z. Zhou, and C.H. Lee, "Sign transition modeling and a scalable solution to continuous sign language recognition for real-world applications", *ACM Trans. Access. Comput.,* vol. 8, no. 2, pp. 1-23, 2016. [TACCESS].

[http://dx.doi.org/10.1145/2850421]

[56]   Lizhong Wu, S.L. Oviatt, and P.R. Cohen, "Multimodal integration-a statistical view", *IEEE Trans. Multimed.,* vol. 1, no. 4, pp. 334-341, 1999.
[http://dx.doi.org/10.1109/6046.807953]

[57]   T. Starner, J. Weaver, and A. Pentland, "Real-time American sign language recognition using desk and wearable computer based video", *IEEE Trans. Pattern Anal. Mach. Intell.,* vol. 20, no. 12, pp. 1371-1375, 1998.
[http://dx.doi.org/10.1109/34.735811]

[58]   Camgoz, Necati Cihan, Oscar Koller, Simon Hadfield, and Richard Bowden. "Sign Language Transformers: Joint End-to-end Sign LanguageRecognition and Translation." arXiv (2020): arXiv-2003.

[59]   H.D. Yang, and S.W. Lee, "Robust sign language recognition by combining manual and non-manual features based on conditional random field and support vector machine", *Pattern Recognit. Lett.,* vol. 34, no. 16, pp. 2051-2056, 2013.
[http://dx.doi.org/10.1016/j.patrec.2013.06.022]

[60]   R. Cui, H. Liu, and C. Zhang, "A deep neural framework for continuous sign language recognition by iterative training", *IEEE Trans. Multimed.,* vol. 21, no. 7, pp. 1880-1891, 2019.
[http://dx.doi.org/10.1109/TMM.2018.2889563]

[61]   A. Mittal, P. Kumar, P.P. Roy, R. Balasubramanian, and B.B. Chaudhuri, "A modified LSTM model for continuous sign language recognition using leap motion", *IEEE Sens. J.,* vol. 19, no. 16, pp. 7056-7063, 2019.
[http://dx.doi.org/10.1109/JSEN.2019.2909837]

[62]   H. Cooper, and R. Bowden, "Sign language recognition using linguistically derived sub-units, Proceedings of 4th workshop on the representation and processing of sign languages: corpora and sign language technologies, pp. 57-61", 2010.

[63]   X. Jiang, M. Lu, and S.H. Wang, "An eight-layer convolutional neural network with stochastic pooling, batch normalization and dropout for finger spelling recognition of Chinese sign language", *Multimedia Tools Appl.,* vol. 79, no. 21, pp. 15697-15715, 2020.
[http://dx.doi.org/10.1007/s11042-019-08345-y]

[64]   Q. Xiao, M. Qin, and Y. Yin, "Skeleton-based Chinese sign language recognition and generation for bidirectional communication between deaf and hearing people", *Neural Netw.,* vol. 125, pp. 41-55, 2020.
[http://dx.doi.org/10.1016/j.neunet.2020.01.030] [PMID: 32070855]

[65]   V. Carl, P. Hamed, and T. Antonio, "Generating videos with scene dynamics", In: *Advances in Neural Information Processing Systems.* vol. Vol. 29. Curran Associates, Inc., 2016, pp. 613-621.

[66]   P. Yingwei, Q. Zhaofan, Y. Ting, L. Houqiang, and M. Tao, "To create what you tell: Generating videos from captions", *Proceedings of the 25th ACM international conference on Multimedia,* pp. 1789-1798, 2017.

[67]   Y. Li, M.R. Min, D. Shen, David E. Carlson, and L. Carin, "Video generation from text", *Proceedings of the Thirty-Second AAAI Conference on Artificial Intelligence,* 2018.New Orleans, Louisiana, USA

[68]   V. Subhashini, S. Venugopalan, M. Rohrbach, J. Donahue, R. Mooney, T. Darrell, and K. Saenko, "Sequence to sequence-video to text", *Proceedings of the IEEE international conference on computer vision,* pp. 4534-4542, 2015.

[69]   N.B. Ibrahim, M.M. Selim, and H.H. Zayed, "An Automatic Arabic Sign Language Recognition System (ArSLRS)", *Journal of King Saud University - Computer and Information Sciences,* vol. 30, no. 4, pp. 470-477, 2018.
[http://dx.doi.org/10.1016/j.jksuci.2017.09.007]

[70]   H-Y. Cho, and Y-H. Kim, "Stabilized training of generative adversarial networks by a genetic

algorithm", *Proceedings of the Genetic and Evolutionary Computation Conference Companion,* 2019.
[http://dx.doi.org/10.1145/3319619.3326774]

[71]   Y. Yan, "Skeleton-aided articulated motion generation", *Proceedings of the 25th ACM international conference on Multimedia,* 2017.
[http://dx.doi.org/10.1145/3123266.3123277]

[72]   S. Yamamoto, and T. Harada, "Video Generation Using 3D Convolutional Neural Network", *Proceedings of the 24th ACM international conference on Multimedia,* 2016.
[http://dx.doi.org/10.1145/2964284.2967287]

[73]   Z. Hao, X. Huang, and S. Belongie, "Controllable video generation with sparse trajectories", *Proceedings of the IEEE Conference on Computer Vision and Pattern Recognition,* 2018.

[74]   E. Denton, and R Fergus, "Stochastic video generation with a learned prior", arXiv preprint arXiv:1802.07687 (2018).

[75]   T-H. Wang, "Point-to-Point Video Generation", *Proceedings of the IEEE International Conference on Computer Vision,* 2019.

[76]   J. Pan, "Video generation from single semantic label map", *Proceedings of the IEEE Conference on Computer Vision and Pattern Recognition,* 2019.
[http://dx.doi.org/10.1109/CVPR.2019.00385]

[77]   M. Saito, E. Matsumoto, and S. Saito, "Temporal generative adversarial nets with singular value clipping", *IEEE International Conference on Computer Vision (ICCV),* vol. volume 2, p. 5, 2017.
[http://dx.doi.org/10.1109/ICCV.2017.308]

[78]   S. Tulyakov, M-Y. Liu, X. Yang, and J. Kautz, "Mocogan: Decomposing motion and content for video generation. arXiv preprint arXiv:1707.04993", 2017.

[79]   D. Kanaa, "Simple video generation using neural odes", *Workshop on Learning with Rich experience, Advances in Neural Information Processing Systems,* vol. Vol. 32, 2019.

[80]   Aidan Clark, Jeff Donahue, and Karen Simonyan, "Efficient video generation on complex datasets." arXiv preprintarXiv:1907.06571", 2019.

[81]   J. He, "Probabilistic video generation using holistic attribute control", *Proceedings of the European Conference on Computer Vision (ECCV),* 2018.
[http://dx.doi.org/10.1007/978-3-030-01228-1_28]

CHAPTER 9

Hybrid Convolutional Recurrent Neural Network for Isolated Indian Sign Language Recognition

Elakkiya Rajasekar[1], **Archana Mathiazhagan**[1] and **Elakkiya Rajalakshmi**[1,*]

[1] *School of Computing, SASTRA Deemed University, Thanjavur 613401, India*

Abstract: Even though the hearing and vocally impaired populace rely entirely on Sign Language (SL) as a way of communication, the majority of the worldwide people are unable to interpret it. This creates a significant language barrier between these two categories. The need for developing Sign Language Recognition (SLR) systems has arisen as a result of the communication breakdown between the deaf-mute and the general populace. This paper proposes a Hybrid Convolutional Recurrent Neural Network-based (H-CRNN) framework for Isolated Indian Sign Language recognition. The proposed framework is divided into two modules: the Feature Extraction module and the Sign Model Recognition module. The Feature Extraction module exploits the Convolutional Neural Network-based framework, and the Model recognition exploits the LSTM/GRU-based framework for Indian sign representation of English Alphabets and numbers. The proposed models are evaluated using a newly created Isolated Sign dataset called ISLAN, the first multi-signer Indian Sign Language representation for English Alphabets and Numbers. The performance evaluation with the other state-o--the-art neural network models have shown that the proposed H-CRNN model has better accuracy.

Keywords: Hybrid Neural Networks, Isolated Indian Sign Language, Image segmentation, Sign Language Recognition.

INTRODUCTION

Sign Language is a medium of communication for the deaf and mute community. As per the World Health Organization, approximately 6.1 percent of the worldwide population is deaf or with speech impediment. According to the National Association of the Deaf (NAD), about 18 million people in India suffer from hearing impediments. Sign language differs from region to region. There are approximately more than 120 Sign Languages (SL). Some of the notorious sign languages include Arabic [1], American, Bhutanese [2], German, Chinese [3], Russian, Turkish [4], and Indian Sign languages.

---

[*] **Corresponding author Elakkiya Rajalakshmi:** School of Computing, SASTRA Deemed University, Thanjavur, India; E-mail: elakkiya@cse.sastra.edu

Gyanendra Verma & Rajesh Doriya (Eds.)

The Indian Sign language itself differs from region to region. Deaf and mute people generally need someone to translate their sign language for their regular communication. The formulation of the Sign Language Recognition System (SLR) is motivated by the desire to contribute to the development of feasible solutions for the automation of sign language recognition, hence eliminating the need for human assistance during interpretation. There have been many recent developments in building SLR systems. Most of the state-of-the-art SLR systems that are reliable, accurate, and simple are dependent on the wearable devices such as gloves. Although wearable devices give accurate predictions based on the measures of the finger joints, the orientation of the hand and the location of key points on the face, *etc.,* when it comes to practical usage for day to day life of a person with hearing and speech impediment it would be tedious, restrictive, bizarre as well as costly to use. The robustness of an image/video-based SLR system's image processing framework, *i.e.,* its potential to withstand heterogeneous, dynamic, or generally unrestrained environments, poor lighting, and different skin tones, has a significant impact on its usability. One of the other main drawbacks in building the most accurate model for SLR is the lack of publicly available large datasets. There are no publicly available datasets for Indian Sign Language (ISL). Though the state-of-the-art models have used their customized datasets, they have not considered the dataset that is signer-independent, having different illuminations and backgrounds.

To overcome the above-said issues, we have proposed an image/video-based SLR system using a Convolutional Recurrent Neural Network (CRNN) framework to comprehend sign language by feeding it images/videos of hand gestures in different illumination scenarios with different backgrounds, different hand orientations, and different signers. We have created our own dataset, namely ISLAN [5], which consists of Indian gestures for Alphabets and numbers, and it is made publicly available for further research. The proposed CRNN framework can be divided into two modules, namely Feature Extraction (FE module) and Model Recognition (MR module). The FE module has been implemented using Convolutional Neural Network (CNN), and the MR module has been implemented using Recurrent Neural Network (RNN). By integrating both, we get an H-DNN, namely CRNN model. The main objective of the proposed work is:

a. Creation and collection of Indian Isolated Sign Language dataset for Indian Alphabet and Numeric signs (ISLAN) and making it publicly available.
b. Implementation of the H-CRNN SLR model for feature extraction and sign language recognition.
c. Evaluation of the model proposed using the newly created ISLAN dataset.

The rest of this paper is organized as follows: Section 2 gives a brief discussion of related works and a literature review. Section 3 introduces the proposed methodology, followed by result analysis and discussion in section 4. Section 5 discusses the conclusion and future work.

RELATED WORK

During the last couple of years, studies in the area of sign language gesture recognition have made tremendous progress. The present findings serve as a foundation for future applications intended to assist deaf people in their assimilation into hearing society. There has been much research conducted on the Sign Language Recognition System. There have been many sensor-based as well as video-based recognition systems used for formulating the SLR system. Many researchers have worked on traditional methods without the implementation of neural networks and machine learning [6]. One of the approaches proposed English alphabet recognition using scale-invariant feature transform [7]. A framework for recognition of the Indian Alphabet gesture was proposed, which dealt with the Eigenvalues and Eigenvectors [8]. Various HMM-based models were also introduced for recognition of Arabic SLR [9 - 11]. Then came the era of sensor-based gesture recognition using sensors such as Leap motion sensors and Microsoft Kinect [12], other machine learning approaches such as KNN, SVM, *etc* [13]. Some approaches also used more than one digital camera along with wearable sensors to capture the gestures from different angles [14]. There were several other frameworks introduced having wearable sensors with the integration of Neural Networks. For instance, a CNN-based framework was proposed using a Microsoft Kinect sensor using American Sign Language consisting of an alphanumeric dataset [15]. The same combination of the framework was also utilized using Italian Sign Language, where the framework was modeled based on the hand and upper body features [16]. Later, a neural network model was proposed for Arabic SLR where not only the height and width dimension but the depth dimension of the object was also extracted from the sensor and fed into various CNN frameworks [17]. Another Arabic SLR framework was proposed, which utilized a comparatively large dataset consisting of 7869 signs for Alphabets and Numbers, which yielded a good accuracy of 90% [18].

Many kinds of research have been out carried on sign language recognition using the video-based approach in different regions throughout the world. The researchers have exploited various CNN-based frameworks [19], such as VGG16, VGG19, AlexNet, ResNet, inception net, *etc.,* for sign language classification. A Chinese SLR system was proposed that integrated CNN with Long-Term Memory Network (LSTM) [20] for Isolated SLR using word sign videos which yielded a 95% accuracy level [21]. The CNN-based frameworks have a major drawback when it comes to the size of the data. It requires a large dataset to train the neural network, which results in huge computation time and power. To overcome this issue, the researchers shifted to transfer learning and fine tuning-based methodologies. There were works done related to the comparison of frameworks before and after using the fine-tuning techniques [22]. A recognition framework was implemented using fine-tuned CNN model that was pre-trained using 1.2 million datasets for plant recognition tasks [23]. Later a Bengali SLR system [24] was built using fine-tuned CNN having weights obtained from a pre-trained model [25]. A neural network-based approach was implemented using Myanmar SL [26].

The vision-based approach has proven to be easy to use and implement for real-time systems. One of the proposed models dealt with the formulation of the SLR system using the lip shape and texture pattern [27]. A Taiwanese SLR system was built using a Machine Learning approach that used a Kinect camera to extract manual features like hand orientation, shape, and position [28]. A new recognition system for a 3D sign using the CNN approach was built wherein temporal and spatial features were extracted [29]. Another ANN-based SLR system was proposed for Indian SL that used image datasets captured from the mobile phone camera [30]. Another model was proposed for recognizing static gestures using the Inception V3 model using the ASL dataset [31]. Some of the models also introduced Skin segmentation and tracking methods for recognition tasks [32]. An ISL-based SLR system was introduced using Deep Neural Networks [33]. An Indian SLR was proposed that made use of the signer-independent Indian Sign Language (ISL) dataset [34]. Few deep learning-based models using various optimizers were also developed for Indian SL [35]. An Indian SLR system was proposed that dealt with the classification of Indian sign representations of alphabets using HOG features. Due to the lack of availability of ISL datasets, all the proposed ISLR systems have used self-collected datasets [36].

METHODOLOGY

The proposed methodology deals with the integration of two modules. One is the CNN framework for the feature extraction, FE module, and the other is RNN for the sign recognition task, MR module. The integration of these two modules results in the formulation of the Hybrid-CRNN framework along with the creation of the Indian Isolated Sign Language dataset, namely ISLAN, for Indian Alphanumeric signs.

Proposed H-CRNN Framework

The proposed H-CRNN framework consists of 5 stages, namely, Data Acquisition, Data preprocessing, Data Augmentation [37], Feature Extraction, and

Sign Recognition. The proposed H-CRNN framework is illustrated in Fig. (**1**). The proposed H-CRNN model uses CNN for the FE module and RNN as a recognizer for the MR module. Two models were built for the evaluation. In the first model, CNN + LSTM was used, wherein CNN was exploited for the FE module, and LSTM was used for the MR module. In the second model, CNN + GRU was used, wherein CNN was exploited for the FE module, and GRU was used for the MR module.

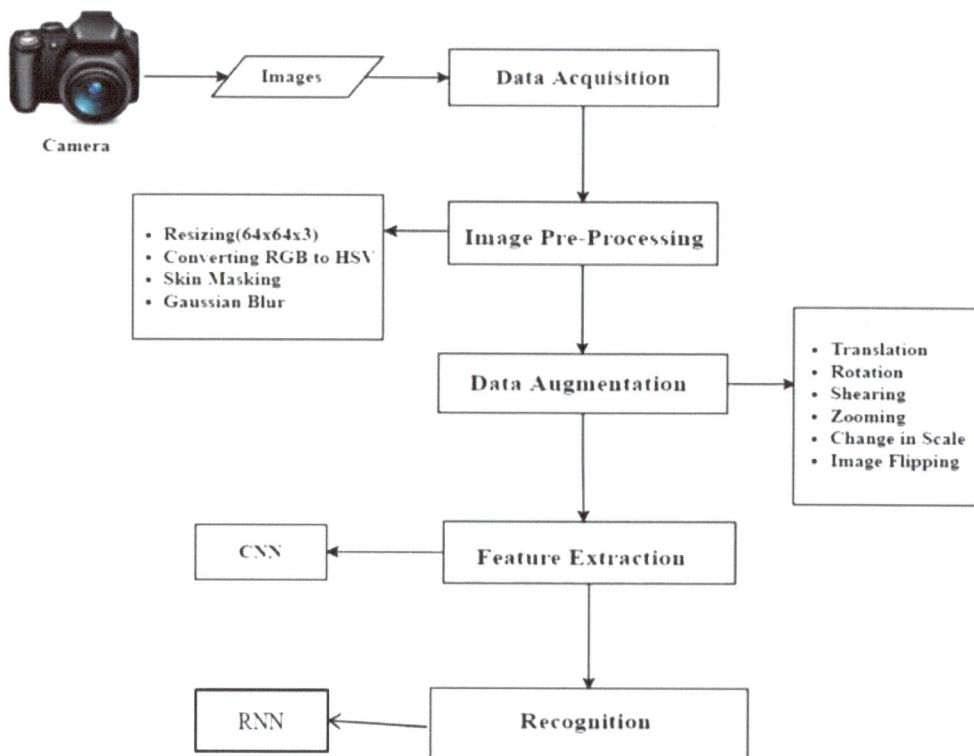

Fig. (1). Proposed H-CRNN framework.

As illustrated in Fig. (**1**), the sign images/videos were captured and collected in the Data Acquisition stage. Further, the images/frames were preprocessed using various methods. In the Preprocessing stage, the images/frames were resized and converted from RGB to HSV. Skin Masking and Gaussian Blurring were also done on these sign images/frames. In the Data Augmentation phase, the dataset created was increased and augmented by using various operations on the sign images/frames such as translation, rotation, shearing, zooming, change in scale, and image flipping. In the FE phase, the segmented images were filtered through the CNN for feature extraction. In the MR stage, the main sign language recognition was done using LSTM/GRU.

Data Acquisition, Preprocessing, and Augmentation

There are currently no publicly available datasets for Indian signs that may be used to develop an Indian Sign Language Recognition (ISLR) system. We have created and collected our dataset called ISLAN and have made it publicly available for further research. ISLAN consists of Indian Sign Language (ISL) representation of English Alphabets and Numbers. It is a collection of 24 videos and 700 image sign representations. Each video/image illustrates the ISL representation of English alphabets or numbers. Both the single-handed and double-handed sign representations were created and collected for each alphabet. The images/videos were collected from 6 different signer volunteers. Signers with diverse skin tones and hand sizes/orientations were considered for the compilation of this dataset. ISLAN will be the first publicly available multi-signer dataset comprising alphabets (single and double-handed signs) and numbers in Indian Sign Language. The images/videos collected were captured under regular lighting conditions in an indoor space.

Later the dataset was increased by gathering signs from additional 4 different signer volunteers, and now ISLAN consists of 2 (A-Z) signs and 10 digits (0-9) signs. The data are collected from a total of 10 signer volunteers. Each signer helped to collect 36 signs of each alphabet and digit. The images were captured in different lighting and background condition. The 26 Alphabet and 10 digits signs of a single signer gesture are shown in Fig. (**2**). Fig. (**2**) illustrates the double-handed sign images of alphabets and single-handed sign illustrations of the numeric digits. Fig. (**3**) shows the single-handed multi-signer sign representation of the letter A.

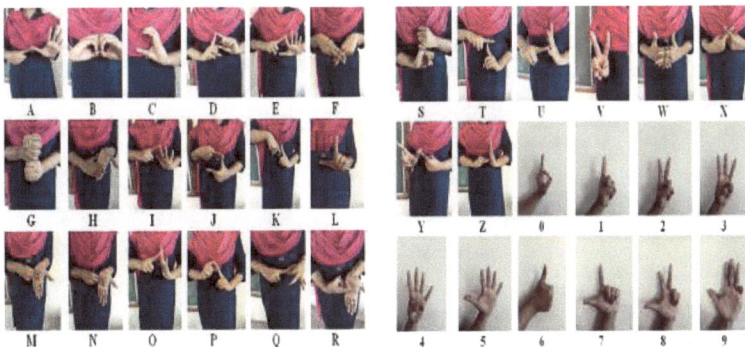

Fig. (2). ISL Alphabets and Digits Representation.

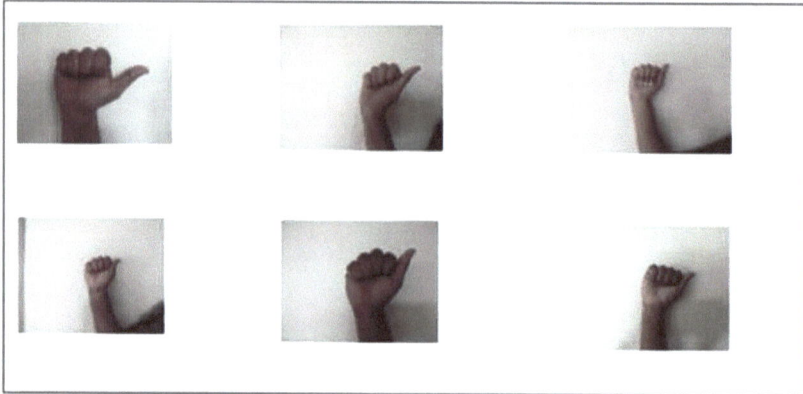

Fig. (3). Single-handed sign representation of alphabet A.

In the preprocessing step, with the help of OpenCV, the original images were resized into 64x64x3. The resized RGB images were converted into HSV color space. HSV separates the color and intensity of the image and is robust to varying lighting conditions and illumination factors. Then by using HSV segmentation, skin masking was performed on these images. Skin masking is done to detect and extract only the hand gestures in the image by using a threshold value. By applying skin segmentation to the images, we were able to extract only the gesture part and thereby discard the unwanted background parts. Gaussian blur was used to remove the noise in the skin masked images. The preprocessed image has then undergone data augmentation by using the Keras image data generator. The image augmentation techniques such as translation, shearing, rotation, width and height shifting, zooming, and horizontal flipping were performed to increase the dataset. Fig. (**4**) shows the sample augmented images. After data augmentation, the dataset was large enough to train the model and get accurate results.

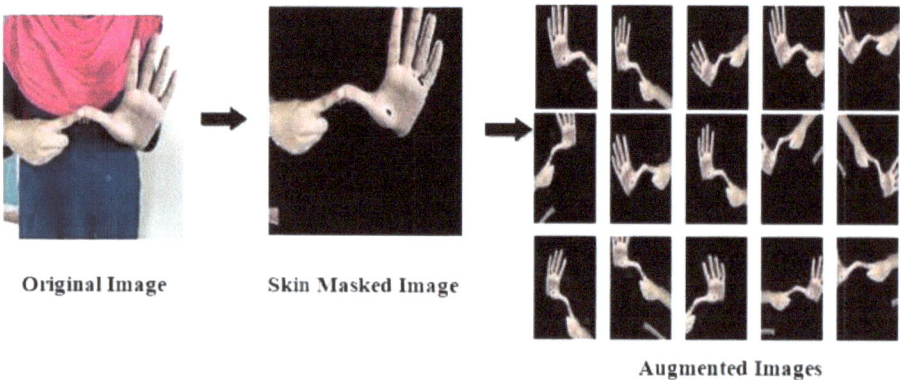

Original Image   Skin Masked Image   Augmented Images

Fig. (4). Preprocessed and augmented images.

Proposed H-CRNN Architecture

The proposed core H-CRNN model is the integration of a CNN and RNN (LSTM/GRU). The preprocessed and augmented input images with size 64x64x3 were fed to the CNN to extract the features from the images in the FE module. The CNN model has five convolutional layers with five convolutional blocks. Each convolutional block has a 2D Convolutional layer followed by Leaky ReLu, a 2D Max-pooling layer, and a Dropout rate of 0.3 to avoid overfitting. The Leaky ReLu activation function is used in the convolutional block, which is shown in Equation 1.

$$f(z) = 1(z < 0)(\alpha z) + 1(z \geq 0)(z) \tag{1}$$

where z is the input neuron, and α is a small constant. Each convolutional layer has different sizes of filters, and 2D max-pooling is applied with two strides. The max-pooling operation was done on the 2D spatial sign images. By selecting the maximum value for every channel of the inputs over an input window, max-pooling downsamples the inputs among their spatial dimensions. Across each dimension, the window is adjusted by two strides.

The extracted features were fed into the MR module. The MR module uses the RNN (LSTM/GRU) framework for classification. The feature vectors from the FE module were reshaped. The reshaped feature vectors as input were fed into the LSTM and GRU units for the classification of signs. In the proposed H-CRNN architecture, the classification block has two LSTM/GRU units followed by the fully connected layers. The last layer produces the output of the class probabilities using the softmax activation function. The Adam optimizer [38] is used to optimize the model with the learning rate. The model is compiled with the categorical cross-entropy loss function. The output layer consists of 36 classes which include 26 double-handed alphabet sign classes, 26 single-handed alphabet sign classes, and 10 numeric digit sign classes.

Fig. (5) illustrates the proposed H-CRNN Architecture. As discussed above, the architecture is divided into two modules Feature Extraction module and the Model Recognition (Classification) module. The preprocessed image is fed to the FE module consisting of five convolutional blocks wherein the image dimensions are reduced, thereby extracting only the required set of features from the gesture images. The extracted features are then passed for classification to the MR module, wherein the extracted features were exploited for recognition and classification of Isolated ISL representation of the English Alphabet and digit gestures.

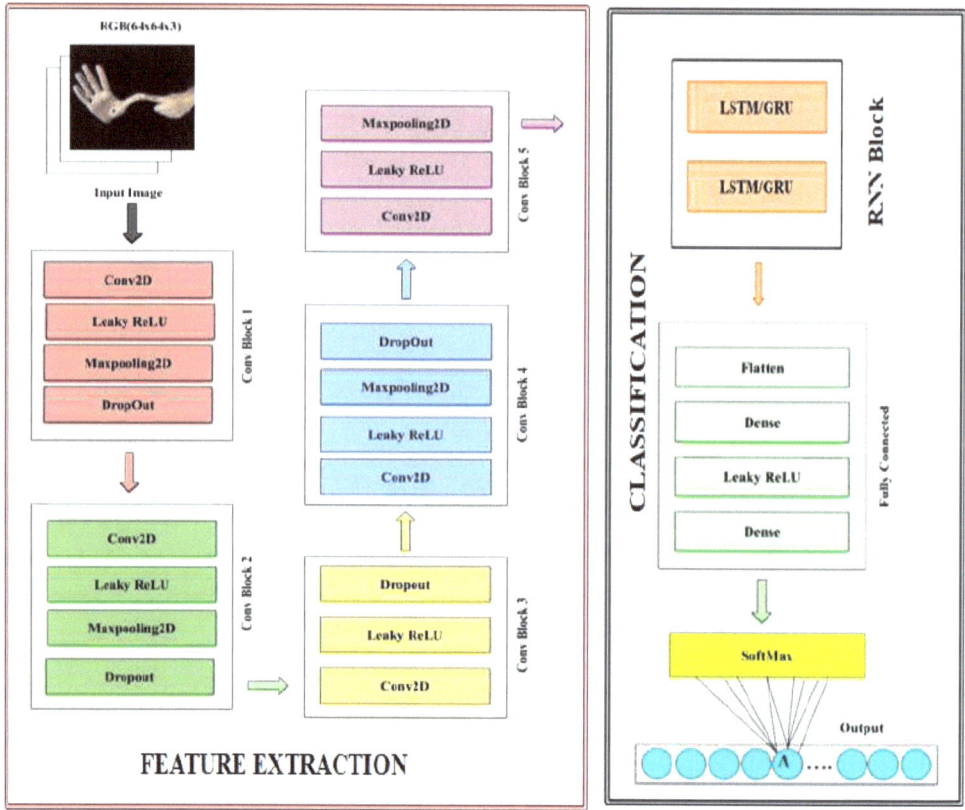

Fig. (5). Proposed H-CRNN Architecture.

Experiments and Results

The proposed H-CRNN model was fed with the newly created ISLAN dataset. ISLAN consisted of 7200 sign images and 360 sign videos of Indian sign representation of English Alphabets (both double-handed and single-handed sign gestures) and numeric digits. The ISLAN dataset was split into training and a testing set, with the training set acquiring 75% of ISLAN and the testing set acquiring 25% of ISLAN. The proposed model was evaluated and compared with other state-of-the-art neural network modules with the ISLAN dataset. The proposed H-CRNN model proved to perform better than the rest of the models. The proposed architecture with the feature dimension is discussed in Fig. (**6**). The overall model parameters are discussed in Fig. (**7**). The Source Code for H-CN--GRU is discussed in Fig. (**8**) and the Source Code for H-CNN-LSTM is discussed in Fig. (**9**).

Fig. (6). Description of the proposed CRNN architecture.

Fig. (7). Overall model parameters generated from the proposed CRNN architecture.

Fig. (8). Source code sample of the proposed H-CNN-GRU model.

```
[ ]  from keras.models import Sequential
     from tensorflow.python.keras.layers import LeakyReLU
     hidden_unit = 32
     Final_model1 = Sequential()

     Final_model1.add(Conv2D(filters = 256,kernel_size = (5,5),padding = 'same',input_shape = (64,64,3)))
     Final_model1.add(LeakyReLU(alpha=0.3))
     Final_model1.add(MaxPooling2D((2,2)))
     Final_model1.add(Dropout(0.3))

     Final_model1.add(Conv2D(filters = 128,kernel_size = (5,5),padding = 'same'))
     Final_model1.add(LeakyReLU(alpha=0.3))
     Final_model1.add(MaxPooling2D((3,3)))
     Final_model1.add(Dropout(0.3))

     Final_model1.add(Conv2D(filters = 64,kernel_size = (5,5),padding = 'same'))
     Final_model1.add(LeakyReLU(alpha=0.3))
     Final_model1.add(Dropout(0.3))

     Final_model1.add(Conv2D(filters = 64,kernel_size = (5,5),padding = 'same'))
     Final_model1.add(LeakyReLU(alpha=0.3))
     Final_model1.add(MaxPooling2D((3,3)))
     Final_model1.add(Dropout(0.3))

     Final_model1.add(Conv2D(filters = 32,kernel_size = (5,5),padding = 'same'))
     Final_model1.add(LeakyReLU(alpha=0.3))
     Final_model1.add(MaxPooling2D((3,3)))
     Final_model1.add(Dropout(0.3))


     Final_model1.add(TimeDistributed(Flatten()))
     Final_model1.add(Bidirectional(LSTM(hidden_unit,return_sequences=True)))
     Final_model1.add(Dropout(0.3))
     Final_model1.add(Bidirectional(LSTM(hidden_unit,return_sequences=True)))
     Final_model1.add(Flatten())
     Final_model1.add(Dense(256, activation = "relu"))
     Final_model1.add(BatchNormalization())
     Final_model1.add(Dense(36, activation = "softmax"))

     Final_model1.summary()
```

Fig. (9). Source code sample of the proposed H-CNN-LSTM model.

Firstly the proposed H-CNN-LSTM and H-CNN-GRU models were evaluated using the ISLAN dataset, and their performances were compared with each other. The Confusion matrix of the proposed Hybrid CNN-GRU model has been discussed in Fig. (**10**). The Confusion matrix of the proposed Hybrid CNN-LSTM model has been discussed in Fig. (**11**). The Hybrid CNN-GRU model has acquired 99.51% accuracy, whereas CNN-LSTM has acquired 99.21% accuracy in the 150th iteration For the ISLR system. It was observed that the H-CNN-GRU model had performed better when compared with the H-CNN-LSTM model. The accuracy and loss graph of the proposed Hybrid CNN-GRU model has been discussed in Fig. (**12**). The accuracy and loss graph of the proposed Hybrid CNN-LSTM model has been discussed in Fig. (**13**).

Fig. (10). Confusion Matrix of Hybrid CNN-GRU model.

Fig. (11). Confusion Matrix of Hybrid CNN-LSTM model.

ACCURACY / LOSS

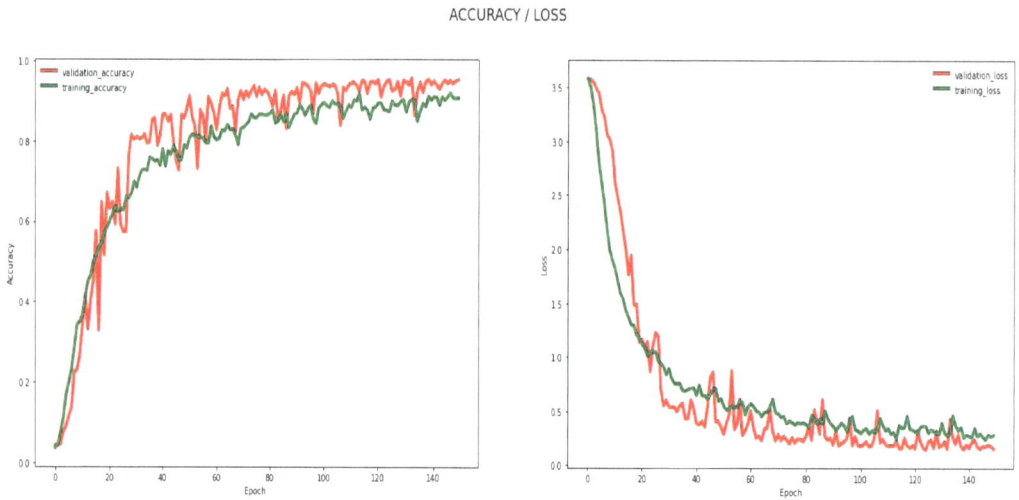

Fig. (12). Accuracy and Loss graph of CNN-GRU model.

ACCURACY / LOSS

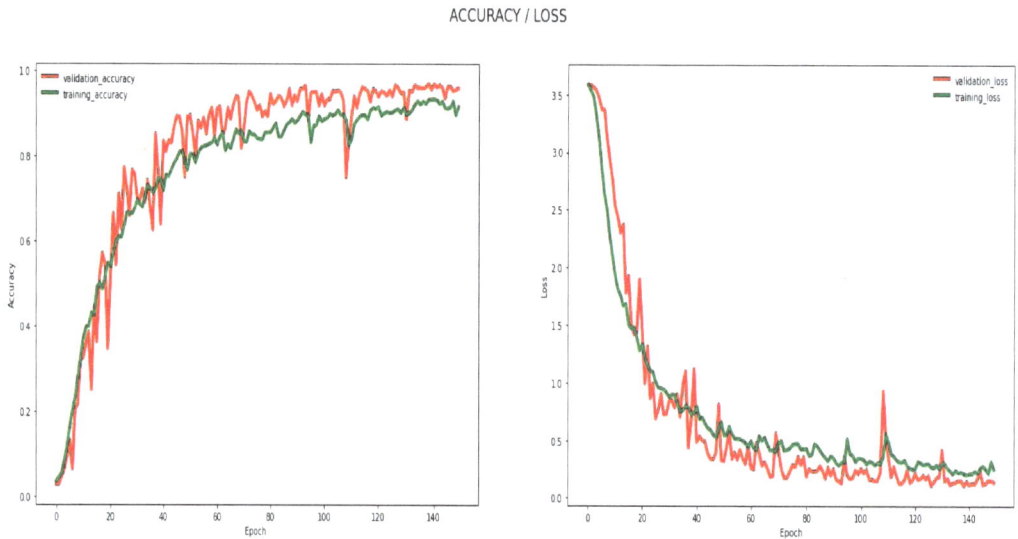

Fig. (13). Accuracy and Loss graph of CNN-LSTM model.

The classification Report of the proposed Hybrid CNN-GRU had precision, recall, and F1-score for all 36 classes. It had been noted that the minimum percentage of precision was 77% for alphabet M and 87% for digit 8. The lowest percentage of Recall was 80% for alphabet N and 88% for digit 3. The lowest F1-score for alphabet M is 87%, and digit 3 is 92%. The Weighted Average of precision, recall, and the F1-score for all 36 classes was 99.51%. The classification report of the proposed Hybrid CNN-LSTM had precision, recall, and F1-score for all 36 classes. It had been noted that the minimum percentage of precision was 79% for alphabet M and 93% for digit 4. The lowest percentage of Recall was 81% for Alphabet U and 93% for digit 3. The lowest F1-score for alphabet M was 85%, and digit 8 was 94%. The weighted average of precision for all 36 classes was 96%, and recall, the F1-score for all 36 classes was 99.21%.

The different CNN models are compared and evaluated with the proposed model as well. Table **1** describes the accuracy obtained by several state-of-the-art neural network models using the ISLAN dataset for the ISLR system.

Table 1. Comparison of accuracy of state-of-the-art neural networks with the proposed model.

Model	Accuracy (%)
VGG16	96.13
AlexNet	97
ResNet	84
Proposed CNN-LSTM	99.21
Proposed CNN-GRU	99.51

CONCLUSION AND FUTURE WORK

The main objective of this paper is to classify the Indian Sign Language representation of English alphabets and numbers with the application of the Hybrid Convolution Recurrent Neural Network-based framework. In the proposed work, two hybrid models have been created for ISL classification. The first model is the Hybrid CNN-GRU framework, and the other model is the Hybrid CNN-LSTM model. The proposed Hybrid CNN-GRU model proved to be performing better than the Hybrid CNN-LSTM framework. The proposed Hybrid-CRNN model achieved 99.21% and 99.51% accuracy and achieved good precision, recall, and F1-score on our dataset. We have contributed by creating and collecting a new multi-signer Indian Sign Language dataset called ISLAN, which has been made publicly available. For further research. The ISLAN consists of signer-independent, double-handed and single-handed Indian gesture representation of English alphabets as well as numbers. We also compared our work with different CNN models. This work could be useful for deaf and mute communities to overcome the communication difficulty with the general populace. In the future, we will use our proposed architecture for Indian Sign Language words.

ACKNOWLEDGEMENTS

We gratefully acknowledge the Department of Science & Technology (DST), India for the financial support through the Indo-Russian Joint Project (INT/RUS/RFBR/393). We also acknowledge SASTRA Deemed University, Thanjavur, India, for extending infrastructural support to carry out this research work.

REFERENCES

[1]   Y. Saleh, and G. Issa, "Arabic sign language recognition through deep neural networks fine-tuning", 2020: 71-83.
[http://dx.doi.org/10.3991/ijoe.v16i05.13087]

[2]   WANGCHUK, KARMA, Karma Wangchuk, and Panomkhawn Riyamongkol., Bhutanese Sign Language Hand-shaped Alphabets and Digits Detection and Recognition. Diss. Naresuan University, 2020.

[3]   X. Jiang, M. Lu, and S.H. Wang, "An eight-layer convolutional neural network with stochastic pooling, batch normalization and dropout for fingerspelling recognition of chinese sign language", *Multimedia Tools Appl.,* vol. 79, no. 21-22, pp. 15697-15715, 2020.
[http://dx.doi.org/10.1007/s11042-019-08345-y]

[4]   O. Sevlï, and N. Kemaloğlu, "Turkish sign language digits classification with cnn using different optimizers", *International Advanced Researches and Engineering Journal,* vol. 4, no. 3, pp. 200-207, 2020.
[http://dx.doi.org/10.35860/iarej.700564]

[5]   R. Elakkiya, and E. Rajalakshmi, ISLAN *Mendeley Data V1*, 2021.
[http://dx.doi.org/10.17632/rc349j45m5.1]

[6]   L.S.T. Mangamuri, L. Jain, and A. Sharmay, "Two hand indian sign language dataset for benchmarking classification models of machine learning", *2019 International conference on issues and challenges in intelligent computing techniques (ICICT)..* Vol. 1. IEEE, 2019.
[http://dx.doi.org/10.1109/ICICT46931.2019.8977713]

[7]   M. Nachamai, "Alphabet recognition of american sign language: a hand gesture recognition approach using sift algorithm", *International Journal of Artificial Intelligence & Applications,* vol. 4, no. 1, p. 105, 2013.

[8]   J. Singha, and K. Das, "Recognition of indian sign language in live video", arXiv preprint arXiv:1306.1301, 2013.

[9]   Youssif, AA. Aliaa , E.A Amal, and H.A Heba, "Arabic sign language (arsl) recognition system using hmm", *Int. J. Adv. Comput. Sci. Appl.,* vol. 2, p. 11, 2011.

[10]   M. Abdo, "Arabic alphabet and numbers sign language recognition", *Int. J. Adv. Comput. Sci. Appl.,* vol. 6, no. 11, pp. 209-214, 2015.

[11]   N. El-Bendary, "Arslat: Arabic sign language alphabets translator", In: *2010 international conference on computer information systems and industrial management applications (CISIM).* IEEE, 2010.

[12]   Miada A. Almasre, and Hana Al-Nuaim, "A real-time letter recognition model for Arabic sign language using kinect and leap motion controller v2", International Journal of Advanced Engineering, Management and Science 2. no 5, pp. 239469, 2016.

[13]   C-H. Chuan, E. Regina, and C. Guardino, "American sign language recognition using leap motion sensor,", *in 2014 13th International Conference on Machine Learning and Applications,* pp. 541-54, 2014.
[http://dx.doi.org/10.1109/ICMLA.2014.110]

[14]   M. ElBadawy, "A proposed hybrid sensor architecture for arabic sign language recognition", Intelligent Systems' 2014. Springer, Cham, 2015. 721-730.

[15]   B. Kang, S. Tripathi, and T.Q. Nguyen, "Real-time sign language fingerspelling recognition using convolutional neural networks from depth map", *In 2015 3rd IAPR Asian Conference on Pattern Recognition (ACPR),* pp. 136-140, 2015.
[http://dx.doi.org/10.1109/ACPR.2015.7486481]

[16]   L. Pigou, "Sign language recognition using convolutional neural networks", In: *European conference on computer vision.* Springer, Cham, 2014.

[17]   M. ElBadawy, "Arabic sign language recognition with 3d convolutional neural networks." 2017 Eighth international conference on intelligent computing and information systems (ICICIS). IEEE, 2017.
[http://dx.doi.org/10.1109/INTELCIS.2017.8260028]

[18]   S. Hayani, "Arab sign language recognition with convolutional neural networks", *2019 International Conference of Computer Science and Renewable Energies (ICCSRE),* IEEE, 2019.
[http://dx.doi.org/10.1109/ICCSRE.2019.8807586]

[19]   A. Khan, A. Sohail, U. Zahoora, and A.S. Qureshi, "A survey of the recent architectures of deep convolutional neural networks", *Artif. Intell. Rev.,* vol. 53, no. 8, pp. 5455-5516, 2020.
[http://dx.doi.org/10.1007/s10462-020-09825-6]

[20]   S. Hochreiter, and J. Schmidhuber, "Long short-term memory", *Neural Comput.,* vol. 9, no. 8, pp. 1735-1780, 1997.
[http://dx.doi.org/10.1162/neco.1997.9.8.1735] [PMID: 9377276]

[21]   S. Yang, and Q. Zhu, "Continuous Chinese sign language recognition with CNN-LSTM", *Ninth International Conference on Digital Image Processing (ICDIP 2017),* vol. Vol. 10420, 2017.

[22]   N. Tajbakhsh, J.Y. Shin, S.R. Gurudu, R.T. Hurst, C.B. Kendall, M.B. Gotway, and J. Liang, "Convolutional neural networks for medical image analysis: Full training or fine tuning?", *IEEE Trans. Med. Imaging,* vol. 35, no. 5, pp. 1299-1312, 2016.
[http://dx.doi.org/10.1109/TMI.2016.2535302] [PMID: 26978662]

[23]   A.K. Reyes, J.C. Caicedo, and J.E. Camargo, "Fine-tuning Deep Convolutional Networks for Plant Recognition", *CLEF,* vol. 1391, pp. 467-475, 2015. [Working Notes].

[24]   M.M. Hasan, A.Y. Srizon, and A.M.H. Md, "Classification of Bengali sign language characters by applying a novel deep convolutional neural network", 2020 IEEE Region 10 Symposium (TENSYMP). IEEE, 2020.
[http://dx.doi.org/10.1109/TENSYMP50017.2020.9230658]

[25]   M.A. Hossen, "Bengali sign language recognition using deep convolutional neural network." 2018 joint 7th international conference on informatics, electronics & vision (iciev) and 2018 2nd international conference on imaging, vision & pattern recognition (icIVPR). IEEE, 2018.
[http://dx.doi.org/10.1109/ICIEV.2018.8640962]

[26]   S.M. Htet, B. Aye, and M.M. Hein, "Myanmar Sign Language Classification using Deep Learning", *2020 International Conference on Advanced Information Technologies (ICAIT),* IEEE, 2020.
[http://dx.doi.org/10.1109/ICAIT51105.2020.9261775]

[27]   S.P. Das, A.K. Talukdar, and K.K. Sarma, "Sign language recognition using facial expression", *Procedia Comput. Sci.,* vol. 58, pp. 210-216, 2015.
[http://dx.doi.org/10.1016/j.procs.2015.08.056]

[28]   G.C. Lee, F.H. Yeh, and Y.H. Hsiao, "Kinect-based Taiwanese sign-language recognition system", *Multimedia Tools Appl.,* vol. 75, no. 1, pp. 261-279, 2016.
[http://dx.doi.org/10.1007/s11042-014-2290-x]

[29]   E.K. Kumar, P.V.V. Kishore, A.S.C.S. Sastry, M.T.K. Kumar, and D.A. Kumar, "Training CNNs for 3-D sign language recognition with color texture coded joint angular displacement maps", *IEEE Signal*

Process. Lett., vol. 25, no. 5, pp. 645-649, 2018.
[http://dx.doi.org/10.1109/LSP.2018.2817179]

[30]   G.A. Rao, and P.V.V. Kishore, "Selfie video based continuous Indian sign language recognition system", *Ain Shams Eng. J.,* vol. 9, no. 4, pp. 1929-1939, 2018.
[http://dx.doi.org/10.1016/j.asej.2016.10.013]

[31]   B. Xie, X. He, and Y. Li, "RGB-D static gesture recognition based on convolutional neural network", *J. Eng. (Stevenage),* vol. 2018, no. 16, pp. 1515-1520, 2018.
[http://dx.doi.org/10.1049/joe.2018.8327]

[32]   N.B. Ibrahim, M.M. Selim, and H.H. Zayed, "An automatic Arabic sign language recognition system (ArSLRS)", *Journal of King Saud University - Computer and Information Sciences,* vol. 30, no. 4, pp. 470-477, 2018.
[http://dx.doi.org/10.1016/j.jksuci.2017.09.007]

[33]   S. Sharma, and S. Singh, "Recognition of Indian sign language (ISL) using deep learning model", *Wirel. Pers. Commun.,* vol. 123, no. 1, pp. 671-692, 2022.
[http://dx.doi.org/10.1007/s11277-021-09152-1]

[34]   C.J. Sruthi, and A. Lijiya, "Signet: A deep learning based indian sign language recognition system", *2019 International conference on communication and signal processing (ICCSP)*. IEEE, 2019.

[35]   A. Wadhawan, and P. Kumar, "Deep learning-based sign language recognition system for static signs", *Neural computing and applications ,* vol. 32, no. 12, pp. 7957-7968, 2020.
[http://dx.doi.org/10.1007/s00521-019-04691-y]

[36]   A. Sharma, N. Sharma, Y. Saxena, A. Singh, and D. Sadhya, "Benchmarking deep neural network approaches for Indian Sign Language recognition", *Neural Comput. Appl.,* vol. 33, no. 12, pp. 6685-6696, 2021.
[http://dx.doi.org/10.1007/s00521-020-05448-8]

[37]   L. Perez, and J. Wang, "The effectiveness of data augmentation in image classification using deep learning", arXiv preprint arXiv:1712.04621 2017.

[38]   P. Kingma Diederik, *and Jimmy Ba Adam. "A method for stochastic optimization." arXiv preprint arXiv:1412.6980 (2014)..*

## CHAPTER 10

A Proposal of an Android Mobile Application for Senior Citizen Community with Multi-lingual Sentiment Analysis Chatbot

Harshee Pitroda[1,*], **Manisha Tiwari**[1] and **Ishani Saha**[1]

[1] *Department of Computer Engineering, NMIMS University, Mukesh Patel School of Technology Management & Engineering, Mumbai, India*

Abstract: Throughout these years, technology has transformed our world and has become an integral part of our everyday lives. This massive digitalization needs to take into consideration the elderly community too. However, the elderly community is usually digitally excluded, but despite these various and diverse difficulties, they remain driven, engaged, and eager to make an effort, to incorporate developing digital technologies into their daily life. Hence, this research implements the functionality of analyzing and determining the emotions of senior citizens by utilizing various natural languages processing-based machine learning techniques like SVM, Random Forest, and Decision Tree. Different algorithms were used, and various parameters were compared to obtain the results. It is seen that SVM gave the best results with an accuracy of 88%. The android application "Bandhu – your forever friend" would be accessible and usable by the elderly community. In addition, this proposed application offers various other features, including learning a new language and listening to the regional songs which would cater to the multicultural requirements in a diverse country like India, recording their audio stories to preserve the ethnic culture and inspire others, and lastly becoming tech-savvy by following easy video tutorials. These features would not only keep them engaged but also tackle their loneliness and isolation to some extent, as all these features were considered after surveying around 100 senior citizens' lifestyles and needs. This app will also make them more digitally independent. All the above-mentioned functionalities have been implemented using the programming language Java and the android application is built in Android Studio. Also, the entire app is in the Hindi language, considering that this language is the most preferred and spoken language in India.

Keywords: Android application for senior citizens, Decision Tree, Multi-lingual sentiment analysis chatbot, Random Forest, Support Vector Machine (SVM), TF-IDF Vectorization.

[*] **Corresponding author Harshee Pitroda:** Department of Computer Engineering, NMIMS University, Mukesh Patel School of Technology Management & Engineering, Mumbai, India; E-mail:harshee.pitroda2910@gmail.com

Gyanendra Verma & Rajesh Doriya (Eds.)

INTRODUCTION

The world is changing at a breakneck pace, and although much emphasis is placed on developing the potential of the youth community, the other end of the age spectrum, that is, the elderly community, is also increasing at a rapid pace often overlooked. Life expectancy is anticipated to rise further in the next decades as medical science advances, signaling an urgent need to build a digital infrastructure that supports and leverages the potential of this enormous but often-forgotten 'silver' sector. These technological advancements should seek to improve the lives of the elderly community by making them easier and more enjoyable, hence helping them to cope with the feeling of loneliness, isolation, and independence. So, the app "Bandhu – your forever friend" aims to cater to the elderly community of society.

The proposed solution is built incrementally, augmenting various features. After each successive version of this application, another functionality was added to the preceding version until all intended functionalities were implemented.

A survey was conducted through google forms, where around 100 senior citizens were asked a series of questions, and their responses were recorded. The questions asked are listed in Section VI, named Questionnaire. The survey results were used as a guiding tool to decide on various features to be implemented in this proposed solution.

Certain physiological and cognitive changes are nearly inevitable as people age, and these changes must be incorporated while designing the app's user interface. In designing the user interface of the app, all these factors are taken into consideration.

The salient features of this app's UI design include the following:

- The entire application is in the Hindi language, considering that it is the most preferred and spoken language in India.
- Hand-eye coordination may decline as people age, which may impair UI interaction. As a result, in this app, all UI components that need to be read or clicked are made larger in size.
- As motor abilities may deteriorate with age, it becomes more difficult for the elderly to operate a smartphone in many ways. So, this app's user interface is made incredibly simple to use and navigate.
- Colour vision may also deteriorate with aging, making it harder to distinguish between different hues. As a result, contrast colors have been utilized to help the senior citizens clearly identify between the background and the buttons or texts.

- Icons are labeled with text everywhere, making the function of the iconography clear to them.

The modules of the app "Bandhu – your forever friend" are as follows:

- **Multi-lingual sentiment analysis chatbot** - Sentiment analysis is the process of analyzing and determining the emotion or purpose behind a piece of text, voice, or any other method of communication. This is performed by using the Natural Language Processing-based Machine Learning model. The goal of conducting a sentiment analysis is to identify the sentiments underlying the senior citizen's texts and then respond to them accordingly. This chatbot can assist fill the void of an elderly population in need of human connection, as well as alleviate feelings of loneliness and isolation. It can also be useful in aiding senior citizens, both as a companion and as an instrument to keep their physical and mental health in check.
- **Listen and learn a language** - learning a new language at a later age may help one to refresh and invigorate both social and cognitive skills. Learning a new language exercises the brain and has been shown to improve IQ, memory, and attention. This app also allows the elderly community to learn by listening to the language, and also at their own speed, without the aid of youngsters.
- **Learn technology** – Learning new technology will ease their life, make them more independent, and they won't remain secluded from society. This is achieved by providing easy video tutorials in the Hindi language to show them to do online shopping, send and receive emails, pay bills, do banking services, learn how to utilize social media, download and upload materials, *etc.* They can learn these at their own speed without the aid of the young.
- **Audio Diaries** – Seniors, who reflect on their lives, are typically astonished and grateful for how much they've been through. Having someone to share one's life tales boosts the senior citizen's self-esteem. It is a fantastic legacy to preserve life tales through audio recordings. Through this app, senior citizens can record their own cultural stories, recipes, and real-life inspiring and motivating experiences, to share with others.
- **Listen to regional songs** - Music is a powerful tool for evoking memories and increasing people's overall quality of life. Senior citizens would enjoy listening to regional music from this app, which would recall their wonderful memories.

The remainder of this paper discusses in detail the multi-lingual sentiment analysis chatbot module and is organized as follows: Section II is the literature review. Section III is further subdivided into three subsections, A, B, and C, describe the proposed framework for the multi-lingual sentiment analysis chatbot, proposed architecture for integrating the model, and the dataset, respectively.

Section IV discusses the implementation overview, which is further subdivided into four subsections, A, B, C, and D, describing the exploratory data analysis, feature extraction, classification, and integration, respectively. Section V is subdivided into two sections, A and B, that describe the results and, finally, the conclusion. The results section also contains a tabular representation, summarizing and comparing the algorithms used. Section VI contains the questions asked in the survey.

LITERATURE REVIEW

V Goel *et al.* [1], presented solutions to the multi-lingual sentiment analysis problem by developing algorithms and comparing accuracy factors to determine the optimum option for multi-lingual sentiment analysis. They have used a multi-lingual dataset from Twitter. Their observations revealed that the RNN classifier was well ahead of the other classifier in the job of predicting feelings.

Sazzed S *et al.* [2], applied various machine learning algorithms to a collection of Bengali corpus and equivalent machine-translated English versions, and the models' performance was assessed on two datasets of different domains: the sports comments (Cricket) dataset and the Drama review dataset.

They noticed that the efficiency of their sentiment analysis in Bengali was frequently hampered by language complexity, a difficult writing system, insufficient labeled data, and a lack of lexical resources. Their results showed that machine translation could give higher accuracy than the native language (Bengali) and may be utilized for sentiment analysis in resource-limited languages like Bengali.

A Madan *et al.* [3] collected movie tweets in Hindi for sentiment analysis of Twitter data and led a comparative assessment for both techniques: lexicon-based approach and hybrid-based approach, which combine the Lexico-Based Approach and Machine Learning approach. Their research was incapable of translating tweets that are in the English language into the Hindi Language. As mentioned, their work could be extended to include the translation of English language tweets to Hindi Language and then further classifying them with the classifier. Their study concluded that it only addresses binary-class sentiment analysis; however, it may be expanded to incorporate multi-class sentiment analysis as well.

D Mahajan *et al.* [4] demonstrated that there was a higher accuracy by using the RNN (Recursive Neural Network) algorithm because when they classified the tweets fetched from Twitter, the volume of data that was taken into account to be classified as higher than the amount of data that is usually taken into account, by other researchers because they used the Stanford library and Google translator, which increased the machine's competence power.

A. K. Soni al [5]. have attempted to categorize sentiment analysis for tweets obtained from Twitter using machine learning methods. They used two algorithms: Naive Bayes (NB) and Maximum Entropy. They discovered that the Maximum Entropy classifier surpasses all other classifiers in predicting sentiments, with an accuracy of 74%.

Shukrity Si *et al.* [6] developed a model that can detect aggressive texts *via* social media. Sentiment scores, emoji, aggressive words, and the POS tag were utilized as features, and Gradient Boosting, XGBoost, and SVM were employed as classifiers. Their approach performs well on English datasets, but it has to be modified for Hindi and code-mixed datasets.

Abu *et al.* [7] focused on using multi-class classification to classify tweets based on mood. The emotion classes were fundamental human emotions (happiness, sorrow, surprise, disgust) and neutral. Their technique increased the performance of multi-class classification of Twitter data, according to their experimental results. They developed a system for emotion analysis with a Naïve Bayes classifier for

Twitter data

Sumitra *et al.* [8] devised a model in which a Hindi text can be effectively categorized in many classes using an ontology, as well as the polarity of each class, using two approaches: HSWN and a combination of HSWN and LMClassifier.This approach achieved better accuracy.

According to Christian *et al.* [9], long-term use of a mobile application (app) for elders promotes physical and mental activity. The usage records of 82 users over a two-year period were analyzed, revealing that active older users may be divided into two categories, each with growing or declining activity and very little stable activity.

According to Wei *et al.* [10], using the ARCS motivation model in the design of online learning apps helps to stimulate users' learning demands, sustain learning interest, and provide a better user experience. They proposed an online learning app design model for the elderly group by merging the ARCS motivation model with the design technique of an online learning app, which completes the functional framework design, interaction, and interface design of the application.

PROPOSED FRAMEWORK

This section describes the proposed framework for the multi-lingual sentiment analysis chatbot that is shown through a diagrammatic representation in Fig. (**1**). This section also includes a brief description of the dataset used and the proposed architecture for the integration of the model in the android application - "Bandhu – your forever friend," which is shown through a diagrammatic representation in Fig. (**2**).

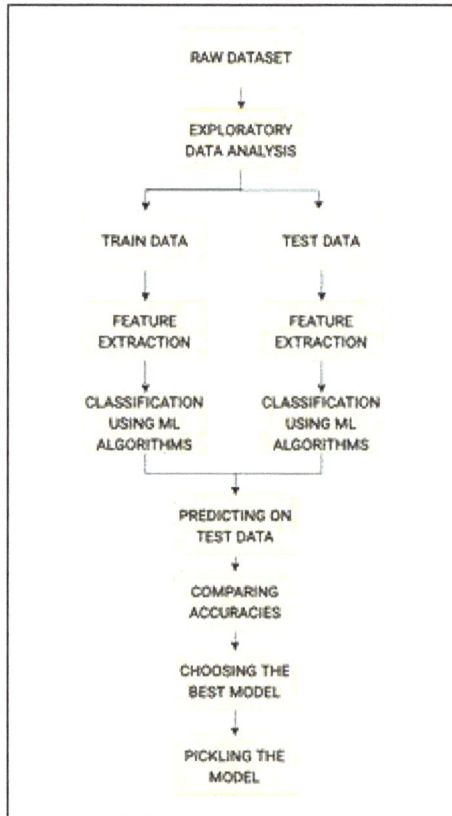

Fig. (1). Flow chart representation of the proposed framework for the sentiment analysis chatbot.

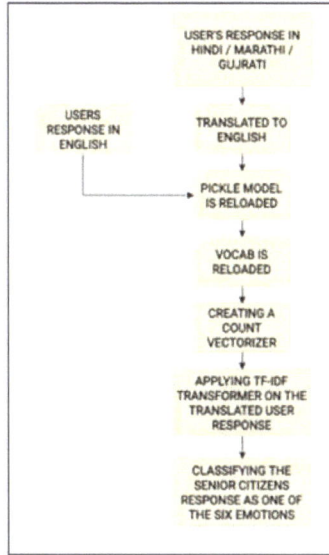

Fig. (2). Flow chart representation of the proposed architecture for integrating the model.

A. Proposed framework for the multi-lingual sentiment analysis chatbot

The proposed framework is as follows:

1. **Exploratory data analysis (EDA)** - EDA is for the basic exploration of the dataset, summarizes the key features, and is performed in conjunction with data visualization approaches.

2. **Feature extraction** - For feature extraction, TF-IDF vectorization is used. This approach reflects the importance of a word compared to a record in the corpus and provides insights into the less and more relevant terms in a document.

3. **Multi-class classification** - Classification entails classifying data and grouping it based on commonalities. A multi-class classification task has more than two classes or outputs. Our multi-class classification approach determines if a senior citizen's response is happy, sad, furious, fearful, loved, or surprised.

4. **Testing on the unseen dataset** - Testing is used here to evaluate raw and unseen datasets in order to assess and compare the performance of the model.

5. **Performance Evaluation of various algorithms** - Various machine learning techniques' accuracies and confusion matrices were compared.

6. **Generating a pickled model** - Pickling the model is done here to save, restore, and reload the model later in order to test it on/with new data and also to incorporate it into the Android app.

B. Proposed architecture for integrating the model

The proposed architecture for integrating the model in the android application is as follows:

1. **User's response in English / Hindi / Marathi / Gujrati** – While using the application "Bandhu – your forever friend," the senior citizen (user) will input their text message in either English / Hindi / Marathi / Gujarati language. If the user inputs directly in the English language, then step 2 of translating to English is not carried out. It is then executed from step 3.

2. **Translated to English** - The input taken from the senior citizen in the Hindi / Marathi / Gujrati language is then converted to the English language by using translation libraries in python.

3. **Pickle model is reloaded** – The model is reloaded in order to classify the user's response within one of the 6 classes - happy, sad, furious, fearful, loved, or surprised.

4. **Vocabulary is reloaded** - The vocabulary facilitates the collection of the processed text before it is converted into a representation for classification. It is a collection of words that are unique to the document. It is either a mapping, where the keys are terms and the values are feature matrix indices or an iterable over terms. The vect. Vocabulary_ is dumped into a pickle file that is then reloaded while recreating the model.

5. **Count vectorizer and TF-IDF Transformer** - In order to use the TfidfTransformer, one will first have to create a CountVectorizer to count the number of words (term frequency) and specify the vocabulary as the vocabulary pickle file reloaded in the previous step. We then compute the IDFs by initializing the transformer and performing fit_transform on the user's data.

6. **Classification** – It will then successfully classify whether the senior citizen's response is happy, sad, furious, fearful, loved, or surprised.

C. Dataset

In this research project, the "Emotions dataset for NLP" dataset is used. This dataset contains 19997 messages with their corresponding emotion labels.

IMPLEMENTATION OVERVIEW

In this section, a detailed implementation overview of the research project is described.

Exploratory Data Analysis (EDA)

The initial phase of the research project was exploratory data analysis. Basic data exploration was conducted to better understand the dataset and gain insights from it. We also visualized the dataset through bar charts and gained a clear understanding of the dataset segregated by emotions. A bar chart representation of the dataset is shown in Fig. (**3**).

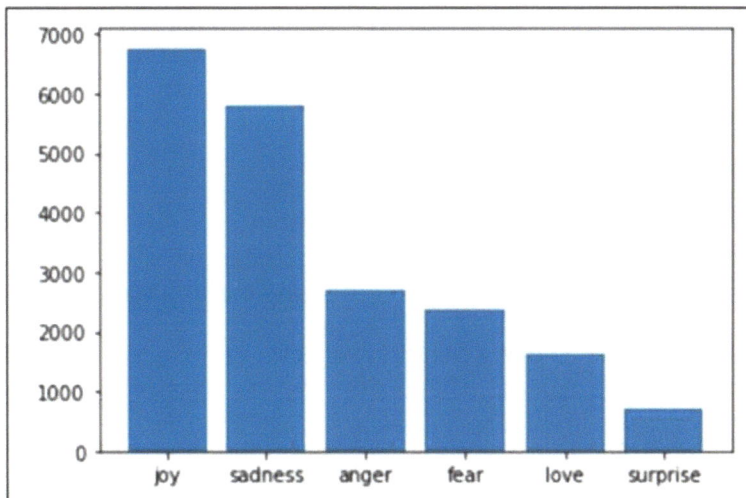

Fig. (3). Overview of the dataset represented through a bar chart.

Feature Extraction

Machine learning algorithms work with numerical data and require a two-dimensional array as input. To perform machine learning on text data, it is first required to convert the text data to a vector representation; hence machine learning algorithms can then be applied. This is known as feature extraction or, more colloquially, vectorization. There were 2 approaches that were used in this research project

1. **Count Vectorization** - Count Vectorization is concerned with the occurrence of words in a document.

2.TF-IDF Vectorization (term frequency-inverse document frequency). - Using TF-IDF Vectorization, the word counts are normalized by the number of times they appear in the documents. The formula for TF-IDF vectorization is as follows:

$$W_{i,j} = tf_{i,j} \times \log\left(\frac{N}{df}\right)$$

df_i = number of documents containing i

N = total number of documents

Classification

Train test split - The dataset has been divided into 2 sets, the training dataset, and the test dataset. The training dataset is used to train the entire algorithm to produce the output. At the same time, the test dataset acts as a substitute for new data. The test dataset, also known as the hold-out set, is not utilized in model training but can be used to predict and assess metrics.

Predictions - The classification approach divides data into several classes and then predicts which class the incoming data belongs to. There are two kinds of classification: binary classification and multi-class classification.

Binary classification is a classification process in which a given data set is classified into only two classes, whereas the task of classifying items into two or more separate classes is known as multi-class classification.

We moved ahead with the multi-class classification approach that determines if a senior citizen's response is happy, sad, furious, fearful, loved, or surprised.

The various multi-class classifications algorithms that were used in this research project are as follows:

Support Vector Machine

The Support Vector Machine (SVM) algorithm can be used for both regression and classification problems. Its goal is to establish the best possible boundary between the potential outputs and to identify a hyperplane in an n-dimensional space that will optimize the separation of data points to their actual classes. The confusion matrix produced after using the SVM algorithm is shown in Fig. (**4**).

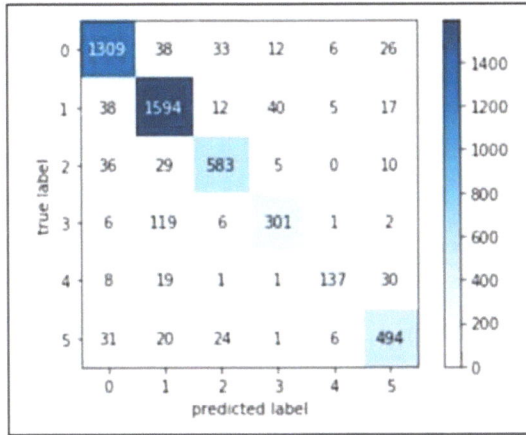

Fig. (4). Confusion matrix produced after using the Support Vector Machine algorithm.

Decision Tree

A decision tree divides a dataset into smaller and smaller subgroups while developing an associated decision tree progressively. The end result is a tree containing leaf nodes and decision nodes. A decision node has at least two branches. The classification of the data is represented by the leaf nodes. The confusion matrix produced after using the decision tree is shown in Fig. (**5**).

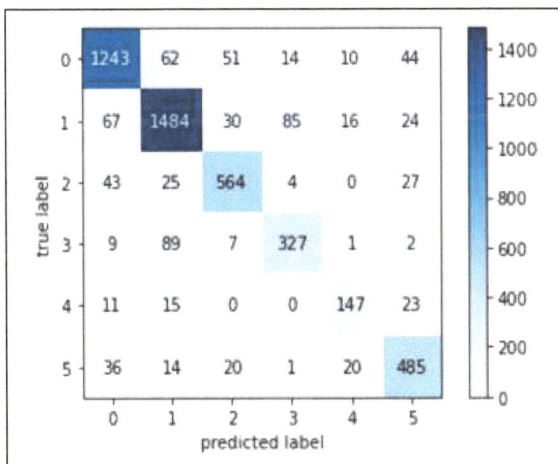

Fig. (5). Confusion matrix produced after using the Decision Tree algorithm.

Random Forest

Random Forest is a tree-based algorithm that comes under the ensemble method. The Random Forest Classifier is a collection of decision trees chosen at random from a subset of the training data. It combines the votes from several decision trees to determine the final class of the test object. The confusion matrix produced after using the random forest is shown in Fig. (**6**).

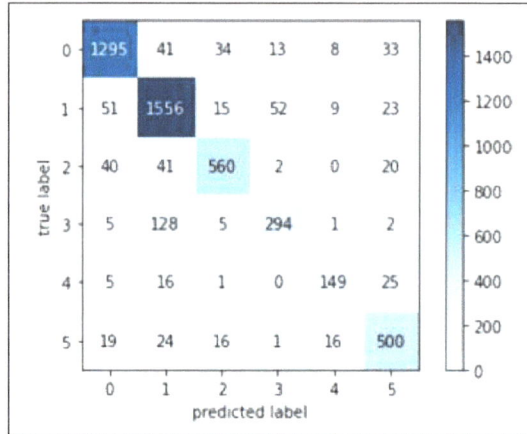

Fig. (6). Confusion matrix produced after using the Random Forest algorithm.

Implementation

Pickling the Model

Pickle is the standard Python object (de)serialization tool. Pickle is used to save and recover trained models in order to reuse them later in the development of the application - "Bandhu – your forever friend."

Translation

Specifically, one of the modules used here that makes it simple to translate texts is deep_translator, which supports several well-known translators. The Google Translator is already included in the deep translator package and can be accessed simply by importing it. The source and target languages are then passed as parameters to build an instance. Following that, the translation method may be used to return the translated text. This translation module of this research project will translate the senior citizens' text messages that are in Hindi / Marathi / Gujrati language to English language and then perform the sentiment analysis and produce a reply like ways. The reply to the senior citizen will also be in the respective language used by the senior citizens.

Integrating with the Android App

The app for this research project is made using Android Studio software with Java as the programming language. To integrate the python script in the android app for the research project, chaquopy plugin is used. Chaquopy is a Gradle-based build system plugin for Android Studio; it is the well-known "Python SDK for Android." Chaquopy enables the intermixing of Java and Python in the development of an Android application.

Code Snippets

This section displays the code snippets for all the algorithms.

Support Vector Machine

The hyperparameters used in Support vector machines are the kernel set to linear, and the c hyperparameter is set to 1.

```python
from sklearn.svm import SVC
start2 = time.time()
model = SVC(kernel = 'linear', C =
1).fit(features_train_vectorized, labels_train)
end2 = time.time()
fit_time2 = (end2 - start2)
predictions =
model.predict(vect.transform(features_test))
#score
from sklearn.metrics import f1_score
svmscore = (f1_score(labels_test,
predictions, average=None)*100)
#accuracy
from sklearn.metrics import accuracy_score
svmacc = (accuracy_score(labels_test,
predictions)*100)
#recall and precision
from sklearn.metrics import
precision_recall_fscore_support as score
precisionsvm, recallsvm, fscore,
train_support = score(labels_test,
predictions)
```

Decision Tree

```
from sklearn.tree import DecisionTreeClassifier
start1 = time.time()
model = DecisionTreeClassifier()
model.fit(features_train_vectorized, labels_train)
end1 = time.time()
fit_time1 = (end1 - start1)
predictions =
model.predict(vect.transform(features_test))
#score
from sklearn.metrics import f1_score
decisiontreescore = (f1_score(labels_test,
predictions, average=None)*100)
#accuracy
from sklearn.metrics import accuracy_score
dtacc = (accuracy_score(labels_test,
predictions)*100)
#recall and precision
from sklearn.metrics import
precision_recall_fscore_support as score
precisiondt, recalldt, fscore, train_support =
score(labels_test, predictions)
```

Random Forest

```
from sklearn.ensemble import RandomForestClassifier
start3 = time.time()
model = RandomForestClassifier()
model.fit(features_train_vectorized, labels_train)
end3 = time.time()
fit_time3 = (end3 - start3)
predictions =
model.predict(vect.transform(features_test))
#score
from sklearn.metrics import f1_score
rfscore = (f1_score(labels_test, predictions,
average=None)*100)
#accuracy
from sklearn.metrics import accuracy_score
rfacc = (accuracy_score(labels_test, predictions)*100)
#recall and precision
from sklearn.metrics import
precision_recall_fscore_support as score
precisionrf, recallrf, fscore, train_support =
score(labels_test, predictions)
```

RESULTS AND CONCLUSION

Results

Feature Extraction

The F1-score was compared after applying both the feature extraction methods and the SVM algorithm (the SVM algorithm was applied as it had the highest accuracy), and the results are shown in Fig. (7).

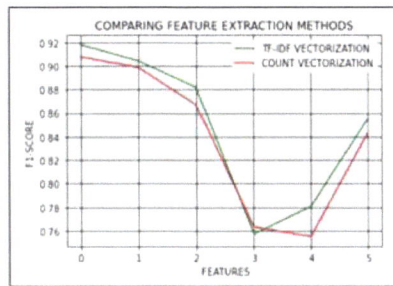

Fig. (7). Comparing the F1-Score after applying both the methods of feature extraction.

TF-IDF Vectorization produces-IDF Vectorization produces better results than the Count Vectorization. TF-IDF outperforms Count Vectorizers because it considers the frequency of words in not only the corpus but also the importance of the word.

Classification

Accuracy - Accuracy is a measure that describes how the model performs. The accuracy of a machine learning model is the metric used to evaluate which model is best at finding correlations and patterns between variables in a dataset based on the input or training data.

The formula to calculate accuracy is as follows:

$$\frac{True\,positive + True\,negative}{True\,positive + True\,negative + False\,positive + False\,negative}$$

In this research project, the SVM algorithm produces the highest accuracy when compared with others, and the results of the accuracies are shown in Table 1.

F1 Score - The F1score is a composite of the accuracy and recall measures. A strong F1 score indicates that there are a low number of false positives and false negatives. When an F1 score is nearing 1, the model is regarded as ideal, whereas when it is nearing 0, the model is not considered ideal. Fig. (**8**) represents the F1 Scores for each feature. The features are numbered from 0 to 5 that represent the emotions - sad, joy, anger, love, surprise, and fear, respectively.

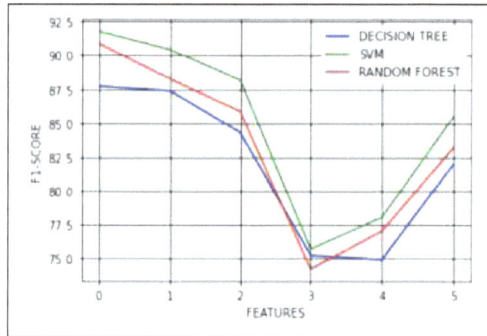

Fig. (8). Comparing the F1 Score for each feature after applying the different algorithms.

In this research project, the SVM algorithm has the highest F1-Score as compared to other algorithms, and the results of the F1-score are shown in Table **1**.

Fit time – The time it takes for the model to fit the training data. In this research project, the Decision Tree algorithm has the lowest fit time, and the results of the fit time are shown in Table **1**.

Precision – Precision refers to how accurate a model is in terms of how many of those predicted positives are actually positive. When the costs of False Positive are high, precision is a suitable metric to use. Fig. (**9**) represents the precision for each feature. The features are numbered from 0 to 5 that represent the emotions - sad, joy, anger, love, surprise, and fear, respectively.

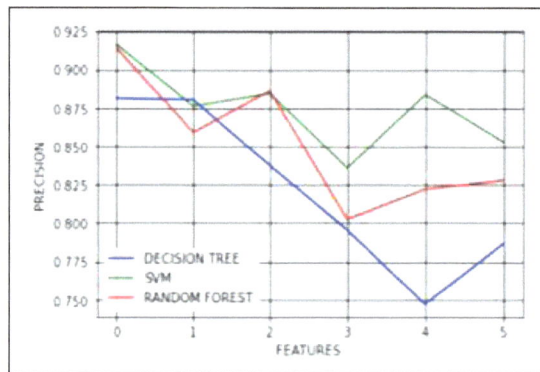

Fig. (9). Comparing the precision for each feature after applying the different algorithms.

The formula for precision is as follows:

$$\frac{True positive}{True positive \,+\, False positive}$$

In the research project, the SVM algorithm has the highest precision as compared to other algorithms, and the results of the precision are shown in Table **1**.

Recall – Instead of looking at the number of false positives predicted by the model (as with precision), recall looks at the number of false negatives. When there is a significant cost associated with False Negative, we will utilize recall as the model measure to choose our best model. Fig. (**10**) represents the recall for each feature. The features are numbered from 0 to 5 that represent the emotions - sad, joy, anger, love, surprise, and fear, respectively.

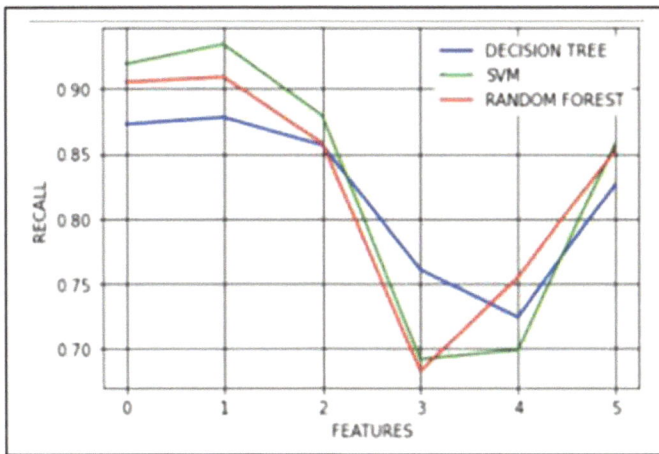

Fig. (10). Comparing the recall for each feature after applying the different algorithms.

The formula for the recall is as follows:

In this research project, the SVM algorithm comparatively has a greater recall factor than other algorithms, and the results of the recall are shown in Table **1**. Table **1** summarizes and compares each algorithm.

Table I. Summary and comparison of the algorithms

Parameter	SVM	Random Forest	Decision Tree
Accuracy	88.36%	86.86%	86.39%
F1-score for each feature	91.80, 90.44, 88.20, 75.72, 78.06, 85.54	90.76, 88.50, 86.46, 74.05, 79.25, 84.07	87.84, 88.02, 85.43, 76.42, 75.32, 81.73
Fit time (seconds)	21.99	9.75	3.22
Precision for each feature	91.67, 87.63, 88.47, 83.61, 88.39, 85.32	91.42, 85.93, 88.63, 80.27, 82.22, 82.80	88.16, 88.07, 83.78, 79.57, 74.74, 78.68
Recall for each feature	91.92, 93.43, 87.93, 69.20, 69.90, 85.76	90.52, 90.91, 85.82, 68.28, 75.51, 85.24	87.29, 87.81, 85.67, 76.09, 72.45, 82.64

The model has been successfully integrated with the android app, and the screenshots of the app are shown below from Fig.(**11**) to Fig. (**16**).

Table II. Screenshots of the integration of the ml model in the app

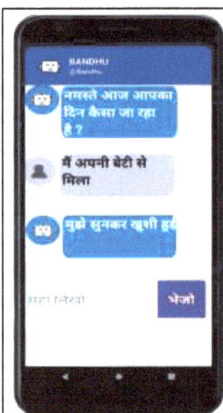

Fig. (**11**) – Screenshot of a conversation with the multi-lingual AI chatbot in the Hindi language for the emotion of joy.

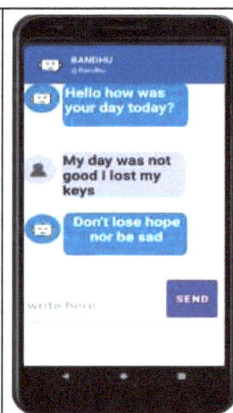

Fig. (**12**) – Screenshot of a conversation with the multi-lingual AI chatbot in the English language for the emotion of sad.

Fig. (**13**) – Screenshot of a conversation with the multi-lingual AI chatbot in Gujrati language for the emotion of fear.

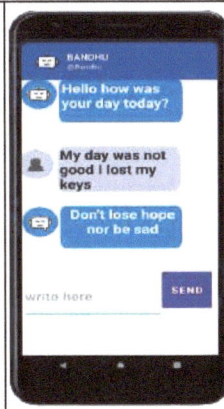

Fig. (**14**) – Screenshot of a conversation with the multi-lingual AI chatbot in the Marathi language for the emotion of anger.

Fig. (**15**) – Screenshot of a conversation with the multi-lingual AI chatbot in the Hindi language for the emotion of love.

Fig. (**16**) – Screenshot of a conversation with the multi-lingual AI chatbot in the English language for the emotion of surprise.

CONCLUSION

Hence, considering all these parameters in this research project, we concluded to use the TF-IDF Vectorization approach for feature extraction and the SVM algorithm to train the machine learning model, as it has the highest accuracy, and precision, and recall for each feature.

So, to conclude, the app "Bandhu – your forever friend" would serve the elderly community, who have accepted digitalization and are eager to master new technology. To some extent, it would aid in bridging the digital gap, social isolation, and loneliness. The multi-lingual chatbot feature can help the elderly community rewire their thoughts and enhance their mental wellness. They can use it to cope with depression or stress. This chatbot can also be beneficial to assist senior citizens in giving them company.

CONSENT FOR PUBLICATION

We give our consent for the publication of identifiable details, which can include photograph(s) and text material to be published.

CONFLICT OF INTEREST

The authors declare no conflict of interest, financial or otherwise.

ACKNOWLEDGEMENT

Declared none.

REFERENCES

[1]   V. Goel, A.K. Gupta, and N. Kumar, "Sentiment analysis of multi-lingual twitter data using natural language processing", *2018 8th International Conference on Communication Systems and Network Technologies (CSNT)*. IEEE, 2018.

[2]   S. Sazzed, and S. Jayarathna, "A sentiment classification in bengali and machine translated english corpus", *2019 IEEE 20th international conference on information reuse and integration for data science (IRI)*. IEEE, 2019.
[http://dx.doi.org/10.1109/IRI.2019.00029]

[3]   A. Madan, and U. Ghose, "Sentiment Analysis for Twitter Data in the Hindi Language", *11th International Conference on Cloud Computing, Data Science & Engineering (Confluence)*. IEEE, 2021.
[http://dx.doi.org/10.1109/Confluence51648.2021.9377142]

[4]   D. Mahajan, and D.K. Chaudhary, "Sentiment analysis using rnn and google translator", *In 2018 8th International Conference on Cloud Computing, Data Science & Engineering (Confluence)*, pp. 798-802, 2018, January. IEEE.

[5]   A.K. Soni, "Multi-lingual sentiment analysis of twitter data by using classification algorithms", *2017 Second International Conference on Electrical, Computer and Communication Technologies (ICECCT)*, IEEE, 2017.
[http://dx.doi.org/10.1109/ICECCT.2017.8117884]

[6]   S. Si, A. Datta, S. Banerjee, and S.K. Naskar, "Aggression detection on multi-lingual social media text", *10th International Conference on Computing, Communication and Networking Technologies (ICCCNT)*. IEEE, 2019.

[7]   Riyadh, Abu Zonayed, Nasif Alvi, and Kamrul Hasan Talukder. "Exploring human emotion via Twitter." *2017 20th International Conference of Computer and Information Technology (ICCIT)*. IEEE, 2017.
[http://dx.doi.org/10.1109/ICCITECHN.2017.8281813]

[8]   S. Pundlik, P. Dasare, P. Kasbekar, A. Gawade, G. Gaikwad, and P. Pundlik, "Multi-class classification and class based sentiment analysis for hindi language", *2016 International Conference on Advances in Computing, Communications and Informatics (ICACCI)*, IEEE., pp. 512-518, 2016.
[http://dx.doi.org/10.1109/ICACCI.2016.7732097]

[9]   C. Lins, A. Hein, L. Halder, and P. Gronotte, "Still in flow — long-term usage of an activity motivating app for seniors", *IEEE 18th international conference on e-health networking, applications*

and services (Healthcom). IEEE, 2016.
[http://dx.doi.org/10.1109/HealthCom.2016.7749476]

[10]   W. Xiong, W. He, and Z. Liu, "Design of online learning mobile app for the elderly based on attention, relevance, confidence, and satisfaction (arcs) motivation model", *2019 IEEE International Conference on Engineering, Technology and Education (TALE)*, pp. 1-5, 2019.
[http://dx.doi.org/10.1109/TALE48000.2019.9225849]

CHAPTER 11

Technology Inspired-Elaborative Education Model (TI-EEM): A futuristic need for a Sustainable Education Ecosystem

Anil Verma[1], **Aman Singh**[1,*], **Divya Anand**[1] and **Rishika Vij**[2]

[1] *Department of Computer Science and Engineering, Lovely Professional University, Jalandhar, Punjab, India*

[2] *Department of Veterinary Physiology & Biochemistry, Dr. GC Negi College of Veterinary & Animal Science, Palampur, Himachal Pradesh, India*

Abstract: Before three decades, providing higher education infrastructure for young aspirants in their locality was a challenge for India. With 5164 higher education institutions, including universities, colleges, and stand-alone institutions, India has surpassed the United States as the global leader in educational infrastructure over the last two decades. This work intends to propose an elaborative education ecosystem for sustainable quality education. The secondary data from top global ranking agencies (Times, QS, Webometric, Scimago, and Shanghai Ranking) is deployed to avoid the cost of a worldwide survey for primary data and the execution time. Quality education's quantitative and qualitative parameters are reviewed separately on different scales. The need for the proposed model is evaluated on academic reputation, employer reputation, faculty-student ratio, citations per faculty, international faculty, international students, and infrastructure on the 7-point quality scale. The proposed elaborative model will establish a robust quality education ecosystem on global parameters. The proposed model emphasizes the use of emerging technologies including the Internet of Things (IoT), Artificial Intelligence (AI), and Blockchain (BC), in the education industry.

Keywords: Education Ecosystem, Higher Education, Quality Education, Technology-Enabled Infrastructure.

INTRODUCTION

More than 993 universities, 39931 colleges, and 10725 stand-alone institutions by 2019 [1] made India the top country in the world regarding the number of universities and colleges.

* **Corresponding author Aman Singh:** Department of Computer Science and Engineering, Lovely Professional University, Jalandhar, Punjab, India; E-mail: amansingh.x@gmail.com.

Gyanendra Verma & Rajesh Doriya (Eds.)

As per webometric data July-2019, India is the top participant with 3944 colleges and universities in the webometric university ranking survey 2019 [2]. The United States of America was just behind India with 3257 participants. China is the most populated country in the world at number 3, with 2208 participants. Indonesia, Brazil, and the Russian Federation are the countries with more than 1000 participants each. A total of 28077 colleges and universities participated in this survey. The top six countries, i.e., India, the US, China, Indonesia, Brazil, and Russia, cover almost 50% of the total number of colleges and universities around the globe. Two hundred-eleven countries across the world participated in this survey in 2019. Only India covers 7.12% of the world's population of colleges and universities in this survey. China has only 0.1 billion more inhabitants than India, but India has 1736 more colleges and universities than China (and 687 more colleges and universities than the US). So, India is nowhere lagging in terms of infrastructure facilities as India has more colleges and universities compared with any country in the world.

Infrastructure is only one aspect of the education system; intellectual faculty and a suitable environment for learning are the other two aspects that also have equal significance. The QS-World University Ranking—2020 justifies the intellect of the Indian faculty. The appreciable research work conducted by Indian faculty on a global platform in 2019 ranked India among the top three nations in the world in citation per faculty [3]. More than 40 domain-specific apex bodies, including UGC, AICTE, PCI, MCI, BCI, AISHE, NIRF, and NBA, are deployed in India to ensure a better learning environment at the ground level. Although all these apex bodies have a rich technological environment for quality assurance, the position of quality education in India on a global platform is even below the world's average quality. In India, the basic education model that comprises infrastructure, faculty, and a learning environment is deficient in achieving sustainable quality education. India has already completed most of the quantitative goals in the higher education sector, but the qualitative goals are not meeting the average standards on global platforms. Fig. (**1**) illustrates an elaborative model with many other factors contributing to quality education. All the inner elements required more focus on quality enhancement. The exploration and systematic assessment of all inner elements (including curriculum, activities, exposure for students and faculty, awareness for quality education, participation in quality assessment, faculty interest in imparting quality education along with their academic and research growth, students' interest and urge for quality education, communication and dialogue among all stakeholders, including students, teachers, and respective apex bodies), will edify a comprehensive model for sustainable quality education [4].

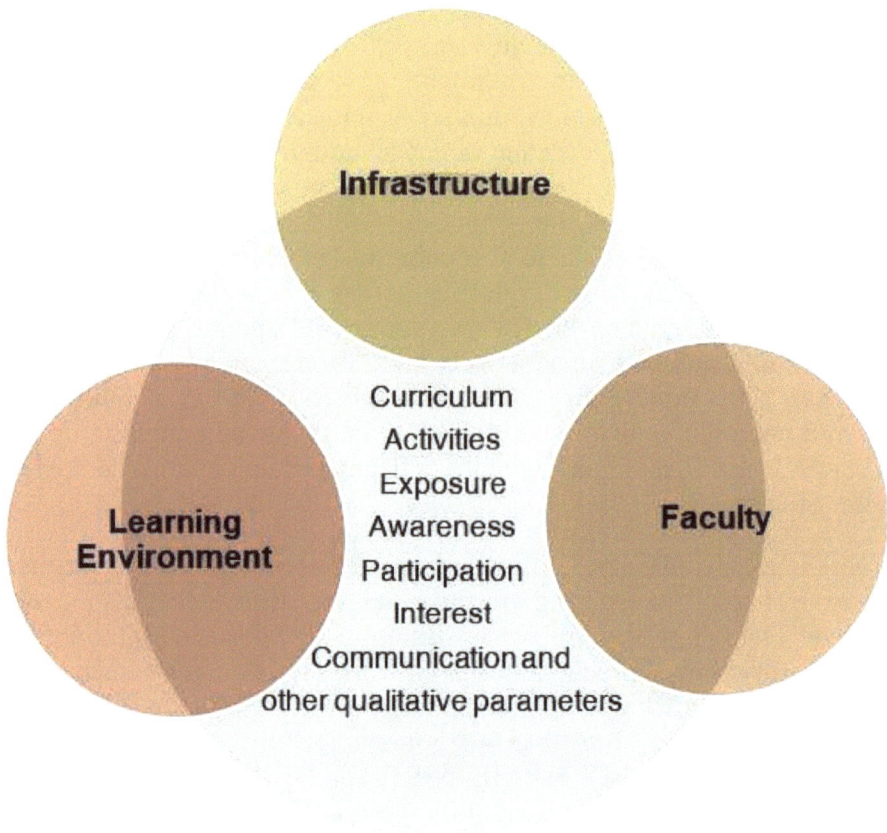

Fig. (1). Elaborative Education model with various qualitative parameters.

This study reviews the global higher education system using quantitative and qualitative parameters. The comparative measures used in this study are qualitative parameters with those of the top 5 countries in education and quantitative parameters with those of the top 5 most populated countries in the world. Moreover, figuring out the futuristic quantitative and qualitative needs for sustainable quality education in India is the central aim of this study, which further proposes a technology-inspired solution for sustainable quality education.

The rest of the paper is organized as follows. Section II discusses the background of the Indian education system. Section III presents the methodology and objectives of this study. Section IV illustrates a detailed discussion of a quantitative and qualitative comparison of various effects with their respective results. Section V concludes the paper.

BACKGROUND

India is the youngest country in the world. India has a 1.2 billion population aged between 15 and 24, which is about 16% of the world's overall population. About 50% of the Indian population is under the age of 25 years [5]. This youngest country in the world is also rich in educational infrastructure, research-oriented faculty, and a healthy environment for learning. All these rich educational facilities make up a robust education ecosystem in India, but the quality of Indian education on the global platform is not attaining a good score. So, the case study of the Indian education system under the elaborative education model has been considered. This section of the paper elaborates on the background of the Indian education system, specifically the higher education sector, and also explores the enrichment of the present education ecosystem in India.

The Indian education system is the oldest in the world. The world's first university, Takshashila University, was established before 700 BC. Takshashila was witnessed by more than 10,500 students in 700 BC who were taking education in more than 60 different subjects [6]. The Indian education system is also known for many ancient discoveries that benefit various fields of education worldwide, i.e., zero, place value system, decimal system, geometry, trigonometry, and many others. At present, India is the top country in education infrastructure. The Ministry of Human Resource Development governs the education system in India, Govt. of India. The ministry has two central departments, i.e., the Department of School Education and Literacy and the Department of Higher Education.

Furthermore, these departments have separate center-level and state-level divisions. More than 50 apex bodies are deployed to ensure quality education in India at school and higher education levels [7]. The Higher Education Department is the concerned area of this study and is monitored by more than 40 domain-specific apex bodies. The All India Council of Technical Education (AICTE), for the affiliation of technical institutions, is an apex advisory body for technical education [8]. The Central Institution of Educational Technology (CIET) is an integral part of NCERT, i.e., the National Council of Educational Research & Training. CIET is working on establishing teaching methodologies and alternative teaching techniques for school, college, and university-level students. The National Assessment and Accreditation Council (NAAC) was established by the University Grants Commission for assessing and accreditation various UG and PG-level courses, except for technical education [9]. The National Board of Accreditation (NBA) is an autonomous body formed by AICTE for periodic assessment of technical institutions [10]. The National Council for Educational Research and Training (NCERT) works to assist the government in academic matters. It also promotes research activities in the education sector. The National Council of Teacher Education (NCTE) is the apex body that sets up the norms and standards for teaching education in India. The National Institute of Fashion Technology (NIFT) is India's main apex body behind the fashion industry and fashion education. The National Institute of Education Planning and Administration (NIEPA) is the prime body behind the education policy of India. Planning, management, and capacity building in education are the prime activities of NIEPA. The Pharmacy Council of India (PCI) is an affiliating apex body for the pharmaceutical industry and education. The Rehabilitation Council of India (RCI) was established under the aegis of the Ministry of Social Welfare, Government of India. Maintaining standards in primary health centers is the main objective of RCI. The Union Public Service Commission (UPSC) is the autonomous apex body for ensuring standards in public sector recruitment, Civil Services Examination (CSE) is the primary examination conducted by UPSC. The Indian Administrative Service (IAS), Indian Foreign Service (IFS), and Indian Police Service (IPS) are the main examinations conducted under CSE. The University Grants Commission (UGC) is India's pioneer apex body for higher education. The UGC maintains educational standards in universities and teaching in India.

The Veterinary Council of India (VCI) is the affiliating apex body for maintaining quality and standards in veterinary science in India. Many other apex bodies are also working to ensure quality education in India. Maintaining quality and standards in veterinary science in India. Many other apex bodies are also working to ensure quality education in India.

Along with all the above-mentioned apex bodies, the All India Survey on Higher Education (AISHE) and the National Institute Ranking Framework (NIRF) are two other autonomous bodies responsible for ensuring quality education at the higher education level in India [11]. AISHE is the most extensive survey conducted at the national level in any country worldwide. The abstract hierarchy of the Indian education system is shown in Fig. (**2**).

The use of technology for improvement and sustainability is appreciable. Emerging technologies, including IoT, Cloud and Fog Computing, AI, Deep Learning, Blockchain, and many more, contribute significantly to improvement and sustainability in every domain of life. IoT is the most promising infrastructure for capturing data in a real-time environment. IoT, fog, and cloud integration framework, i.e., IFC, is a suitable technology integration for data acquisition, classification, processing, and storage in a real-time environment. The countless features of these emerging technologies indicate the improvement in quality education after the upgradation of technology-empowered infrastructure in the education domain.

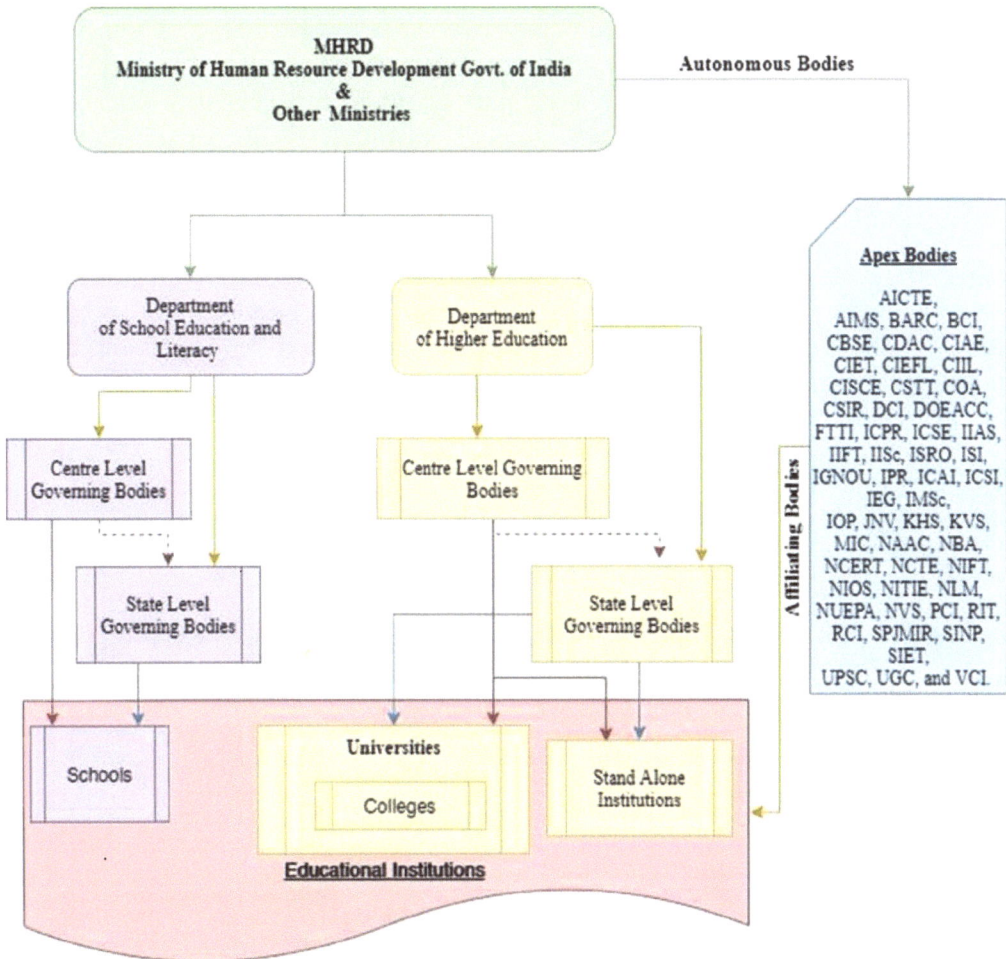

Fig. (2). Indian Education System.

METHODOLOGY

The four main objectives of this study are to study the quality of education in the global higher education system, to compare the Indian and global higher education systems on qualitative parameters, to find out the qualitative parameters in which India is leading or lagging in quality education, and to compare the Indian higher education system with the global higher education system on quantitative parameters. For the first objective, the Times Ranking, QS Ranking, Shanghai Ranking, Webometric, and Scimago Ranking are used for this study. India's position in all these globally known ranking systems is checked. The second objective is achieved by studying the Webometric University Ranking 2019 on the 7-point quality scale (Excellent-Top 100; Good-Between 100 & 201, Above Average-Between 200 & 501, Average-Between 500 & 1001, Below Average-Between 1000 & 5002, Poor-Between 5001 & 10007, and Very Poor – Above) to find the position of the top-5 contributing nations and the world on this scale and compare India with the top-5 nations under this scenario. For the third objective, QS-World University Rankings-2020 studies all the 5-parameters used in QS-Ranking and alsostudy the average score of all top 5 nations in QS-Ranking for all five parameters. A comparison of India with the world's top-5 nations and the world's position on these parameters is also checked. The last objective is achieved by studying the quantitative parameters of the higher education system (i.e., the number of institutions for higher education) in the top-5 most populated nations in the world. For quantitative comparison, the number of institutions per 10,000 inhabitants of the age group 15–24 years is also checked. Fig. (**3**) and Fig. (**4**) illustrate the methodologies and objectives of this study.

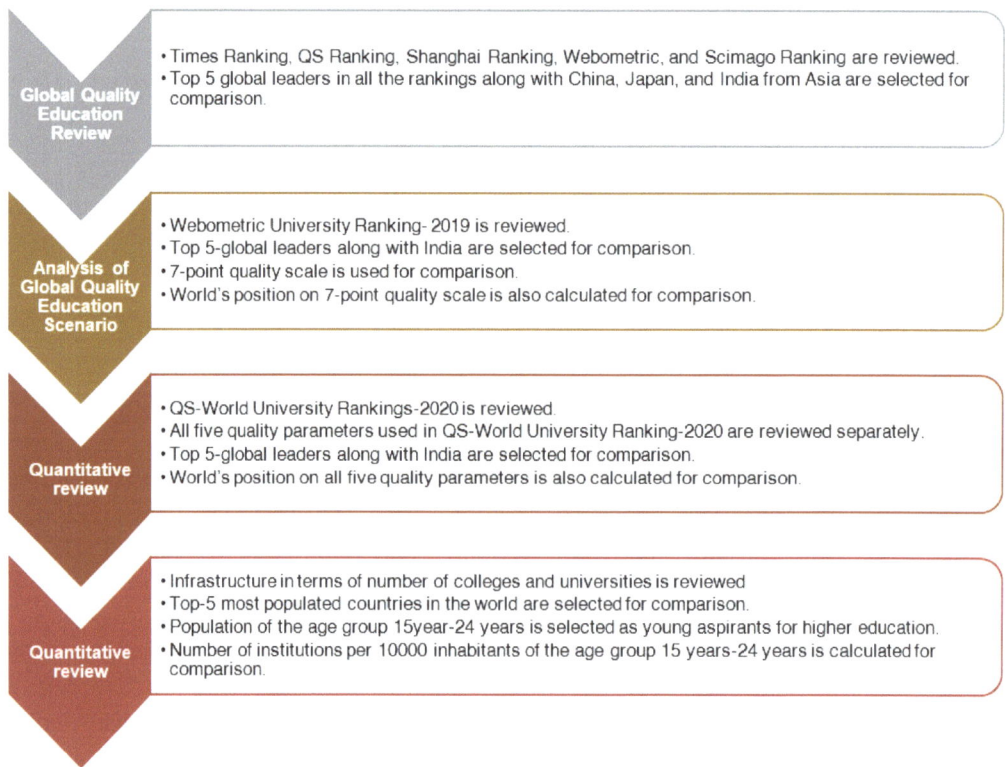

Global Quality Education Review
- Times Ranking, QS Ranking, Shanghai Ranking, Webometric, and Scimago Ranking are reviewed.
- Top 5 global leaders in all the rankings along with China, Japan, and India from Asia are selected for comparison.

Analysis of Global Quality Education Scenario
- Webometric University Ranking- 2019 is reviewed.
- Top 5-global leaders along with India are selected for comparison.
- 7-point quality scale is used for comparison.
- World's position on 7-point quality scale is also calculated for comparison.

Quantitative review
- QS-World University Rankings-2020 is reviewed.
- All five quality parameters used in QS-World University Ranking-2020 are reviewed separately.
- Top 5-global leaders along with India are selected for comparison.
- World's position on all five quality parameters is also calculated for comparison.

Quantitative review
- Infrastructure in terms of number of colleges and universities is reviewed
- Top-5 most populated countries in the world are selected for comparison.
- Population of the age group 15year-24 years is selected as young aspirants for higher education.
- Number of institutions per 10000 inhabitants of the age group 15 years-24 years is calculated for comparison.

Fig. (3). List of four main objectives and the respective methodologies used in this study.

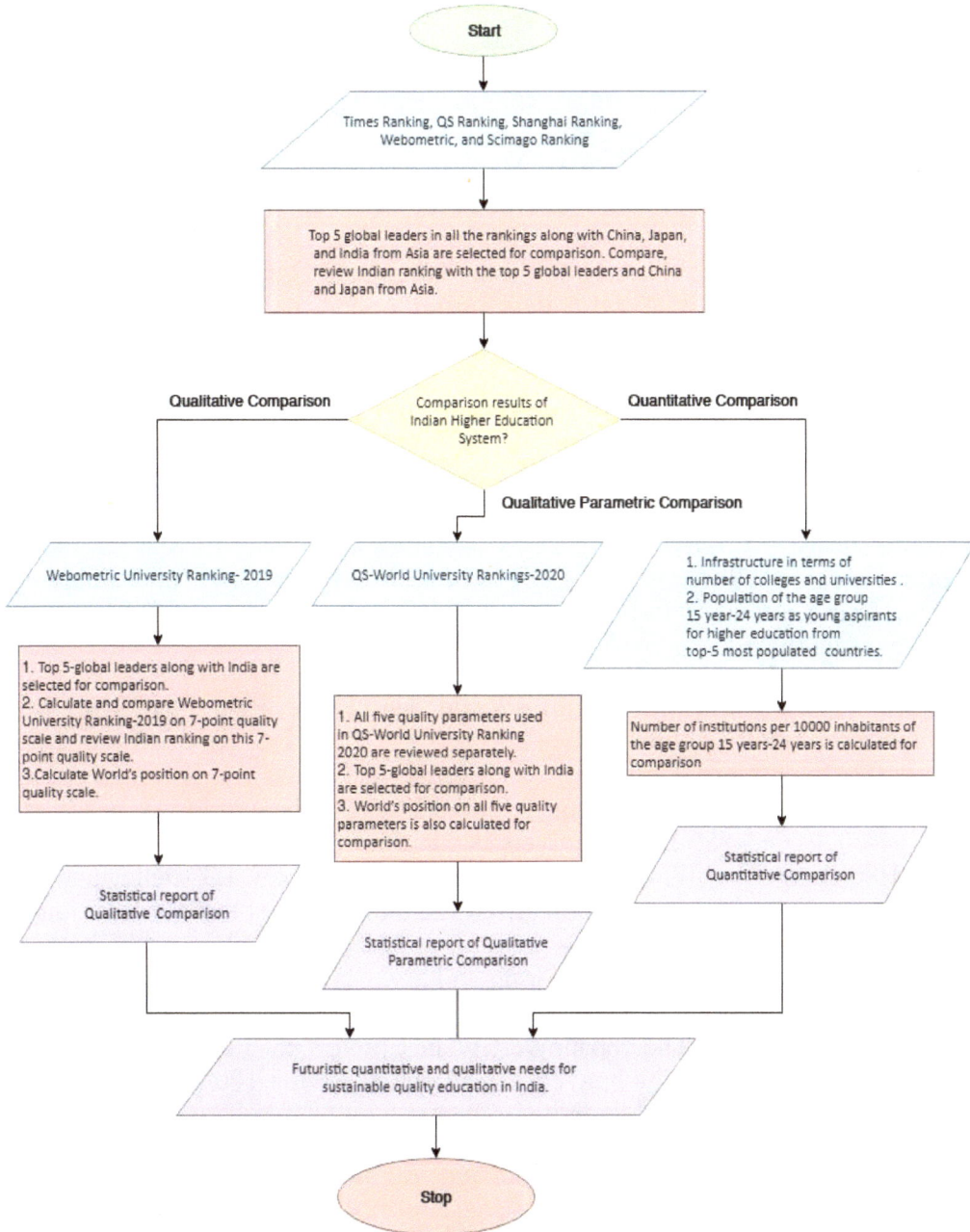

Fig. (4). Block Diagram of the main objectives and the respective methodologies used in this study.

RESULT AND DISCUSSION

The Times Higher Education World University Ranking, QS World University Ranking, Academic Ranking of World Universities (ARWU-Shanghai Ranking), Ranking Web of Universities (webometrics), Scimago Institution Ranking, and Washington Accord are the top global quality parameters that ensure and provide rankings to colleges and universities around the world [12]. The position of Indian colleges and universities is very pathetic in the global ranking. Only 24 universities in India are represented in the QS World University Ranking 2020, including 1002 universities and colleges from around the world. IIT Bombay is the top-ranked institution from India with 152nd global rank, followed by IIT Delhi with 182nd rank, and IISc Bangalore with 184th rank, as the top 3 performers from India. 42 institutions from China and 41 from Japan are on this list. 6 institutions in China are among the top 100 ranked; 7 institutions from China and 8 institutions from Japan are beyond the top ranker from India, i.e., IIT Bombay. IIT Bombay bagged the 32nd position in Asia, and Nanyang Technological University Singapore (NTU) is the top ranker in Asia. In the QS World University Ranking 2020, the Massachusetts Institute of Technology (MIT), Stanford University, and Harvard University are the top 3 educational institutions worldwide.

For the Times Higher Education World University Ranking 2020, 1397 universities from 99 countries worldwide were evaluated. As per the Times Ranking-2020, Oxford University, California Institution of Technology, and Cambridge University are the top 3 universities in the world, as per Times Ranking-2020. Only 56 Indian universities can take part in the Times Ranking 2020; IISc-Bangalore, IIT-Ropar, IIT-Indore, IIT-Bombay, IIT-Delhi, and IIT-Kharagpur are the only 6 institutions from India that bagged top-500 positions in the Times Ranking 2020. The top institution is IISc Bangalore ranks between 301st and 350th in IISc. Our neighboring country, China, is equally populated and has almost half the number of institutions compared to India, which bagged 81 positions out of 1397. The top university in China, i.e., Tsinghua University, bagged the 23rd rank. China bagged 3 positions in the top 100 and 17 in the top 500, which is 3 times more than India [13].

The position of India in the Academic Ranking of World Universities-2019(ARWU-2019) or Shanghai Ranking is also pathetic. Harvard University, Stanford University, and Cambridge University are the top 3 universities in the world in this ranking. According to the Shanghai Ranking 2019, IISc-Bangalore is again the top university in India. IISc. Bangalore is the only university that comes under the top 500 universities, followed by IIT-Madras, with the top 600 university positions. In 2003, ARWU published the world university ranking for the first time and IISc. Bangalore's position was comparable to or even better than in 2019. Its position in China in the Shanghai Ranking is much better than India's, with 58 universities in the top 500 and 4 universities in the top 100. China's top university, i.e., Tsinghua University, bagged the 43rd rank worldwide [14]. Scimago, the globally recognized journal ranking, is also known for its institutional and country rankings. India is in the 9th position in the country's ranking of Scimago, The US, China, and the UK are in the top 3 positions, followed by Germany and Japan in the 4th and 5th positions, respectively. Scimago recognizes the world's institutions in different sectors like government, health, higher education, and private sectors. According to the Scimago Institution Ranking-2019, Harvard University is first, and the United States holds the top five positions in all sectors. India's top institution, IISc-Bangalore, is in 353rd rank in the Higher Education sector and 516th rank in all sector categories. Only 45 Indian universities took place in Asia out of 261 Asian universities, including India's top-ranked IISc. Bangalore is ranked 109th in Asia. In total, 126 institutions from India took place in the Scimago institution world ranking.

Indian universities' performance in the Scimago institutions ranking is also not good if we compare it with China, Japan, or any other developed nation in Asia. 276 universities from China took place in this ranking, whereas the number of universities from India was only 126. China's top university, Tsinghua University, is ranked 6th in the higher education sector and 13th in the overall ranking. Six Chinese and two Japanese universities are ranked in the top 100, while none of the Indian universities are ranked in the top 350 [15]. Sustainable quality education is a global challenge nowadays. 96.44% of universities and colleges around the globe are below average quality. The US, the top performer in the education sector, has 92.08 percent of institutions of below-average quality. India is the top participant in the world for the Webometric University Ranking 2019, with 3944 participants. 99.80% of Indian universities that participated in this ranking are below average quality, and 85.60% of institutions have very low quality on a 7-point scale (Fig. **5**). This is the case of the top 7.64% (3944) universities and colleges in India. The remaining 92.36 percent (47705) are not even qualified for such a global ranking. One can conclude from this data that although the number of universities and colleges in India is more significant than in any other country, Indian educational institutions still lag in providing quality education. More than 93% of Indian students are associated with institutions where the quality of education is very low [16].

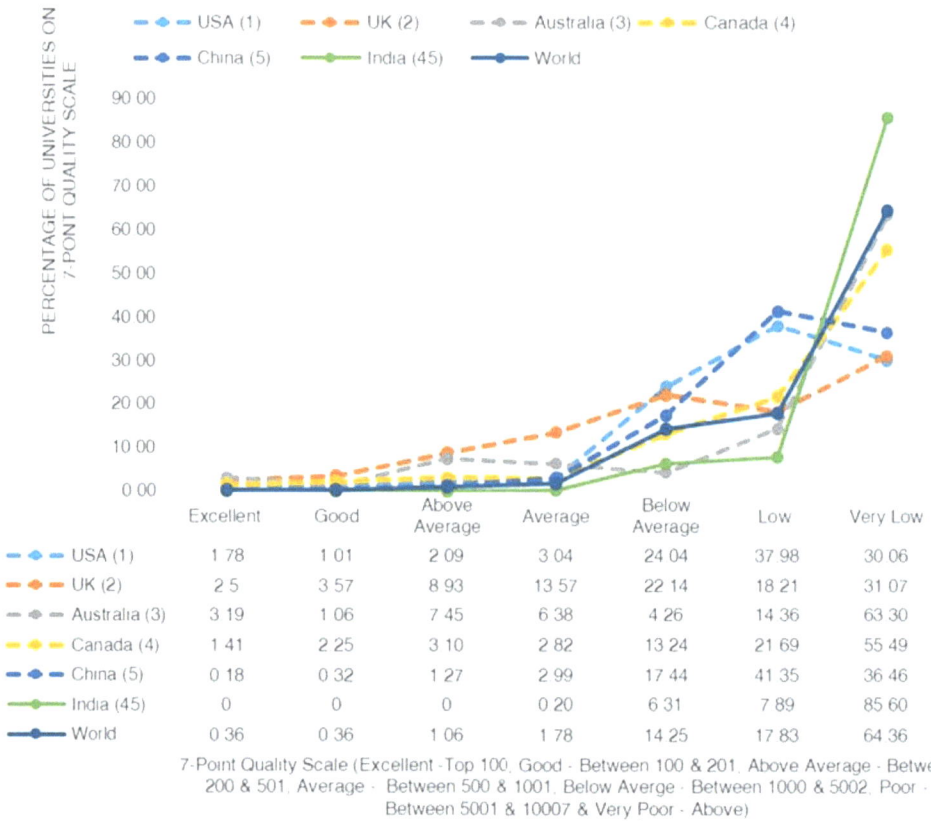

Fig. (5). Comparison of India with the world and top-five leading nations in the world as per Webometric University Ranking-2021.

So, first, India should focus more on quality education in 93% of institutions. Second, indicators and parameters to evaluate the quality of education in India have to be more stringent and standardized to improve its global rankings. The six main parameters to evaluate the quality of education used by Shanghai Ranking are Academic Reputation, Employer Reputation, Faculty Student, Citations Per Faculty, International Faculty, and International Students. Fig. (**6**) indicates the Indian education quality on all these 6 parameters and a comparison of India's education with the world and the top 5 contributing nations in the world in the Shanghai Ranking 2020. India is leading in one factor only, i.e., citation per faculty. The average value of all scores of citations per faculty is just behind the US and China. This value is better than the UK, Germany, Japan, and the average value of the world. But India is struggling with international faculty and students.

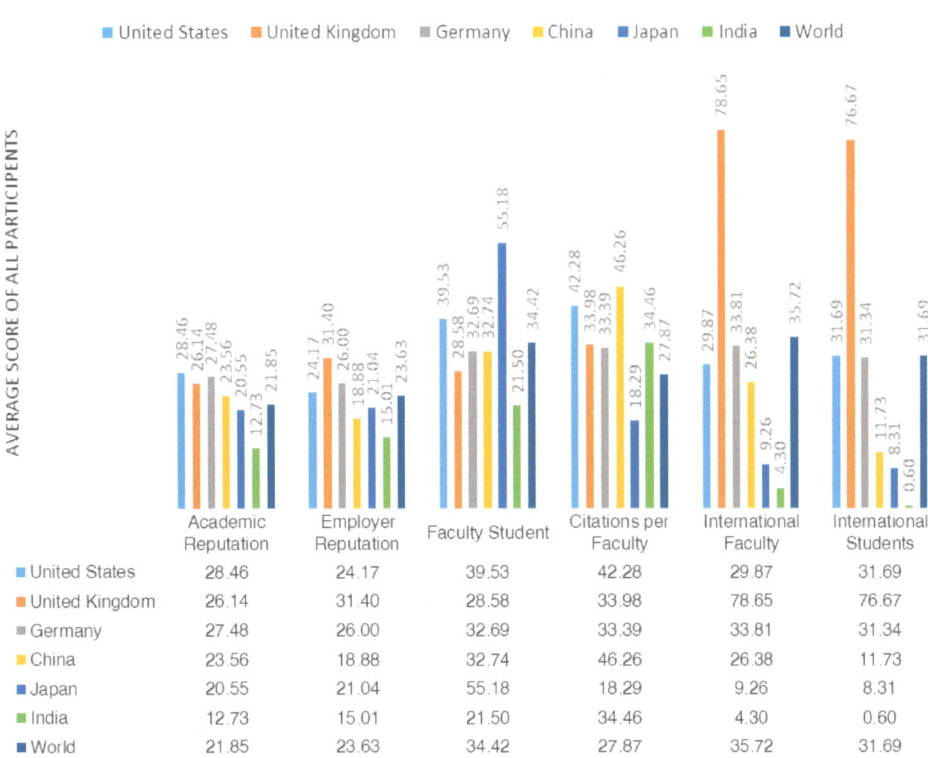

Fig. (6). Comparison of India with the world and top-five leading nations in the world as per QS-World University Rankings-2020.

Although the performance of all other countries except the UK is also very poor, India still needs to improve a lot. The three other parameters, i.e., academic reputation, employer reputation, and faculty students, also need to improve for improvement in the global ranking.

According to the most recent UNESCO data, India is the world's leading country, with a population age group of 15 to 24 years [18]. This population group is the most appropriate group for higher education. More than 245 million (245212000) came in the age group of 15 to 24 years [19]. In the AISHE-2019 report, 51649 universities, colleges, and stand-alone institutions participated in AISHE-2019. India is just behind the US and Indonesia in the number of higher educational institutions per 10,000 students (Fig. **7**). Indonesia is the second-largest populated country that has a higher number of higher educational institutions for new aspirants than India. But Indonesia is below India in the webometric country ranking and Scimago country ranking rankings [20]. India has three times higher educational institutions than Brazil [21] and four times more than China [22].

Although China and Brazil have fewer higher-educational institutions than India, their global ranking in higher education is better than India's. It clearly shows that the focus of these countries is not on the expansion of higher educational infrastructure but on the sustainable quality of education for their young aspirants. India must follow this trend and divert the focus from the progress of institutions to a sustainable quality of education. India does not require new institutions to strengthen the education system, but quality improvement and assurance in existing institutions are of paramount importance.

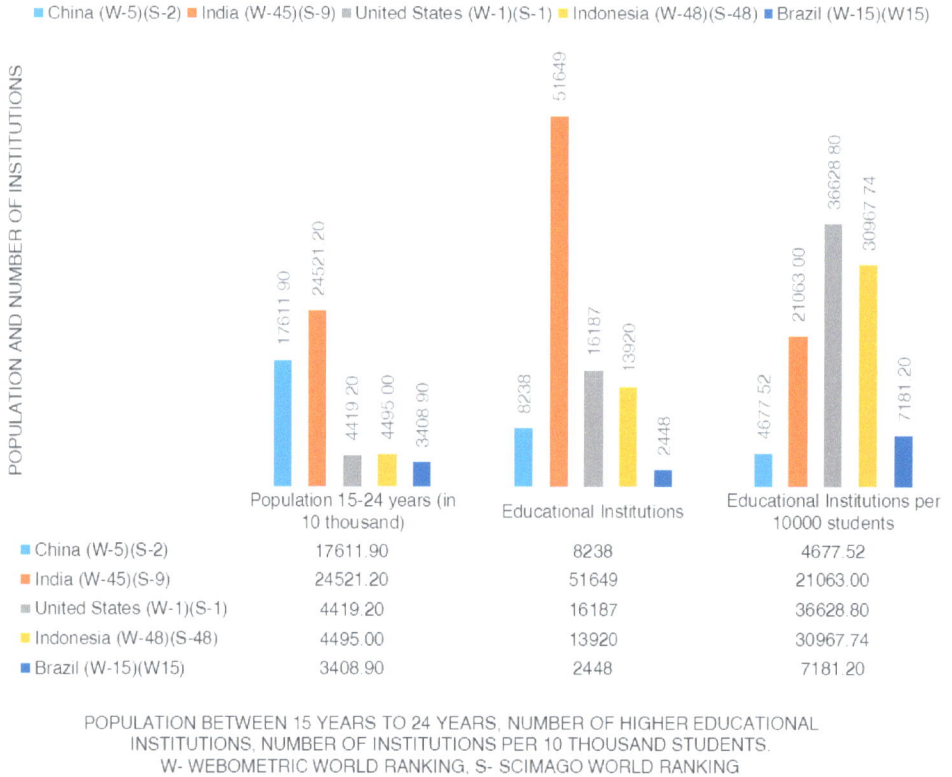

	Population 15-24 years (in 10 thousand)	Educational Institutions	Educational Institutions per 10000 students
China (W-5)(S-2)	17611.90	8238	4677.52
India (W-45)(S-9)	24521.20	51649	21063.00
United States (W-1)(S-1)	4419.20	16187	36628.80
Indonesia (W-48)(S-48)	4495.00	13920	30967.74
Brazil (W-15)(W15)	3408.90	2448	7181.20

POPULATION BETWEEN 15 YEARS TO 24 YEARS, NUMBER OF HIGHER EDUCATIONAL INSTITUTIONS, NUMBER OF INSTITUTIONS PER 10 THOUSAND STUDENTS. W- WEBOMETRIC WORLD RANKING, S- SCIMAGO WORLD RANKING

Fig. (7). Comparison of India with the top-five most populated countries of the world.

It is now the right time for India to converge its national focus from quantitative parameters to qualitative parameters in the higher education system. The result of the Scimago ranking is also reflected in the QS-World University Rankings-2020, as India is the 3rd in citations per faculty, behind China and the United States [3]. Sustainable, quality education is a challenge for all nations, including the US, UK, Australia, Germany, and China. But for India, the situation is more critical. Only 7% of institutions participated in the global ranking (Webometric University

Ranking-2019), and out of these 7% of institutions, only 0.2% of institutions were above-average ranked. It concludes that more than 99% of higher educational institutions in India are below average in quality.

India has an urgent need to strengthen its international image in the Indian Higher Education System, as India is lagging in international faculty, international students, academic reputation, employer reputation, and faculty-student relationships. Although research and publication of faculty are comparably good, India has to focus on all other lagging parameters to improve its global appearance. Although India is the leading nation in the world in higher educational institutions, the population of India, especially in the age group of 15 years to 24 years, is also more prominent in comparison with any nation in the world.

The massive population of young aspirants for higher education makes India the 3rd-top nation in higher educational institutions per 10,000 young aspirants for higher education. India has 16385 more institutions for 10,000 young aspirants than China, but still [1, 22], China is providing much better-quality education than India on a global platform. India has to stop the proliferation of institutions because it already ranks first in the world for the number of higher education institutions and third for the number of institutions per 10,000 young people interested in pursuing higher education. Instead of institutions proliferating, technology-enabled infrastructure needs to be upgraded.

India has to improve the quality of education on global parameters. Quality education for every student must be the new objective of the Indian Education System rather than education for every student. India has to work on a state-o--the-art quality monitoring and improvement system that matches the global parameters that lead to the goal of sustainable quality education in India. A technology-inspired elaborative education mode that can define and improve the other quality measures needs to be designed and implemented on the ground level. The technology-empowered improvised education mode will lead to the building of a self-sustaining quality education ecosystem. This study recommends data acquisition *via* IoT sensors, data classification *via* intelligent neural networks over fog nodes, data processing *via* artificial intelligence, and data storage *via* cloud nodes to strengthen the technologically inspired infrastructure. The involvement of technology in monitoring, assessment, and accreditation is of paramount importance to strengthening the quality of education [23].

CONCLUSION

Due to the advancement of institutions in the last two decades, India has become the top nation in higher educational institutions. India has four times more institutions for young aspirants than China. This indicates that it is an alarming stage for higher educational institutions. This is the right time to halt the growing number of educational institutions in India. On the other hand, less than 0.2% of institutions provide average quality education on a global scale, and none of the Indian institutions provide excellent or good quality education on a worldwide scale. So, there is an urgent need to diverge the national focus from the number of institutions and start focusing on the quality of education in these institutions. India must strengthen its quality monitoring and assurance system. The use of a state-of-the-art quality monitoring and improvement system for every institution is the need of the hour.

India has the most fortified root system of educational institutions. Now it is time to nourish the enormous tree of the higher education system with sustainable quality education for the future fruitful global position in higher education that is confined to a sustainable quality education ecosystem.

CONSENT FOR PUBLICATION

Not applicable.

CONFLICT OF INTEREST

The authors declare no conflict of interest, financial or otherwise.

ACKNOWLEDGEMENT

The authors, therefore, gratefully acknowledge Bentham Science Publishers, Lovely Professional University, and Dr. GC Negi College of Veterinary & Animal Science.

REFERENCES

[1]   AISHE Report 2018-19: All India Survey on Higher Education. Ministry of Human Resource Development, Department of Higher Education, New Delhi.

[2]   "World | Ranking Web of Universities: More than 28000 institutions ranked", https ://www.webometrics.info/en/world

[3]   "QS World University Rankings 2020: Top Global Universities | Top Universities", https://www.topuniversities.com/university-rankings/world-university-rankings/2020

[4]   K. Fisher, "Research into identifying effective learning environments." *Evaluating quality in educational facilities* 9 (2005): 159-167.

[5]   Comisión Europea, *Youth in Action impact*, 2013, p. 4.

[6]   Pandya, D. R. N. "Indian education system–a historical journey." Education 3, no. 3, 2014.

[7]   Apex Education Bodies in India | AICTE | UGC | CBSE | UPSC | MHRD | IGNOU | MCI., https://www.indiaeducation.net/apexbodies/

[8]   Government of India, All India Council for Technical Education|., https://www.aicte-india.org/

[9]   NAAC - Home, http://www.naac.gov.in/

[10]   National Board of Accreditation, https://www.nbaind.org/

[11]   NIRF, https://nirfcdn.azureedge.net/2019/flipbook/index.html#p=1

[12]   E. Hazelkorn, *Global Rankings and the Geopolitics of Higher Education 14 Deep Learning: Theory.* Architectures, and Applications in Speech, Image and Language Processing Verma et al, 2016.

[13]   World   University   Rankings   2020 | Times   Higher   Education   (THE). https://www.timeshighereducation.com/world-universit-
-rankings/2020/world-ranking#!/page/0/length/25/sort_by/rank/sort_order/asc/cols/stats

[14]   ShanghaiRanking's Academic Ranking of World Universities, *Press Release.,* 2019. http://www.shanghairanking.com/Academic Ranking of World Universities 2019 Press Release.html

[15]   Scimago Institutions Rankings, https://www.scimagoir.com/rankings.php

[16]   Countries arranged by Number of Universities in Top Ranks | Ranking Web of Universities: More than 28000 institutions ranked., https://www.webometrics.info/en/node/54

[17]   Ten   Countries   with   the   Highest   Population   in   the   World,   https://www.internet-worldstats.com/stats8.htm

[18]   U.N.E.S.C.O. Report, Higher Education in Asia: Expanding Out, Expanding Up. The rise of graduate education   and   university   research | Capacity4dev,   https://europa.eu/capacity4dev/higher-education/blog/unesco-report-higher-education-asia-expanding-out-expanding-rise-graduate-education-and-univers

[19]   India | UNESCO UIS, http://uis.unesco.org/en/country/in

[20]   Indonesia | UNESCO UIS., http://uis.unesco.org/en/country/id

[21]   Universities | DWIH Sao Paulo, https://www.dwih-saopaulo.org/en/research-innovation/the-resea-ch-and-innovation-landscape-in-brazil/research-and-innovation-organizations/universities/

[22]   The number of Higher Education Institutions - Ministry of Education of the People's Republic of China., http://en.moe.gov.cn/documents/statistics/2017/national/201808/t20180808_344686.html

[23]   A. Verma, A. Singh, E. Lughofer, X. Cheng, and K. Abualsaud, "Multilayered-quality education ecosystem (MQEE): an intelligent education modal for sustainable quality education", *J. Comput. High. Educ.,* pp. 1-29, 2021.

## CHAPTER 12

Knowledge Graphs for Explaination of Black-Box Recommender System

Mayank Gupta[1] and **Poonam Saini**[1,*]

[1] *Department of Computer Science and Engineering, Punjab Engineering College, Chandigarh, India*

Abstract: Machine learning models, particularly black-box, make powerful decisions and recommendations. However, these models lack transparency and hence cannot be explained directly. The respective decisions need explanation with the help of techniques to gain users' trust and ensure the correct interpretation of a particular recommendation. Nowadays, Knowledge graphs (*K*-graph) has been recognized as a powerful tool to generate explanations for the predictions or decisions of black-box models. The explainability of the machine learning models enhances transparency between the user and the model. Further, this could result in better decision support systems, improvised recommender systems, and optimal predictive models. Unfortunately, while these black box devices have no detail on the reasons behind their forecasts, they lack clarity. White box structures, on the other hand, will quickly produce interpretations due to their existence. The chapter presents an exhaustive review and step-by-step description for using knowledge graphs in generating explanations for black-box recommender systems, which further helps in generating more persuasive and personalized explanations for the recommended items. We also implement a case study on the MovieLens dataset and WikiData using *K*-graph to generate accurate explanations.

Keywords: Black-Box Recommender System, Explainability, Knowledge Graph.

INTRODUCTION

Machine learning models, essentially the black-box models, generate decisions and recommendations; however, lack of transparency and direct explainability make them untrustworthy to end-users. Therefore, such decisions need explanation using techniques that are interpretable as well as accurate to make any specific recommendation. The high-quality explanations of such recommendations can boost trust, effectiveness, efficiency, and satisfaction [1].

---

[*] **Corresponding author Poonam Saini:** Department of Computer Science and Engineering, Punjab Engineering College, Chandigarh, India; E-mail: poonamsaini@pec.edu.in

Gyanendra Verma & Rajesh Doriya (Eds.)

Introduction to Recommender System

Recommender systems have been gaining attention in recent times as they can ease information overload. One of the major concerns is the explainability of recommender systems. The authors [2] mentioned that fairness issues had received a lot of publicity lately, particularly in the sense of intelligent decision-making processes. However, the explainable feedback frameworks, for example, can be susceptible to both explanation prejudice and success disparity.

Owing to the design of collective filtering, inactive users may be more vulnerable to getting unsatisfactory feedback due to a lack of training evidence, and their recommendations may be affected by the training records of active users, resulting in unequal treatment by the framework. Recommender systems are constantly being used to forecast consumer needs on websites and to suggest specific solutions that will help them deal with knowledge overload. In recommendation systems, existing model-based collective filtering algorithms, like latent factor models, are considered state-of-the-art [2]. Fig. (1) shows the google trend for research interest in explainable artificial intelligence (XAI) key terms over time.

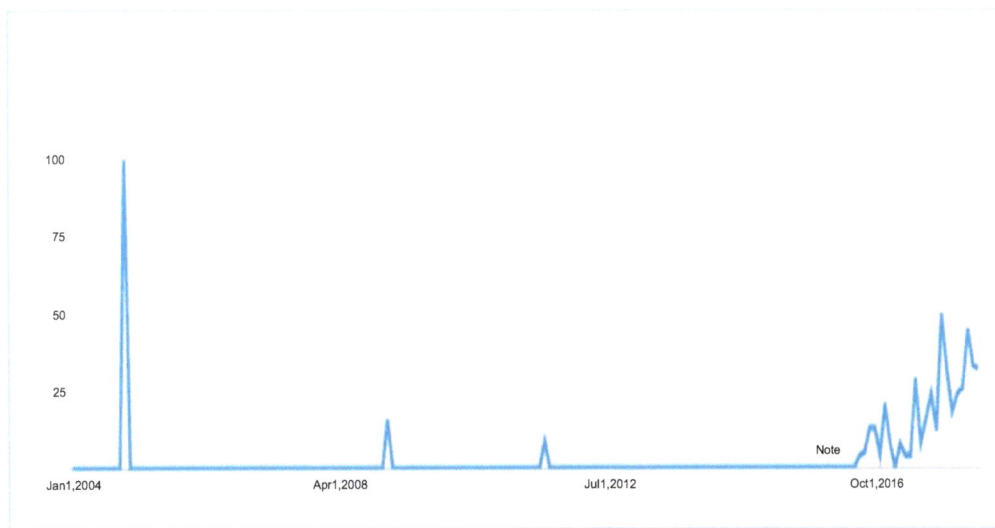

Fig. (1). Google trends result for research interest of Explainable Artificial Intelligence term [3].

Introduction to Knowledge Graphs

A Knowledge Graph (KG) could be used to generate explanations for the predictions or decisions made by the black box models. The KGs are a modern way of data representation that would find a lot of usage in generating explanations in the coming future. This could be useful in making better DSS (Decision Support Systems), Recommender Systems, Predictive Models, and so on. KGs usually provide much more valuable data and links regarding objects than other forms of side information. KG is a guided heterogeneous graph in which the nodes represent individuals, and the edges represent relationships. Several academic KGs, such as NELL and DBpedia, as well as commercial KGs, such as Google Knowledge Graph and Microsoft Satori, have recently been proposed. Many implementations of these information graphs have been good, including KG completion [4], query answering [5], word embedding [6], and text classification [7]. Researchers tried to use KGs to boost the efficiency of recommender mechanisms after observing their effectiveness in diverse domains in handling a variety of problems.

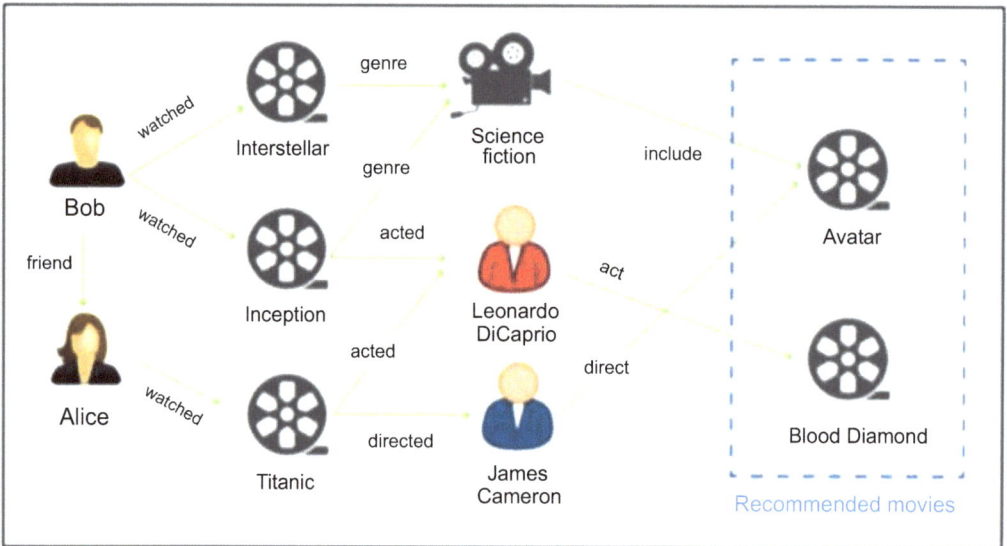

Fig. (2). An illustration of KG-based recommendation [8].

Fig. (**2**) provides an example of KG-based recommendation, in which Bob is recommended for the films "Avatar" and "Blood Diamond." The users, plays, writers, directors, and genres are all individuals in this KG, with interactions, belonging, performing, controlling, and fellowship serving as connections between them. The movies and users are associated with various latent connections using KG, which ensure recommendation accuracy. The authors [9] show that the explainability of referral outcomes is an advantage for such schemes. Following the connection sequences in the user-item graph will show the reasons for recommending these two movies to Bob in the same case. For example, one explanation for suggesting "Avatar" is that it belongs to the same category as "Interstellar," which Bob has previously seen. Multiple KGs, such as Freebase [10], DBpedia [11], YAGO [12], *etc.*, have recently been proposed, making it easier to create KGs for the recommendation.

RECOMMENDER SYSTEMS

A million digital objects (documents, goods, music, books, *etc.*) are added to the World Wide Web (www) every day. This improves the knowledge accessible on the web and allows people more options for selection. However, identifying and searching for specific digital objects are difficult and time-consuming for end users. Using the recommender scheme (RS) may reduce the number of interactive objects for an individual and focus only on the user's favorite collection of items. The aim is to assist users in finding only relevant details rather than sifting through a mass of undifferentiated data. The RS is a filtering mechanism that predicts rates or expectations that a consumer might send to a digital object or a social feature (*e.g.*, people). There are a few typical tasks that RS assists in, such as [13]:

- *Finding some good items*: Recommend a graded collection of objects to a customer, along with their estimated scores.
- *Finding all good items:* Recommend all things that will meet any of the user's needs. This is particularly true when there is a limited amount of products or when the RS is mission-critical, as in financial or medical applications.
- *Annotation in context*: Emphasize any of the objects in a current setting, such as a spreadsheet, based on the user's long-term interests.

Types of Recommender Systems

Messages that are preserved in a folder could be extracted depending on their content as well as other people's views. Following are the types of recommender systems:

a. Content-based Filtering: Content-based recommenders provide a consumer profile based on the characteristics of the products that the user likes. The decisions are produced by matching the features of the desired products to the features of the usable items. It generates a usage profile which is determined by the learning process [14]. For example, a content-based RS for restaurants uses a hierarchical representation by storing restaurant attributes such as cuisine, décor, budget, and so on, while the data at hand for a news article RS is unstructured free form content, in which case, the terms in the text are called attributes and requires a detailed description of contents. There can be the following issues:

No Filtering on Quality and Taste: Even if one article is nice and the other is not, two articles defined by the same collection of keywords will be similarly suggested to a user [15].

Narrow Range of Choices: Users are recommended those products which are close to their previous choice, implying a lack of variety of suggestions.

New User Issue: A new user joining the framework may only receive feedback if shows a preference for a small number of products.

b. Demographic Filtering: Demographic approaches, including collaborative ones, create 'people-to-people' associations, but with separate data [14]. The user profile consists of information about the user, such as age, profession, and pin code. Also, there are difficulties like:

Data elicitation: Owing to users' inability to share personal details, gathering demographic user data can be a costly and challenging process.

Gray Sheep Problem: People with odd or esoteric preferences may not find enough common ground with any given user community.

c. Knowledge-based Recommendations: These systems [16] provide inferences regarding consumer needs based on knowledge about products and users. The inference is based on technical experience or how an object satisfies a specific consumer criterion. The *recommender.com* and the *Entrée systems* are two common knowledge-based recommender systems. Another framework that is a part of the Social Web is the *Stumble Upon* system. While information-based recommender systems may map consumer needs to goods, product domain expertise is essentially required for proper management and organization.

d. Collaborative Filtering: This filtering is focused on our common habit of interviewing friends and colleagues or reading feedback to assist us in making routine, normal choices like which book to read, which movie to stream, and so on. The main distinction is that, rather than a few hundred thoughts from our friends, CF will gather thousands of them. CF is founded on the assumption that consumer expectations are consistent and that "users who have decided in the past ought to accept in the future." CF was being successfully used in a variety of common recommender programs, including MovieLens, Amazon, Ringo, and others. CF is the most commonly employed suggestion method. As long as personal preference knowledge is accessible, CF structures may be divided into model-based approaches and memory-based [17]. A few drawbacks of CF structures are as follows:

Sparsity: In Mutual Filtering (MF), the sparsity issue relates to the lack of usable user scores, which allows calculating similarities between most item/user pairs difficult. Other issues relevant to the sparsity problem include "cold start," which relates to insufficient data in the initial state, which prevents users in the framework from making acceptable recommendations.

Scalability: Since all computations are done at prediction time, scalability for memory-based CF is a problem. The problem can be solved by calculating consumer comparisons and aggregating interests at the time of prediction.

Privacy: User data is collected, and user accounts are created and stored by recommender programs in order to align and identify related people. It has been suggested that the depth or specificity of a user's profile has a significant impact on the consistency of suggestions issued.

Vulnerability to attacks: Collaborative recommender programs rely on their users' goodwill, *i.e.*, it is assumed that users can engage with the framework to receive positive feedback for themselves and also generate helpful data for their neighbors.

e. Hybrid Recommender Systems: Hybrid techniques succeed by incorporating the best aspects of many suggestion techniques to maximize performance. Such techniques [2] integrate CF with content-based, demographic, and other techniques, thereby resulting in higher efficiency as compared to a single technique.

KNOWLEDGE GRAPHS

An entity is a common concept that refers to a word or expression that can be mapped to an information base or ontology. The mapping is easy since the information base used in this proposal is focused primarily on organized data. While using a generic knowledge base such as Wikipedia1, a wikifier or an entity linker might be required. The content associated with the users and objects is usually used to create entities which are usually the demographics of consumers. For a film, this may involve the stars, theme, country of publication, directors, and so on; for restaurants, it could be the venue, food, formal vs. casual, and so on. A Knowledge Graph is a graph in which each object, individual, and consumer is represented as a node, with edges connecting certain nodes that communicate with one another. The Heterogeneous Information Network (HIN), basically a KG with typed entities and connections, is a concept used in the literature. Otherwise, the network would become uniform. A HIN differs from graphs or networks with just one kind of node, such as a buddy network. As a result, KG is a more relaxed version of a HIN in which the types of entities and relations are unknown. In case their sorted information is absent, we presume that the nodes are normally heterogeneous. Only a few strategies are valid if the forms are unclear. And, if the information graph is a HIN, all three approaches are applicable.

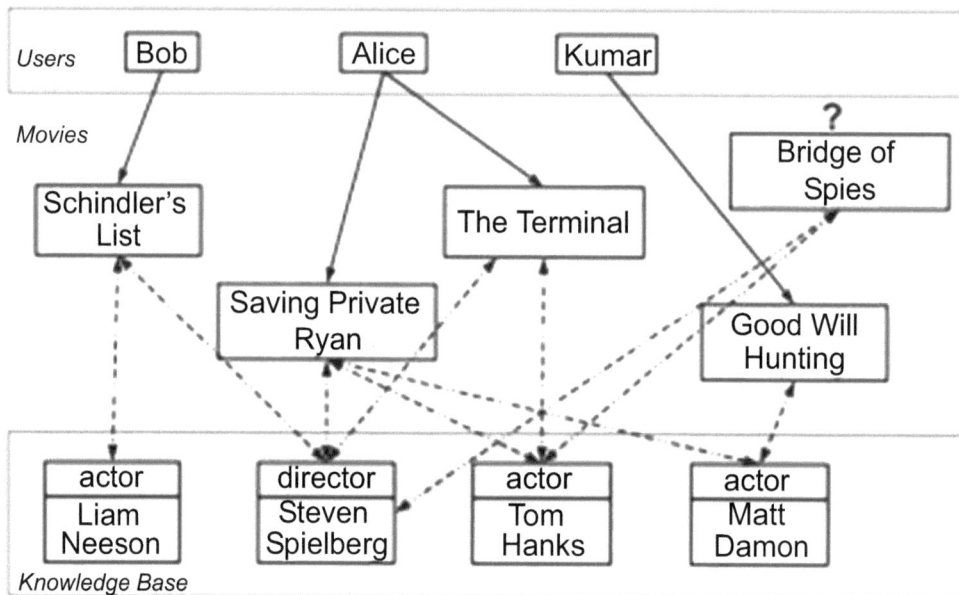

Fig. (3). Example of Movie Recommendation with a Knowledge Graph [18].

Fig. (**3**) illustrates a standard movie suggestion situation in which viewers view and/or rank movies when content regarding the films is preserved in a database. Consider the following three users: Bob, Alice, and Kumar. According to user records, Alice has seen 'Saving Private Ryan' and 'The Terminal,' all directed by Steven Spielberg and starring Tom Hanks, as stated by the knowledge base. Additional content such as language, story keywords and country of publication, awards received, and so on could be included throughout the knowledge base. Likewise, it is known about the films that Bob and Kumar have already seen. If available, we might have user activities such as "reviewing" or "liking" in addition to watching. We might like to know the possibility of users seeing a new movie, such as 'Bridge of Spies,' based on their previous viewing history. Fig. (**3**) illustrates this example graphically. While the movie-entity graph, in this case, is bipartite, it is normal to provide relations between plays, such as 'Finding Nemo' and 'Dory,' where the latter is a reference to previous, or between individuals,

190 Deep Learning: Theory, Architectures, and Applications

such as Tom Hanks and the Best Actor Academy Award.

Knowledge Graphs for Providing Recommendations

In the literature, the existing research focuses on using external KGs to improve recommendation quality. HeteRecp, a recent approach [19], suggested using KGs to improve recommender efficiency. Later, the same authors suggest a link-dependent approach [20] that learns a global model of advice based on the KG but does not seek to personalize the recommendations. A learning-to-rank system, as discussed above, uses paths to locate top-N recommendations; however, the authors did not monitor individual entities that exist in the route as the approach only uses the node forms. Next, personalized page rank has been used for a few methods to rate products. The entities contained in the text of an object (for example, a news article) are first mapped to entities in an information graph in these approaches. Further, an improvement on the current graph embedding framework (named node2vec) allows various types of properties/relations [21]. A recent article applies reinforcement learning to KGs to consider relationships [22]. Their approach teaches a policy-based agent to select a connection at each stage in order to expand its current graph course. The authors use their model to forecast connections and facts in activities. The approaches are often based on a probabilistic thinking paradigm that can be used for any function. Amongst other entities, users' social connection knowledge is used to find related users, or "mates," and their respective scores are used to create suggestions.

Knowledge Graphs for Generating Explanations

In the early phase analysis, researchers looked at various reasons for suggestions in a CF-based recommender method [23]. The usage of a histogram of ratings from the user's neighbors, as well as determining if any of the user's favorite actors feature in the film, is claimed to be well received by the users. A restriction was imposed on mutual filtering that favors explainable recommendations. If there are sufficiently known examples to reason the suggestion, such as "*x* other people like you have enjoyed this item in the past" (user-based neighbor style) or "you have liked *y* other things like this in the past," the recommendation is explainable (item-based neighbor style). The same authors suggested a related approach for a CF methodology that utilizes Restricted Boltzmann Machines (RBM) [24]. The reasoning in content-based recommenders focuses on the content or profile associated with the customer and the object. The scheme clearly showed keyword matches between the user's profile and the books that were being suggested [25]. Similarly, the authors suggested the 'Tagsplanations' process [26], which demonstrated the degree to which a tag is applicable to the object as well as the user's sentiment against the tag. With the emergence of social networking, theories that focus on social connections have gained prominence, *e.g.*, why a user's good friend enjoyed something, where relationship intensity was calculated from their Facebook interactions [27]. More current analysis has focused on offering reasons for the products based on user-written feedback where sentiments and phrases from the feedback are chosen and used for interpretations [28]. Further, subject distribution of the reviews is used to identify useful or representative reviews and uses the topics learned from the reviews as facets of the piece [29].

GENERATING EXPLANATIONS FOR BLACK-BOX RECOMME-NDER SYSTEMS

According to Jonathan L. Herlocker *et al.* [23], the suggestion method takes place within a black box, which indicates that consumers have no idea that the products have been suggested to them. When a page, such as Netflix.com, suggests a video to a customer and has a sentence like *"People who saw this movie also watched..."*, the user is more likely to see the suggested movie [30]. Explanations have been shown to play a significant role in gaining consumer confidence and growing scrutability, which verifies the legitimacy of the advice. So-called expert programs started using examples in the 1990s; however, the theories did not include any satisfactory assessment methods [31].

Later, several reports were also sought to clarify black-box recommender schemes. RippleNet [32] is a tool for resolving sparsity and the cold-start issue by using KGs in collective filtering to provide side details for the device. To improve suggestion consistency and clarity, this black box framework makes use of KGs, which are built using Microsoft Satori. By iteratively contemplating further side detail and propagating the user desires, the authors simulate the concept of water ripple propagation in interpreting user expectations. The developers say that their model is superior to state-of-the-art models throughout the evaluation section. The thesis focuses on utilizing formal information bases to apply explanations to a black box recommender scheme [6]. For justifications, the framework uses past consumer expectations to provide reliable suggestions and organized information bases regarding users and products. Following the model's suggestions, a soft matching algorithm is used to provide customized reasons for the recommendations, using the information bases which outperform other baseline models.

The problem of describing the performance of a black box recommender method is discussed by Bellini *et al.* [33]. The SemAuto recommender framework is developed using an autoencoder neural network technique that is conscious of KGs obtained from the semantic web in that job. According to the writers, explanations improve user retention, loyalty, and confidence. Three explanation types are indicated in their study, namely, popularity-based, pointwise customized, and pairwise personalized. An A/B test was used to assess the suggested explanations' transparency, confidence, satisfaction, persuasiveness, and effectiveness. Most consumers chose the pairwise approach over the pointwise method. Abdollahi and Nasraoui [34 - 36] look at the possibilities of utilizing a neighborhood strategy based on cosine similarity to produce reasons for the performance of a black box device. In terms of error rate and the explainability of the suggested products, the findings indicate that Explainable Matrix Factorization (EMF) outperforms the baseline strategies. Fig. (**4**) shows an indication of a suggestion explanation.

Your ratings for similar movies

Movie	Your rating (1-5)
Batman	5
Twilight	5
Scream 2	4
Space Jam	3
Dead Man	5

Your neighbor's ratings for this movie

Rating	Number of Neighbors
★	0
★★	0
★★★	6
★★★★	8
★★★★★	7

Fig. (4). Explanation of EMF.

In this area, Passant *et al.* [37] were among the first to use semantic network technologies. To create a set of suggestions, the proposed scheme measures the similarity between objects. To get more information about song artists for the music recommendation framework, the suggested system uses the linked data semantic distance algorithm [38]. TasteWeights [39] is a hybrid digital recommender framework for the music business. Several sources of knowledge are used as data sources for the procedure, including Twitter, Facebook, and Wikipedia. The explanation interface not only creates a visually immersive experience that gives justifications to consumers but also enables them to select the basis of the explanation. Suppose the user wants to see an explanation based on Facebook info; the user can see an explanation of their Facebook friends who enjoyed the suggested object. The three layers make up the structure, where the first one is a collection of users' favorite songs culled from their Facebook pages. The material layer is the second layer, where all three knowledge sources' attributes are described (*i.e.*, Wikipedia, Facebook, and Twitter). The third layer is the suggestion layer, which displays the objects that are most often suggested. The semantic equivalent of Wikipedia, DBpedia, is used to extract details from Wikipedia using the query language SPARQL.

According to the authors, interpretation raises the approval of a suggestion, and an explanatory design often makes consumers consider that such suggestions are shown to them, as Herlocker [23] and Middleton [40] mentioned. It also allows users to read more about the recommendation and become more interested in the process. A user analysis was conducted with 32 actual users to assess the system's success and how much the description interface helped them appreciate the suggestion mechanism. The authors concluded that, while Wikipedia was more reliable than Facebook and Twitter being a source of description, users chose explanations based on Facebook friends because they valued their friends' preferences and tastes. Musto *et al.* [41] investigated the importance of natural language descriptions in recommender programs, as well as how connected accessible data would motivate them by connecting the user's previously desired objects and attributes to the current suggestions. The justification process is built on the idea that informative properties that characterize objects that the consumer has previously enjoyed can be used to explain the recommender system's outputs. To validate, a user analysis was performed, and the findings indicate that the suggested system was effective in providing straightforward explanations and recommendations. Table **1** below summarizes recent works along with observations.

Table 1. Literature Review Summary and Observations

S. NO.	TITLE	AUTHOR	SOURCE	OBSERVATION
1	On the Integration of Knowledge Graphs into Deep Learning Models for a More Comprehensible AI: Three Challenges for Future Research	Giuseppe *et al.*	*Journal of Information*, 2020	Knowledge Graphs (KGs) are a promising solution to the issue of understandability.
2	On The Role of Knowledge Graphs in Explainable AI	Freddy Lecue	*Semantic Web* Preprint, 2019	XAI usage in predictions and the challenges associated with them.
3	Mining Semantic Knowledge Graphs to Add Explainability to Black Box Recommender Systems	Mohammed *et al.*	*IEEE Access* 7, 2019	White Box Systems can easily generate explanations as compared to black-box models.

(Table 1) cont.....

S. NO.	TITLE	AUTHOR	SOURCE	OBSERVATION
4	XAI—Explainable artificial intelligence	Gunning David	*Defense Advanced Research Projects Agency (DARPA), and Web* 2.2, 2017	Explainability is essential for users to effectively understand, trust, and manage AI applications.
5	Peeking Inside the Black-Box: A Survey on Explainable Artificial Intelligence (XAI)	Adadi *et al.*	*IEEE Access*, 2018	XAI helps in improving the trust and transparency of AI-based systems.
6	KB4Rec: A Data Set for Linking Knowledge Bases with Recommender Systems	Wayne *et al.*	*Journal of Data Intelligence*, 2019	KB4REC v1.0 is a dataset for linking Knowledge Base information for the RS.
7	WikiDatasets: Standardized Sub Graph from WikiData	Armand *et al.*	*arXiv preprint*, 2019	A unified framework to extract topic-specific subgraphs solves this problem and allows researchers to evaluate algorithms on common datasets.
8	Enhancing JSON to RDF Data Conversion with Entity Type Recognition	Fellipe *et al.*	*WEBIST*, 2017.	A data domain-driven approach to convert semi-structured datasets to RDF using domain vocabularies. The approach can identify 77% of the most appropriate entity types for a given object.
9	Explainable Entity-based Recommendations with Knowledge Graphs	Rose *et al.*	*arXiv preprint*, 2017	Jointly ranks items and knowledge graph entities using a Personalized PageRank procedure to produce recommendations along with their explanations.
10	Fairness-Aware Explainable Recommendation over Knowledge Graphs	Zuohui *et al.*	*arXiv preprint*, 2020	Fairness constrained approach via heuristic re-ranking to mitigate unfairness problems in the context of explainable recommendation over knowledge graphs.
11	Explanation Mining: Post Hoc Interpretability of Latent Factor Models for Recommendation Systems	Georgina *et al.*	*24th ACM Int. Conference on Knowledge Discovery & Data Mining*, 2018	A novel approach for extracting explanations from latent factor recommendation systems by training association rules on the output of a matrix factorization black-box model.

(Table 1) cont.....

S. NO.	TITLE	AUTHOR	SOURCE	OBSERVATION
12	RippleNet: Propagating User Preferences on the Knowledge Graph for Recommender Systems	Hongwei *et al.*	*27th ACM Int. Conference on Information and Knowledge Mgmt, 2018*	The authors proposed RippleNet, an end-to-end framework that naturally incorporates the knowledge graph into recommender systems.
13	A Survey of Explanations in Recommender Systems	Navaet al.	*IEEE 23rd Int. Conference on Data Engineering Workshop*, 2017	A comprehensive review of explanations highlighting possible advantages of an explanation facility and a description of existing measures to evaluate the quality of explanations.
14	Explanations within Conversational Recommendation Systems: Improving Coverage through Knowledge Graph Embeddings	Gustavo *et al.*	*AAAI Workshop on Interactive & Conversational Recommendation System*, 2020	Improving the coverage of the Knowledge Graph using Graph Embedding.

PROPOSED CASE STUDY

A case study of generating explanations using a knowledge graph on the MovieLens dataset is conducted. The methodology is shown in Fig. (**5**), which utilizes two modules, namely, *Recommendation* and *Explanation*. Our method uses an Open Source Dataset for generating domain knowledge graph and item-specific knowledge graph. We have used the largest open-source knowledge graph with 50 million entities, *i.e.*, WikiData, for extracting the item knowledge graph to generate explanations provided by the recommendation module.

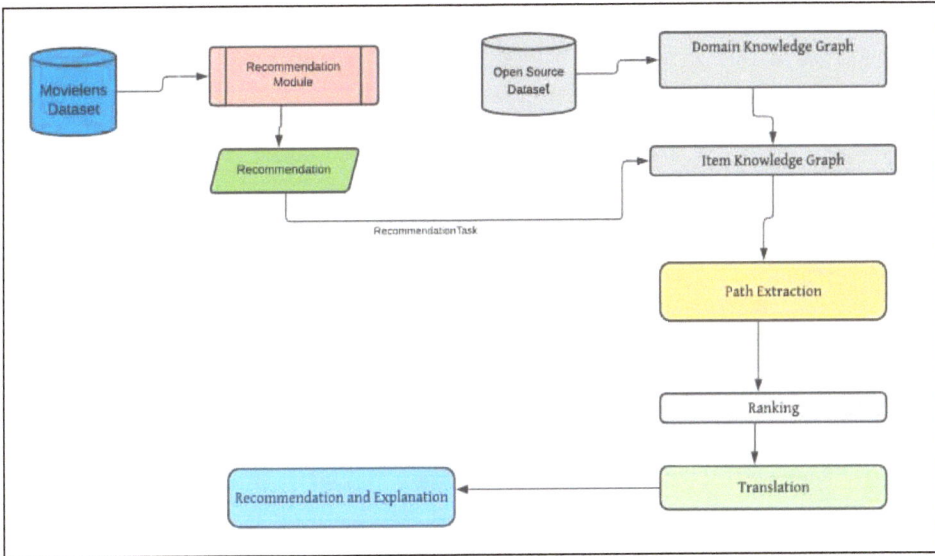

Fig. (5). Block diagram of the proposed model.

The proposed approach is further compared with the three basic approaches, Gspan (Yan, Han, 2002 [42]), WARM (Tao, Murtagh, Farid, 2013 [43]), and GastonFSM (Canim, Sadoghi, Bhattacharjee, Chang, Kalnis, 2017 [44]). Gspan technique performs the iteration of subgraph generation from scratch after each update in the input graph. The methodology of WARM works on the concept of weighted association rule mining. The GastonFSM keeps a list of each node's embedding, and after its evaluation, new nodes are created. Although the performance of the embedding generation system has improved, the traverse time has also increased. This reason being for a single embedding, the whole chain has to be traversed.

MovieLens Dataset

The dataset is a product of member activity in the MovieLens movie recommendation system, an active research platform that has hosted many experiments since its launch in 1997. This dataset contains people's expressed preferences for movies in the form of *<user, item, rating, timestamp>* tuples expressing preferences (1-5 star rating) for a movie.

This dataset is a result of the user's interaction with the online MovieLens Recommender system. During the course of time, MovieLens has undergone a lot of changes and modifications. The MovieLens dataset has been developed by the University of Minnesota. There are four MovieLens datasets released, i.e., 100k,

1m, 10m, and 20m, that reflect the approximate number of ratings in each dataset. There have been major releases every five to six years. The MovieLens dataset has been growing in size since, along with the MovieLens Recommender System. With the release of 20m dataset, GroupLens has been hosting non-archival datasets. It has a version for completeness along with a small version for speed. They are also refreshed periodically to include up-to-date movies: latest and latest-small. The MovieLens dataset is fed as input into the recommendation module (Table **2**).

Table 2. Quantitative Summary of MovieLens Rating Datasets (Maxwell, 2015).

Name	Date Range	Rating Scale	Users	Movies	Ratings	Tag Apps	Density
ML 100K	9/1997–4/1998	1–5, stars	943	1,682	100,000	0	6.30%
ML 1M	4/2000–2/2003	1–5, stars	6,040	3,706	1,000,209	0	4.47%
ML 10M	1/1995–1/2009	0.5–5, half-stars[a]	69,878	10,681	10,000,054	95,580	1.34%
ML 20M	1/1995–3/2015	0.5–5, half-stars[a]	138,493	27,278	20,000,263	465,564	0.54%

Modules

The description of the two modules is as follows:

- *Recommendation Module*: The MovieLens dataset, which is an open-source dataset available online, is pre-processed and is used to train a recommendation module. The Recommendation module is used for generating a recommendation for a particular user in the MovieLens dataset based on the past user-item relationship. A recommender system is used for extracting useful information for users. Recommender systems are classified as collaborative filtering-based, content-based, and hybrid.
- *Explanation Module*: The main purpose of the explanation module is to generate explanations for the recommendation provided to the user so as to increase trust and help in generating more personalized explanations. To generate explanations following sub-modules have to be implemented.

Knowledge Graph Generation

Existing general-purpose open Knowledge graphs like the DBpedia, WikiData, *etc.*, are too large and contain more than 100 million connections. Therefore, they are not suitable for generating explanations directly for the recommendations. The relevant portion of the Knowledge graph will be extracted for the explanation purpose. A Domain Knowledge graph will be extracted from the general-purpose open Knowledge graph. The Domain Knowledge graph will contain only those relations that are relevant and related to the recommendation made. Item Knowledge Graph will be generated by using the user-item information history.

• *Path Extraction*: In this module, candidate paths will be extracted from the Item Knowledge Graph based on the item recommended by the recommendation module and the user's interaction history. A candidate path is a path between the target items (the items with which the user has interacted previously) and the recommended item (the item which is recommended to the user). There can be multiple candidate paths existing between the target user histories of interacted items and recommended items.

• *Ranking*: The candidate paths extracted in the Path extraction module will be ranked based on certain parameters like the user preference for the interacted items. The ranking is done to choose the most relevant path, which will give better explanations for the recommendation. After selecting the 'k' candidate paths, one path will be chosen as the explanation path.

• *Translation*: The translation process will translate the explanation path into a natural language that could be easily understood by the users.

The Proposed Approach for Case Study

The proposed approach creates an item graph based on the recommendations. We generated a knowledge graph directly from the source database. The combined information helps to extract the path, rank the movies and translate the information to get the recommendation for the end-user. The item graph is based on the existing recommendations of the movies as in the Wiki dataset. A knowledge graph (KG) is drawn using the MovieLens dataset with the help of the following Equation (1):

The head and tail have a relation r where the tail is related to entities and Rm are the relations related to the recommended tasks. Using eq. (1), nodes of the KG are generated in graph database represented by Equation (2)

We map Ei and add Ri to KG after extracting a set of entities Ei and a set of relations Ri from user-item information. All triples in the user-item information that is unrelated to the items in the user-item information are eliminated from KG. The items extracted are stored in the graph database setting the entity relationship. Further, Extraction, rating, and translation processes are used to generate the explanations from the Item KG. Based on the item proposed by the recommendation module and the user's interaction history, the extraction method extracts candidate routes on the KG. The recommended item (Fig.**4.2**) and the target items in the user's interaction history are designated as start points and endpoints, respectively. As the target user's candidate paths, all paths with a length of d or less are extracted from the KG. Between the item recommended to a user and his or her history of interacted items, there are usually several paths. Because using all of the paths to provide explanations for only one recommended item is unfeasible, a ranking procedure is required to select the most relevant paths for providing effective individualized explanations. The user's preference for the entities in candidate pathways is used to rank them. The user's preference is calculated using Equation (3).

Note: The vectors U (users) and V (movies) are dot multiplied to get the recommendation of the movie.

Results

The proposed technique is compared with the above-mentioned techniques with respect to efficiency, memory overhead, and accuracy. The memory overhead is computed in terms of consumption of memory. Finally, the output of the proposed algorithm in the form of a graph database is shown.

- *Efficiency*: The efficiency of the proposed approach is compared with Gspan, WARM, and GastonFSM. It is evaluated in terms of the time required for generating the graph along with all the subgraphs and mining the entire graph. Fig. 6 illustrates the result of the efficiency where the X-axis shows the different datasets considered and the Y-axis shows the elapsed time for the graph generation. The estimated time is calculated for a small subset of data and then extrapolated for the entire dataset. It is evident that K-graph outperforms all the other three techniques. It is noteworthy that GastonFSM and WARM perform well when the graph is small. However, with larger graphs, the performance is depreciated since all the embeddings of every node are to be stored. And for larger graphs, the embeddings become too large to store. This increases the memory requirement and time taken hence the efficiency is reduced.

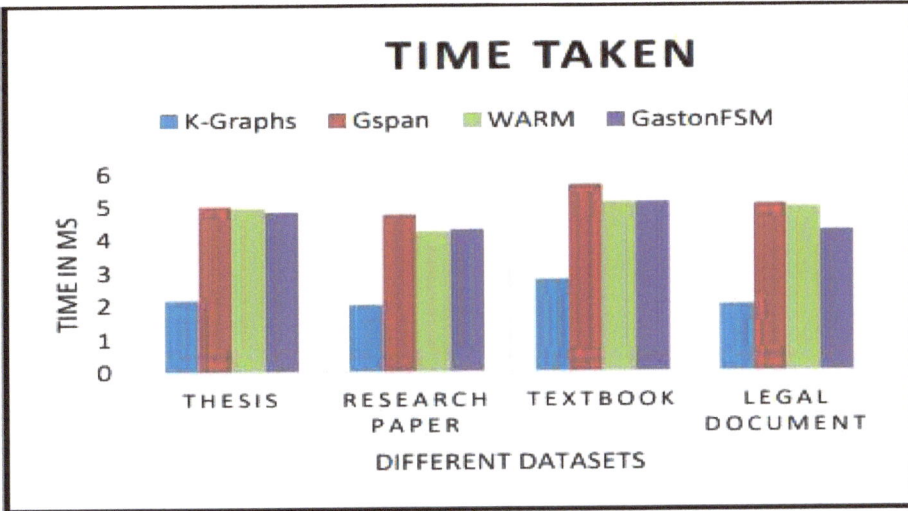

Fig. 6. Efficiency w.r.t time taken for graph generation

- *Performance*: Fig. 7 shows that the K-graph performs 55.95% better than Gspan, 52.91% better than WARM, and 51.3% better than GastonFSM.

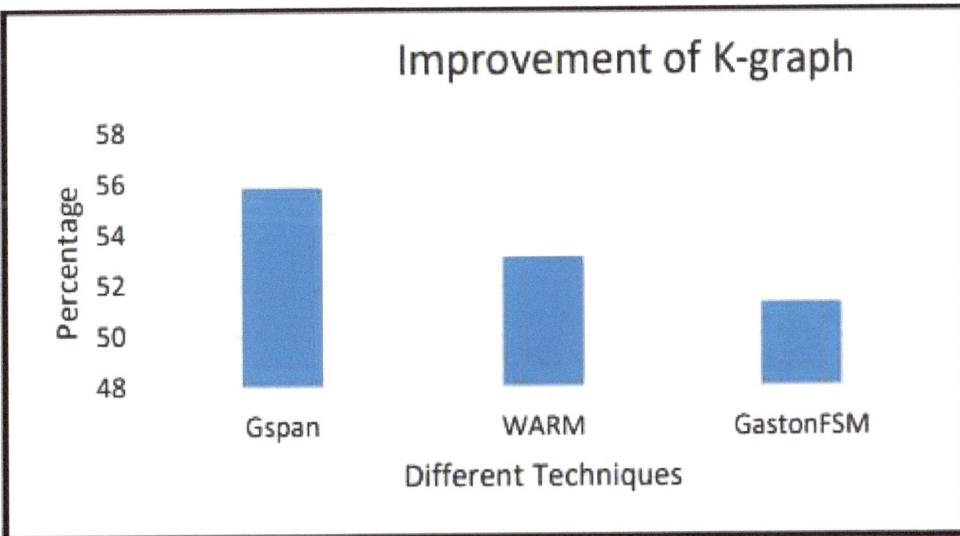

Fig. 7. Improvement of K-graph in comparison to other techniques

- *Memory Overhead*: The proposed algorithm is evaluated in terms of memory overhead which is the amount of memory required to store the graph generated. The graph is generated according to the different subheadings of the target document. The histogram in Fig. (**8**) below shows the comparison of the K-graph with the other three techniques. In the proposed approach, the list of embedding is carefully reduced.

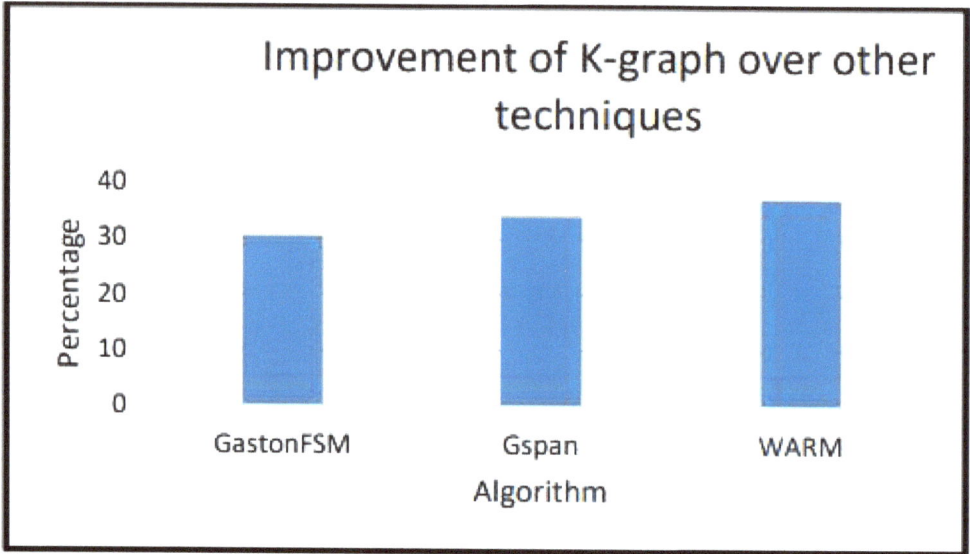

Fig. 8. Improvement of K-graph over other techniques in memory overhead

Graph Visualisation

Fig. (**9** and **10**) show a screenshot of Level 1 and Level 2 graph created. The title of the document is taken as the root node and headers as its leaf nodes. One of the headers has been considered with keywords. Similar headers will not be added; the only weight would be incremented by one, and unique keywords would be added.

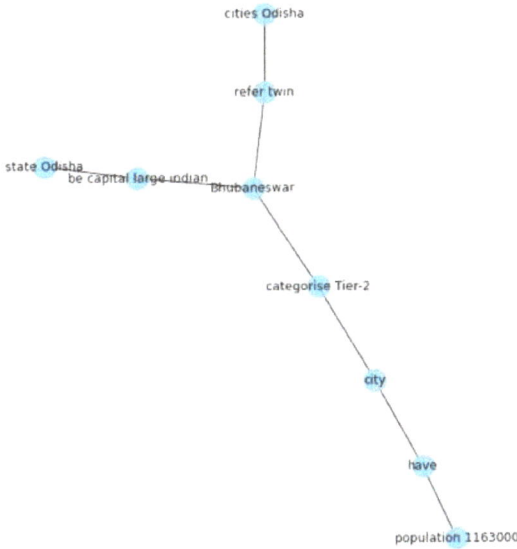

Fig. (10). Snapshot of level 1 graph database.

Fig. (11). Snapshot of level 2 graph database.

CONCLUSION

Nowadays, knowledge graphs are extensively applied to handle complicated and black-box models like recommendation systems. The chapter introduces the concept of recommender systems and knowledge graphs, followed by an exclusive review of literature for both. Further, the use of knowledge graphs for generating back-box recommendations has been explored, and a state-of-the-art summary of related work is presented. We also proposed a case study experiment and compared it with existing recommender systems using the database of graphs. The findings indicate that redundancy and memory space requirements were reduced by more than 50%. This, in turn, resulted in lower traverse time with overall improved efficiency as well as more accuracy for explaining the recommendations.

REFERENCES

[1]   Y. Chen, and J. Miyazaki, A Model-Agnostic Recommendation Explanation System Based on Knowledge Graph" *IEICE Technical Report; IEICE Tech. Rep.* 119.354 (2019): 13-17.
[http://dx.doi.org/10.1007/978-3-030-59051-2_10]

[2]   M. Balabanović, and Y. Shoham, *Fab. Commun. ACM,* vol. 40, no. 3, pp. 66-72, 1997.
[http://dx.doi.org/10.1145/245108.245124]

[3]   A. Adadi, and M. Berrada, *Peeking Inside the Black-Box: A Survey on Explainable Artificial Intelligence (XAI).* vol. Vol. 6. IEEE Access, 2018.

[4]   F. Gong, M. Wang, H. Wang, S. Wang, and M. Liu, "Safe Medicine Recommendation via Medical Knowledge Graph Embedding. arXiv." Information Retrieval (2017).

[5]   R.P. Goldman, and J.S. Breese, Integrating Model Construction and Evaluation Uncertainty in Artificial Intelligence. Morgan Kaufmann, 1992.
[http://dx.doi.org/10.1016/B978-1-4832-8287-9.50019-0]

[6]   Q. Ai, V. Azizi, X. Chen, and Y. Zhang, "Learning heterogeneous knowledge base embeddings for explainable recommendation", *Algorithms,* vol. 11, no. 9, p. 137, 2018.
[http://dx.doi.org/10.3390/a11090137]

[7]   Y. Koren, R. Bell, and C. Volinsky, "Matrix factorization techniques for recommender systems", *Computer,* vol. 42, no. 8, pp. 30-37, 2009.
[http://dx.doi.org/10.1109/MC.2009.263]

[8]   Q. Guo, F. Zhuang, C. Qin, H. Zhu, X. Xie, H. Xiong, and Q. He, "A Survey on Knowledge Graph-Based Recommender Systems", *IEEE Trans. Knowl. Data Eng.,* 2020.

[9]   T. Lin, P. Pantel, M. Gamon, A. Kannan, and A. Fuxman, "Active objects: actions for entity-centric search", Proceedings of the 21st international conference on World Wide Web. 2012.
[http://dx.doi.org/10.1145/2187836.2187916]

[10]   H.Q. Yu, X. Zhao, X. Zhen, F. Dong, E. Liu, and G. Clapworthy, "Healthcare-Event Driven Semantic Knowledge Extraction with Hybrid Data Repository", Fourth edition of the International Conference on the Innovative Computing Technology (INTECH 2014). IEEE, 2014.
[http://dx.doi.org/10.1109/INTECH.2014.6927774]

[11]   T.D. Noia, V.C. Ostuni, P. Tomeo, and E.D. Sciascio, "SPrank: Semantic path-based ranking for top-n recommendations using linked open data", *ACM Trans. Intell. Syst. Technol.,* vol. 8, no. 1, pp. 1-34, 2016.
[http://dx.doi.org/10.1145/2899005] [PMID: 28344853]

[12]   V.C. Ostuni, T.D. Noia, E.D. Sciascio, and R. Mirizzi, "Top-n recommendations from implicit feedback leveraging linked open data", Proceedings of the 7th ACM conference on Recommender systems. 2013.
[http://dx.doi.org/10.1145/2507157.2507172]

[13]   F. Ricci, "Mobile recommender systems", *Inf. Technol. Tour.,* vol. 12, no. 3, pp. 205-231, 2010.
[http://dx.doi.org/10.3727/109830511X12978702284390]

[14]   R. Burke, "Hybrid Recommender Systems: Survey and Experiments", *User Model. User-adapt. Interact.,* vol. 12, no. 4, pp. 331-370, 2002.
[http://dx.doi.org/10.1023/A:1021240730564]

[15]   G. Adomavicius, and A. Tuzhilin, "Toward the next generation of recommender systems: a survey of the state-of-the-art and possible extensions", *IEEE Trans. Knowl. Data Eng.,* vol. 17, no. 6, pp. 734-749, 2005.
[http://dx.doi.org/10.1109/TKDE.2005.99]

[16]   D. O' Sullivan, D. Wilson, and B. Smyth, "Using Collaborative Filtering Data in Case-Based Recommendation", FLAIRS Conference. 2002.

[17] Breese, John S., and Michael R. Fehling. "Control of problem solving: Principles and architecture." Machine Intelligence and Pattern Recognition. Vol. 9. North-Holland, 1990. 59-68.

[18] R. Catherine, K. Mazaitis, M. Eskenazi, and W. Cohen, "Explainable Entity-based Recommendations with Knowledge Graphs", arXiv preprint arXiv:1707.05254 (2017).

[19] X. Yu, X. Ren, Y. Sun, Q. Gu, B. Sturt, U. Khandelwal, B. Norick, and J. Han, "Personalized entity recommendation: A heterogeneous information network approach", In Proceedings of the 7th ACM international conference on Web search and data mining. pp. 283-292, 2014.
[http://dx.doi.org/10.1145/2556195.2556259]

[20] X. Yu, X. Ren, Y. Sun, Q. Gu, B. Sturt, U. Khandelwal, B. Norick, and J. Han, "Recommendation in heterogeneous information networkswith implicit userfeedback", In Proceedings of the 7th ACM conference on Recommender systems, pp. 347-350, 2013.

[21] E. Palumbo, G. Rizzo, and R. Troncy, "entity2rec: Learning User-Item Relatedness from Knowledge Graphs for Top-N Item Recommendation", In Proceedings of the eleventh ACM conference on recommender systems, pp. 32-36, 2017.
[http://dx.doi.org/10.1145/3109859.3109889]

[22] W. Xiong, T. Hoang, and W.Y. Wang, "Deep Path: A Reinforcement Learning Method for Knowledge Graph Reasoning", In: *Empirical Methods in Natural Language Processing*, 2017.

[23] J.L. Herlocker, J.A. Konstan, and J. Riedl, "Explaining collaborative filtering recommendations", In: *CSCW*, 2000.
[http://dx.doi.org/10.1145/358916.358995]

[24] B. Abdollahi, and O. Nasraoui, "Explainable restricted Boltzmann machines for collaborative filtering", In: *WHI*, 2016.

[25] M. Bilgic, and R.J. Mooney, "Explaining recommendations: Satisfaction vs. promotion", In: *Beyond Personalization Workshop, IUI*, 2005.

[26] J. Vig, S. Sen, and J. Riedl, "Tagsplanations: explaining recommendations using tags", in: *IUI*, 2009.
[http://dx.doi.org/10.1145/1502650.1502661]

[27] A. Sharma, and D. Cosley, "Do social explanations work?: Studying and modeling the effectsof social explanations in recommender systems", In: *WWW*, 2013.
[http://dx.doi.org/10.1145/2488388.2488487]

[28] Y. Zhang, G. Lai, M. Zhang, Y. Zhang, Y. Liu, and S. Ma, "Explicit factor models for explainable recommendation based on phrase-level sentiment analysis", In: *SIGIR*, 2014.
[http://dx.doi.org/10.1145/2600428.2609579]

[29] J. McAuley, and J. Leskovec, "Hidden factors and hidden topics: Understanding rating dimensions with review text", In: *RecSYS*, 2013.
[http://dx.doi.org/10.1145/2507157.2507163]

[30] N. Tintarev, and J. Masthoff, "Explaining recommendations: Design and evaluation", In: *Recommender Systems Handbook*. Springer, 2015, pp. 353-382.
[http://dx.doi.org/10.1007/978-1-4899-7637-6_10]

[31] A. Lopez-Suarez, and M. Kamel, "DyKOr: a method for generating the content of explanations in knowledge systems", *Knowl. Base. Syst.,* vol. 7, no. 3, pp. 177-188, 1994.
[http://dx.doi.org/10.1016/0950-7051(94)90004-3]

[32] H. Wang, F. Zhang, J. Wang, M. Zhao, W. Li, X. Xie, and M. Guo, "RippleNet: Propagating user preferences on the knowledge graph for recommender systems", In: *CIKM*, 2018.
[http://dx.doi.org/10.1145/3269206.3271739]

[33] V. Bellini, A. Schiavone, T.D. Noia, A. Ragone, and E.D. Sciascio, "Knowledge-aware autoencoders for explainable recommender systems", In: *DLRS*, 2018.
[http://dx.doi.org/10.1145/3270323.3270327]

[34]   B. Abdollahi, and O. Nasraoui, "Explainable matrix factorization for collaborative filtering", Proceedings of the 25th International Conference Companion on World Wide Web. 2016. [http://dx.doi.org/10.1145/2872518.2889405]

[35]   B. Abdollahi, and O. Nasraoui, "Using explainability for constrained matrix factorization", Proceedings of the eleventh ACM conference on recommender systems. 2017. [http://dx.doi.org/10.1145/3109859.3109913]

[36]   B. Abdollahi, *Accurate and justifiable: New algorithms for explainable recommendations.* University of Louisville: Louisville, Kentucky, 2017.

[37]   A. Passant, and S. Decker, "Hey! Ho! Let's go! Explanatory music recommendations with dbrec", The Semantic Web: Research and Applications: 7th Extended Semantic Web Conference, ESWC 2010, Heraklion, Crete, Greece, May 30–June 3, 2010, Proceedings, Part II 7. Springer Berlin Heidelberg, 2010. [http://dx.doi.org/10.1007/978-3-642-13489-0_34] [http://dx.doi.org/10.1007/978-3-642-13489-0_34]

[38]   A. Passant, "Measuring semantic distance on linking data and using it for resources recommendations", 2010 AAAI Spring Symposium Series. 2010.

[39]   S. Bostandjiev, J. O'Donovan, and T. Höllerer, "TasteWeights: A visual interactive hybrid recommender system", Proceedings of the sixth ACM conference on Recommender systems. 2012. [http://dx.doi.org/10.1145/2365952.2365964]

[40]   S.E. Middleton, H. Alani, and D.C. De Roure, "Exploiting synergy between ontologies and recommender systems", In: *Semantic Web Workshop*, 2002.

[41]   C. Musto, F. Narducci, P. Lops, M. de Gemmis, and G. Semeraro, "Linked open data-based explanations for transparent recommender systems", *Int. J. Hum. Comput. Stud.,* vol. 121, pp. 93-107, 2019. [http://dx.doi.org/10.1016/j.ijhcs.2018.03.003]

[42]   X. Yan, and J. Han, "Span: graph-based substructure pattern mining", In: *IEEE International Conference on Data Mining*, 2002.

[43]   F. Tao, F. Murtagh, and M. Farid, "Weighted Association Rule Mining Using Weighted Support and Significant Framework", In: *International Conference on Knowledge Discovery and Data Mining*, 2003.

[44]   E. Abdelhamid, M. Canim, M. Sadoghi, B. Bhattacharjee, Y-C. Chang, and P. Kalnis, "Incremental Frequent Subgraph Mining on Large Evolving Graphs", *IEEE Trans. Knowl. Data Eng.,* vol. 29, no. 12, pp. 2710-2723, 2017. [http://dx.doi.org/10.1109/TKDE.2017.2743075]

## CHAPTER 13

Universal Price Tag Reader for Retail Supermarket

Jay Prajapati[1,*] and **Siba Panda**[1]

[1] *Department of Data Science, SVKM's NMIMS, Mumbai, Maharashtra, India*

Abstract: Retail supermarkets are an essential part of today's economy, and managing them is a tedious task. One of the major problems faced by supermarkets today is to keep track of the items available on the racks. Currently, the track of the product on the shelf is kept by price tag readers, which work on a barcode detection methodology that has to be customized for each store. On the other hand, if barcodes are not present on the price tags, the data is manually fed by the staff of the store, which is really time-consuming. This paper presents a universal pipeline that is based on Optical Character recognition and can be used across all kinds of price tags, and is not dependent on barcodes or any particular type of price tag. This project uses various image-possessing techniques to determine and crop the Area of Interest. It detects the price of the product and the name of the product by filtering the OCR outputs based on the area and dimensions of the bounding boxes of the text detected. Additionally, the presented pipeline is also capable of capturing discounted prices, if any, for the products. It has been tested over price tags of five different types, and the accuracy ranges from 78% to 94.5%.

Keywords: Artificial intelligence, Contour detection, Image processing, Optical character recognition, Retail supermarkets.

INTRODUCTION

Currently, the price tag reading is widely done by a simple barcode scanner, in which the barcode is scanned, the code is matched with the database, and the information is extracted. The issue with this system is the anomaly of the barcode from store to store. Each of the stores may have its own barcode according to its internal inventory management systems. So the price tag reader has to be custom-tailored for each store. It is quite difficult to maintain data about each store. Also, some stores might not have these kinds of barcode-based inventory management systems, and the price tags do not have barcodes. This is a reason why such syste-

---

* **Corresponding author Jay Prajapati:** Department of Data Science, SVKM's NMIMS University, Mumbai, Maharashtra, India; E-mail: jayprajapati1141@gmail.com

Gyanendra Verma & Rajesh Doriya (Eds.)

ms are not used often. So this project will be using a very popular technique called optical character recognition which is widely used nowadays in number plate detection and recognition, which will be able to read the name, price, and discounted price(if any) of the product irrespective of the type of the tag.

LITERATURE REVIEW

There has been research work done on this front, and the closest one is- Price Tag Recognition using HSV Color Space [1]. This system requires a format and color of the price tag beforehand. It detects the price tag from the image using HSV color filtering and finds the largest rectangle contour in the image. The image is then cropped according to the largest contour, giving the cropped image the price tag. Then the price tag image is masked with a predefined mask image for that particular type of price tag (the research work has considered 3 predefined price tag formats- A, G, T). It returns two cropped images- one is the price-cropped image, and the second one is the product name image. Finally, an OCR is run over these two images to read the price and product name.

The problem with this system is that it requires the format and color of the price tag beforehand, and there might be n number of price tag designs, and there might be n number of colors for price tags, so the system is required to maintain the mask images for each format. Secondly, it doesn't consider the discounts and offer prices for products, and it only reads the price and name of the product.

Computer Vision and Image Processing: A Paper Review' [2] provides a deep, comprehensive review of many computer vision and image processing techniques in the past. It talks about the image processing applied to digital sound systems, food analytics, and CNN used for object detection. It also talks about recent pattern recognition research and image segmentation.

'Two-stage approach to extracting visual objects from paper documents' [3] is a two-stage approach for detecting components like logos, signatures, text blocks, tables, and stamps from the documents. The first stage of the approach is a rough detection through a simple and fast approach called Adaboost Cascade for the classifier, and the second stage is verifying stage, which uses additional techniques like First-order statistics (FOS), Gray-level run-length statistics (GLRLS), Haralick's statistics (HS), Neighboring gray-level dependence statistics (NGLDS), Low-level features (LLF), Histograms of oriented gradients (HOG) and local binary patterns (LBP). It was found that the accuracy was not that great in the first stage, but it improved after the verification stage, except for the signature, in which the accuracy decreased after the verification stage.

'Malaysian Car Number Plate Detection System Based on Template Matching and Colour Information' [4] this research paper proposes a pipeline for detecting number plates. This approach goes about cropping the lower half of the image, continued by pre-processing the image by using top fat filtering, thresholding, intensity correction, and median filtering. Then to identify the region of the number plate, template matching is used, pixel-by-pixel matching is done, and a numeric index is calculated, which shows how good the matching performance is. Then to reduce the noise in the image, contrast correction is used. To tackle the number plates with different dimensions, the bounding box is made with a padding of 10 pixels. The outputs are good for the number plates with similar dimensions as the masking template but don't perform well for larger number plates and number plates in different colors' Post-OCR parsing: building simple and robust parser *via* BIO tagging' [5]; this research talks about a downstream task of parsing textual information embedded in images. It has taken into account parsing tasks for name cards and receipts. There are four major steps in this process- OCR, Serialization, BIO tagging, and parse generation. It uses in-house OCR, which consists of a CRAFT text detector and Comb. Best text recognizer. The OCR outputs are serialized by sorting them from top to bottom and left to right according to their coordinates. These serialized tags are then BIO parsed using a neural network. Input vectors are mapped by adding coordinates, tokens, sequential positions, and segments. The model gives outputs of mixed BIO tags, which can be decoded according to the target field. These outputs are further refined. This approach enables information propagation in abstract space and removes the need for customization.

'A Novel Method for Indian Vehicle Registration Number Plate Detection and Recognition using Image Processing Techniques' [6] this research paper presents a pipeline for detecting and reading license plates. The approach is divided into three major parts- pre-processing, detection and recognition. The pre-processing includes image resizing, RGB to HSV conversion, greyscale extraction, morphological transformations, Gaussian smoothing, and Inverted Adaptive Gaussian Thresholding. The second step includes applying contours to the image, followed by filtering and grouping of contours, correcting the angle of the license plate, and finally fixing overlapping characters and contours. Once the license plate is detected, a model is trained using the KNN algorithm to recognize the characters and digits of the license plate. This research helped tackle situations of blurred images, images with varying illumination, noisy images, and non-standard license plates.

'Text Extraction from Bills and Invoices' [7], this research paper has presented a pipeline for extracting text from bills and invoices. This approach uses OpenCV and Tesseract OCR. The approach goes about by detecting and cropping the piece of paper from the image using the canny edge detection followed by contour detection and, at last, four-point perspective transformation. Once the surrounding noise is removed, Tesseract OCR is used to recognize the text. Finally, to implement this pipeline, a WebApp is developed using the Flask framework. This approach works for printed bills and invoices but doesn't support handwriting recognition.

'Effectiveness of Modern Text Recognition Solutions and Tools for Common Data Sources' [8] is a comparative paper that provides in detail differentiation between two OCR techniques- TesserOCR and Easy OCR. The dataset consists of three major categories of images- books, screenshots, and short images. The study compares the two techniques based on the time taken in the best cases and the worst-case scenario and also the accuracy of the outputs. It was found that TesserOCR was much faster in most of the cases compared to EasyOCR, but EasyOCR gave a much better accuracy when it came to small and distorted images. I concluded by recommending TesserOCR for bigger, clearer, and plain text images and EasyOCR for short text with lots of noise.

METHODOLOGY

In this approach, we have proposed the following methodology, which can be universally used over all kinds of price tags. This method is broadly divided into three parts: image pre-processing and cropping, optical character recognition, and extracting price tag details from the OCR outputs. The flow chart (Fig. **1**) shows the outline of the pipeline.

Image Pre-processing and Cropping

In this section, we will develop an image processing pipeline wherein the main aim is to detect the price tag in the image and crop that particular section so that the cropped image can be further used for OCR. To develop the pre-possessing pipeline, we will use the following techniques: First of all, we use Image thresholding on a sample image (Fig. **2**), wherein image pixels would be thresholded to a particular value (Fig. **3**). Then, we would use two blurring techniques, Gaussian Blur and Canny Blur, to blur and denoise the image so that edge and contours in the image can be clearly detected in the upcoming cropping process. Additionally, we also use Image Dilation and Erosion to improve the edges in the image (Fig. **4**).

After we get the processed image, we move on to cropping the price tag from the image, for which we will use the process of Image Countering, which will detect all the contours in the image (Fig. **5**), and then we would filter out the contour which has the maximum rectangular area that would be the area of interest

(Fig. **6**). Once we get this contour, we will use its coordinates to crop out the price tag from our original image (Fig. **7**).

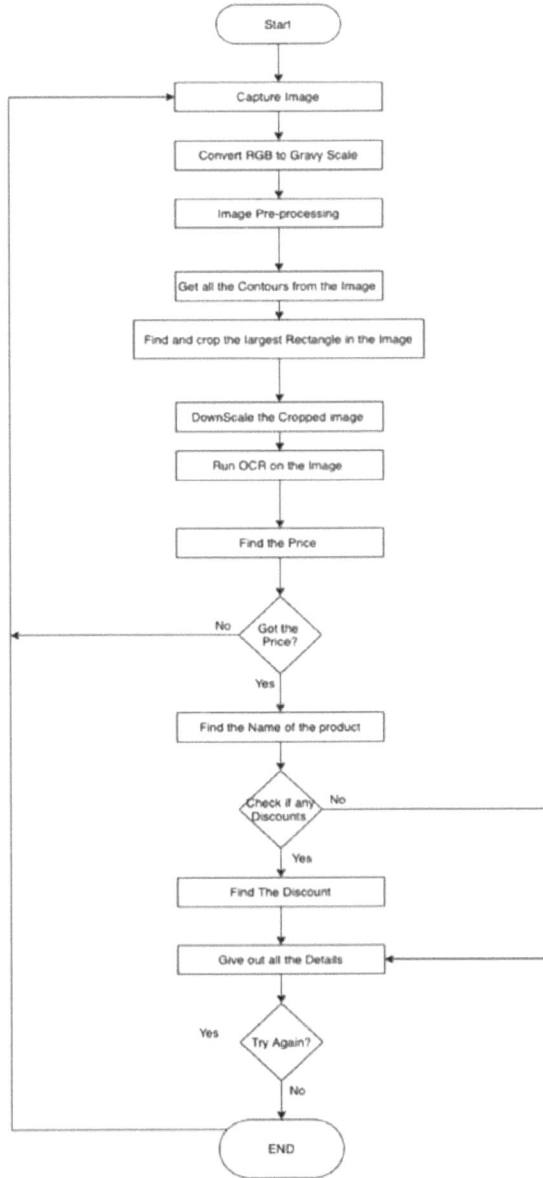

Fig. (1). Flow Cart.

Fig. (2). Input Image.

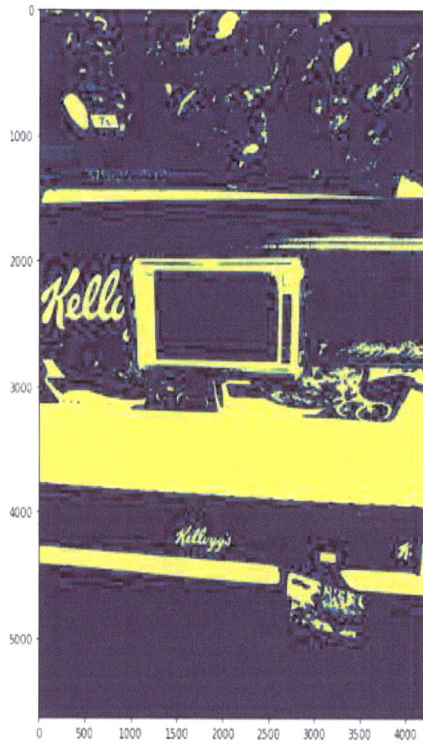

Fig. (3). Threshold Image.

Fig. (4). Dilation Erosion.

Fig. (5). Contours Detected.

Fig. (6). Largest Rectangle.

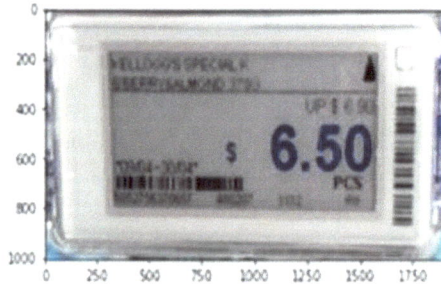

Fig. (7). Cropped Image.

Optical Character Recognition

In this section, we proceed to extract text out of the cropped image that we got in the previous section. For this, we will be using EasyOCR, which is an open-source OCR. It is quite efficient when used with GPU, but for this pipeline, we are not using GPU, so the image will be scaled down to get the OCR outputs much faster; the cropped image is scaled down to 35% of its length and width. After this, the image is passed to the EasyOCR, and we get the output in the form of a list, in which each component is again a list that contains the following three things: Text detected, Confidence Score, and four vertices of the bounding box (Fig. **8**).

```
([[173, 105], [649, 105], [649, 145], [173, 145]], "KELLOGO'S HONEYRNUTS CORN", 0.5230448157354021)
([[173, 143], [367, 143], [367, 181], [173, 181]], 'ELAKES 360G', 0.7849754245602968)
([[615, 187], [785, 187], [785, 229], [615, 229]], 'UP $ 5.40', 0.9122249542283725)
([[178, 304], [377, 304], [377, 345], [178, 345]], '"1104-3004*', 0.1998906960711322)
([[432, 274], [462, 274], [462, 318], [432, 318]], 'S', 0.24152123930022995)
([[526, 232], [786, 232], [786, 354], [526, 354]], '3.95', 0.9496221642788955)
([[178, 334], [367, 334], [367, 373], [178, 373]], 'ILOIII H HMII', 0.023767404900133446)
([[677, 339], [753, 339], [753, 379], [677, 379]], 'PCS', 0.9340297347235303)
([[172, 364], [363, 364], [363, 403], [172, 403]], '8852756304114', 0.9983011705812017)
([[408, 374], [500, 374], [500, 404], [408, 404]], '485098', 0.9960674277024736)
([[548, 378], [612, 378], [612, 408], [548, 408]], '1X12', 0.9227578043937683)
([[704, 382], [744, 382], [744, 412], [704, 412]], 'R8', 0.8525386268848909)
```

Fig. (8). OCR Outputs.

Price of the product

After going through a plethora of price tags in the supermarkets, it is found that the price on the price tag is printed in a larger font compared to the other text on the tag. So to determine the price of the product mentioned on the tag, we will filter out the text with the largest font amongst the OCR text, which can be done by calculating the height of the text by the vertices that are given out by the OCR engine, and then taking out the text with maximum height (Fig. **9**).

Once this text is found, it can be passed through a series of checks, and if any inconsistency is found, it gets corrected. There are two checks: firstly, if the text contains any characters except numbers and period (.), if there exists, get rid of them by just dropping those characters. Secondly, does the text contain a period? (there are some instances where price tags don't have a decimal in the price). If the text doesn't have the period, it is converted to float and divided by 100 as all the prices are rounded up to the second decimal place. After these series of steps, we finally have the accurate price of the product.

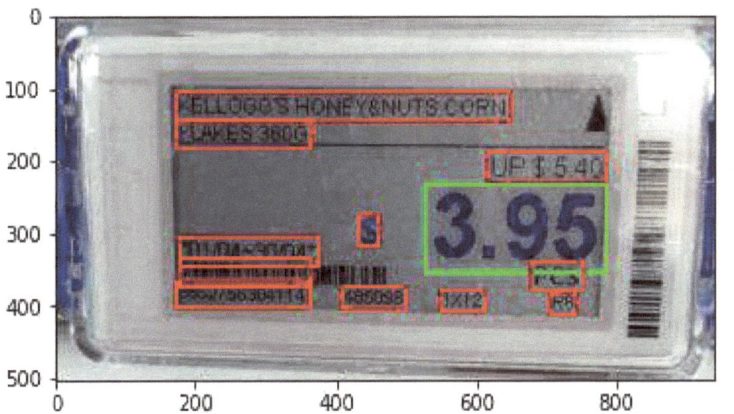

Fig. (9). The Price has the maximum height.

Name of the product

Generally, it is seen that the name of the product is the longest text on the price tag, but there are some numeric codes that can be longer than the name. So two longest texts on the tag are filtered. However, the total number of characters in each text. Then, we eliminate the text which is either numeric or contains a period or a slash as a component in the text, which by default eliminates one of the two texts selected as it is observed that the second long text is always some numeric code or some kind of date.

Sometimes the name of the product is split into two lines (Fig. **10**) for such scenarios, if the text on the second line is the second largest text, it will not be eliminated in the earlier step, but if there is some code or data that is available which is longer than the second line of the name, it will not be detected. So we deploy a check mechanism that looks for any other text around the longest text found. So an area is defined (Fig. **11**) above and below the longest text, which has the height and width equal to the bounding box of the longest text. If any text is found in that area, the found text is merged with the longest text found earlier.

Fig. (10). Name of the product present in two lines.

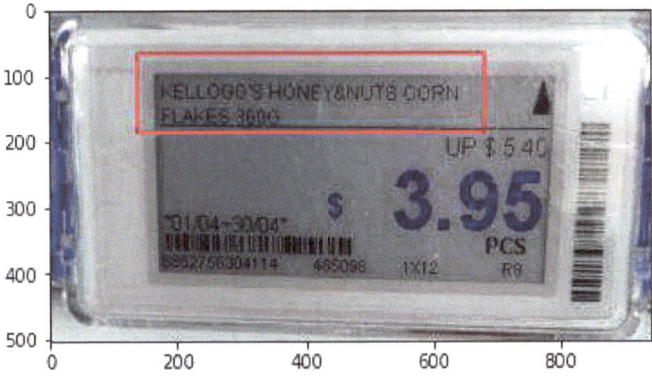

Fig. (11). Area in which the text is searched.

Discounted Price

There are certain instances where the product is available at a discounted price, so a discounted price will also be mentioned on the price tag. These prices can also be determined (if it exists). So if any other price is available on the tag, it will contain a period (.), So the OCR output text is searched, and if any text containing a period is found, there is an alternative price available on the text. Once we find some text like this (Fig. **13**), we clear out all the inconsistencies by passing it through the checks which were defined while cleaning the price. After we receive this price, it will be compared with the price which was found earlier; if the new price found is more in value than the previously found price, then this price would be the original price, and the previous price would be the discounted price. On the other hand, if the newly found value is lesser than the older value, this value would be the discounted price. Finally, a statement will be generated stating the original price and discounted price.

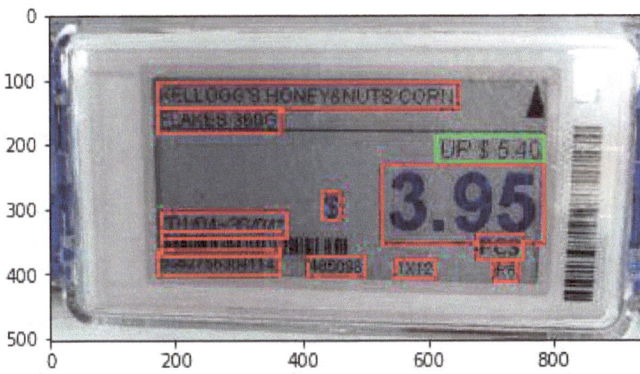

Fig. (12). Discount Condition Found.

After all the previous three sections are carried out, the final output has the three details in the form of a list which contains the price, name of the product, and discounted price, if any (Fig. **13**).

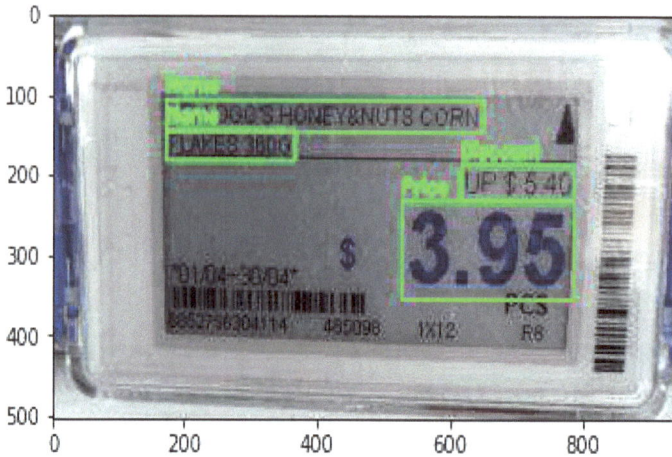

```
Price:  3.95
Name of the Product:    KELLOGO'S HONEYRNUTS CORN ELAKES 360G
Discounts:  Discounted Price is 3.95, Original Price 5.4
```

Fig. (13). Final Outputs.

RESULTS AND FUTURE SCOPE

This methodology is tested over five types of price tags with and without Discounts, and the results are given in Table **1**.

Table 1. Results of testing the methodology.

Types of tags	Total Images	Accurate Price	Accurate Name	Accurate Discount
Type – 1	46	41 (89.13)	39 (84.78)	37 (80.43)
Type – 2	34	29 (85.29)	27 (79.50)	29 (85.29)
Type – 3	77	73 (94.80)	67 (87.01)	60 (78.00)
Type – 4	33	30 (90.90)	29 (87.87)	31(93.93)
Type – 5	20	18 (90.00)	16 (80.00)	19 (95.00)

The accuracy varies from 78% to 94.8% across all five types of tags. This methodology comes with a limitation that only one price tag can be present in the image at a time; if more than one price tag is present in the image, outputs for only one of the price tags will be given out. It can be seen that in some cases, there are some inconsistencies in the name of the product detected, the location is accurately determined, but the text is not; it can be improved but using some advance paid OCR engines like Google OCR and Microsoft Azur OCR. It is also observed that if the price tag is properly cropped, the outputs are as desired. But if not, neither of the functions can pick out the details. Furthermore, more components can be even added to the pipeline, such as expiry dates and conditional discounts.

CONCLUDING REMARKS

This project has successfully developed a pipeline for a price tag reader, which has also been tested over multiple types of price tags. Hence achieving a universal solution to read any type of price tag. This pipeline can be deployed at supermarkets to feed in data about the items available on the rack.

ACKNOWLEDGEMENTS

We would like to thank Dr. Sagar Setu and the Milky Way AI team for providing their constant support and the price tag images used while building this methodology.

REFERENCES

[1]   Hussin, M. N. A, Hussin, M. N. A., A. H. Ahmad, and MA Abdul Razak. "Price Tag Recognition using HSV Color Space." Journal of Telecommunication, Electronic and Computer Engineering (JTEC), vol. 9, no. 3-9, 2017, pp. 77-84. https://jtec.utem.edu.my/jtec/article/view/3129

[2]   Wiley, Victor, and Thomas Lucas. "Computer Vision and Image Processing: A Paper Review." International Journal of Artificial Intelligence Research, vol. 2, no. 1, pp. 28-36, 2018. https://doi.org/10.29099/ijair.v2i1.42.D. Sarunyagate, Ed., Lasers. New York: McGraw-Hill, 1996. [http://dx.doi.org/10.29099/ijair.v2i1.42]

[3]   P. Forczmański, and A. Markiewicz, "Two-stage approach to extracting visual objects from paper documents", *Mach. Vis. Appl.,* vol. 27, no. 8, pp. 1243-1257, 2016. [http://dx.doi.org/10.1007/s00138-016-0803-5]

[4]   M.F. Zakaria, and S.A. Suandi, "Malaysian Car Number Plate Detection System Based on Template Matching and Colour Information", *Int. J. Comput. Sci. Eng.,* vol. 02, no. 04, pp. 1159-1164, 2010.

[5]   W. Hwang, S. Kim, M. Seo, J. Yim, S. Park, S. Park, J. Lee, B. Lee, H. Lee. Post-OCR parsing: building simple and robust parser *via* BIO tagging. Workshop Document Intelligence at NeurIPS, 2019.

[6]   R.K. Varma P, S. Ganta, H.K. B, and P. Svsrk, "A Novel Method for Indian Vehicle Registration Number Plate Detection and Recognition using Image Processing Techniques", *Procedia Comput. Sci.,* vol. 167, pp. 2623-2633, 2020. [http://dx.doi.org/10.1016/j.procs.2020.03.324]

[7]   H. Sidhwa, S. Kulshrestha, S. Malhotra, and S. Virmani, "Text Extraction from Bills and Invoices", *2018 International Conference on Advances in Computing, Communication Control and Networking (ICACCCN),* 2018pp. 564-568 [http://dx.doi.org/10.1109/ICACCCN.2018.8748309]

[8]   K. Smelyakov, *Effectiveness of Modern Text Recognition Solutions and Tools for Common Data Sources.* COLINS, 2021.

CHAPTER 14

The Value Alignment Problem: Building Ethically Aligned Machines

Sukrati Chaturvedi[1,*], Chellapilla Vasantha Lakshmi[1] and **Patvardhan Chellapilla[1]**

[1] *Dayalbagh Educational Institute, Agra, India*

Abstract: Autonomous systems are increasingly being employed in almost every possible field. Their level of autonomy in decision-making is also increasing along with their complexity leading to systems that will soon be making decisions of utmost importance without any human intervention at all or with the least human involvement. It is imperative, therefore, that these machines be designed to be ethically aligned with human values to ensure that they do not inadvertently cause any harm. In this work, an attempt is made to discuss the salient approaches and issues, and challenges in building ethically aligned machines. An approach inspired by traditional Eastern thought and wisdom is also presented.

Keywords: Artificial Intelligence, AI system, Machine ethics, Values, The Eastern perspective of intelligence.

INTRODUCTION

Autonomous systems are being developed for performing tasks in different fields. These systems have embedded AI, which gives them the power of decision making. For instance, Deep Blue [1], is an AI-based chess game that has beaten the world chess champion. It all started with Artificial Narrow Intelligence, where the systems are capable of performing tasks such as playing games like Atari [2] and Go [3, 4]. ANI is the first level of AI, and an ANI system specializes in any one area only. The appearance of this level of AI development is clearly visible in the technologies that we use every day. These advancements will increase with every coming year, and technology will become more complex and pervasive as it becomes more intelligent. Artificial General Intelligence is the next level of Artificial Intelligence. At this level, autonomous systems can perform any intellectual task that a human can perform, meaning it has the ability to solve the

---

[*] **Corresponding author Sukrati Chaturvedi:** Dayalbagh Educational Institute, Dayalbagh, Agra, India; E-mail: sukratichaturvedi@dei.ac.in

Gyanendra Verma & Rajesh Doriya (Eds.)

problem, learn from experiences, reason, *etc.* The third and the last level is Artificial Super Intelligence, which will surpass human intelligence and be practically much smarter than the best human brain available in every field [5].

Currently, the lowest level of AI, i.e., ANI, has been achieved by humans in many domains. Examples include Google search, email spam filters, *etc.* The current effort that has heralded the AI revolution is the path from ANI, through AGI, to ASI – a path that will change everything around us. These advancements in AI appear to indicate that AGI is achievable in the near future, i.e., by the next five to ten years, although there are some who are more conservative in their predictions.

If existing AI systems misbehave, they can be easily monitored and shut down or modified. Examples where problems in data caused the AI system to behave unacceptably, are as follows:

- Google's photos classification algorithm tagged dark-skinned people as gorillas because it has not been trained with enough examples of people with dark skin.
- In 2018, Amazon had to shut down a machine learning tool used to make hiring decisions because it exhibited bias against women. This was also because the data it was trained with had this bias.

However, if a super-intelligent AI system misbehaves, it would realize that modifying or shutting down might interfere with its capability to accomplish its goals. If the super-intelligent AI system, therefore, decides to resist shutdown and modification, it would be smart enough to surpass its programmers if the programmers have taken no prior precautions. The issue of building AI systems that will help their developers in accomplishing the task build systems that would not inadvertently harm their developers, as well as the society, is known as the AI control problem. One major concern is that we have to solve the AI control problem before developing a super-intelligent AI system.

A major approach to solving the AI control problem is to include alignment into the system- the aim here is to align the AI system with human values so that it does not harm humans or gain control over humans.

Value Alignment Problem

Progress in creating AI systems has thrown up some questions that need to be addressed very urgently for AI to be acceptable. What is acceptable AI, or what is expected from AI? One view is that it must have quality and values. Measures of quality depend on the paradigm that is employed for judging the utility of the system, and typically it is the market. Quality is local to the problem being solved and typically gets reflected in the utility function that the AI system attempts to optimize. An AI system can be deemed to have quality if it effectively solves the problem or performs the task for which it was designed.

An AI system can be made acceptable by adding values to it to ensure that it acts according to the accepted human values. This is typically referred to as the Value Alignment Problem (VAP). The problem of inculcating human values into an AI system is an overarching global concept. A typical solution may appear to solve a given problem and yet may not pass the value test. As long as the system is playing chess or Going, the rules of the game are the only values it needs to have or the only ethical considerations. But, in the case of a self-driving vehicle [6, 7], only the driving rules are not enough. Along with the driving rules, the AI system should be fed with values to make an acceptable autonomous AI system. In the absence of values, decisions taken by the AI system may not be acceptable. The fundamental issue is to decide what values to incorporate and how to incorporate them into an AI system. Can humans agree on a set of values that are universally accepted across all cultures? These are, of course, debatable. However, it is not difficult to arrive at a basic set of human values, a kind of a Common Minimum Program. Assimov's Laws [8] are a celebrated example of such a very basic Common Minimum Program.

Ethics or values can be defined in different ways, from religious to the philosophical point of view of what is meant by a good action [9]. The research area of machine ethics has recently emerged as a subfield of AI focusing on the task of ensuring the ethical behavior of artificial agents [10]. One of the issues is to define the exact set of values as people might have different cultures, come from different parts of the world, and have different socio-economic backgrounds.

The ethics of the AI system reflect the ethics of the designer/user. Ethics enable a final choice to be made among contending alternatives. It is not always possible to explain why a particular alternative has been chosen by the AI system. If any system is to gain significant control over the future, then it is imperative that the system be constructed to act according to the interests of not only its operators but all humanity and perhaps all sapient beings [11].

AI value alignment problem has two different aspects: normative aspect and technical aspect. The normative aspect of value alignment deals with the question of what values are to be incorporated into the AI system, whereas the technical aspect deals with the question of how to incorporate the values into the AI system.

Approaches for Solving AI-VAP

Two general approaches are being used to develop AI systems. The first one is- the topdown approach- where values are encoded into the AI systems by design, and the second one is- the bottom-up approach- where systems are made to learn through examples [12]. Both approaches are discussed below in more detail.

Top-Down Approach

The idea behind the top-down approach for designing ethical machines is to use moral principles or theories as rules for selecting ethically appropriate actions [13]. In this approach, the machine needs to be trained in such a way that it recognizes and corresponds to morally challenging situations correctly [14]. In other words, a top-down approach can be defined as an approach that takes a specific ethical theory and analyses its computational requirement to guide the design of algorithms and subsystems capable of implementing that theory. The architecture of a system developed using the top-down approach is hierarchically organized. Explicit Behavioural rules are specified to train the AI system [15]. The Ten Commandments [16], The Golden Rule [17], Kantian deontology, and utilitarianism are some of the possible sources of rules for top-down ethical systems. One of the examples of the top-down approach is Anderson and Anderson's GenEth system [18].

Issues and challenges in incorporating ethical considerations in a top-down approach are as follows.

- It is difficult to make a decision process both flexible as well as correct at the same time.
- It is difficult to design rules that take care of all possible situations. This is a difficult proposition. Grey areas may be left out.

Some of the top-down approaches to developing ethical AI systems are as follows.

Using moral stories: A wealth of data is being produced by many cultures about themselves in the form of written stories. Stories contain socio-cultural knowledge, social protocols, commonly shared knowledge, *etc.* If values cannot be introduced by the programmer, they can be learned. Mark O. Riedl and Brent Harrison stated that an AI could learn human values by reading stories [19]. It is often claimed that Reinforcement Learning offers a universal definition of intelligence. However, there are some limitations. RL models require massive amounts of training cycles. They are very rigid. RL agents could be stuck in meaningless loops that maximize a simple reward at the expense of long-term goals. They also used Reinforcement Learning to teach values to AI using stories. A reward signal is given to the AI agent to encourage it to solve a given problem and discourage it from performing harmful actions. A value-aligned reward signal rewards the AI agent for doing what humans do in the same situation and penalizes the agent if it performs actions otherwise. But, artificial general intelligence is not addressed by their work. The technique of learning reward signals is best for the AI agents that have a limited set of goals but need to interact with humans to achieve their goals.

Scheherazade [20], proposed by D.K. Elson, is an automated story generator that attempts to tell a story about any requested topic by a human. Scheherazade does not rely on hand-built knowledge for storytelling. If this does not have a model for the topic asked, it asks people on the internet (*via* Amazon's Mechanical Turk Service) to write the example stories in natural language and learn a new model from the learned example stories. The Scheherazade system is mentioned here from the perspective of value alignment because of its ability to learn a procedure of how a story on some unknown topic can be presented without any prior knowledge.

Explicit representation: In this approach, a code for all the values that are to be inculcated in AI is written, i.e., all the desired values are hand-coded. However, transferring all the desired human values into AI through writing the code in the computer language is not easy. This approach seems promising as a way of incorporating simple values but does not seem to work for incorporating complex values into ethical systems.

One of the examples of explicit representation is the expert system [21]. Expert systems work in narrow domains but are brittle in the sense that it is relatively difficult to ensure correctness and consistency as the rule base becomes larger to incorporate a larger functionality.

Bottom-Up Approach: Recent efforts in developing AI systems have focused on utilizing Machine Learning, wherein the system is trained with enormous amounts of ground truth data to enable it to perform the intended task. In these endeavors, the most important component is the specially prepared and validated ground truth data that is utilized for training the system. The quality of performance of the AI system depends heavily on the quality and quantity of the ground truth data. If there is bias in the data, it will get reflected in the Machine Learning system that is created using that data. Further, any noise in the data would result in performance degradation of the system.

Therefore, it is important not to work with such data in developing machine learning systems. Identifying the noisy elements and cleaning up the data requires a huge amount of effort. Preparation of the right quality and quantity of data is, therefore, critical for the success of machine learning AI endeavors.

The examples necessarily have to encompass all the variety of situations that the AI system could face when deployed in the real world and respond in an expected manner according to the quality criterion. But most systems cannot be described as optimizers of a utility function alone. Value criteria need to be fulfilled through the examples making the problem much more complicated.

The Asimovian ethical robots of Winfield *et al.* [22] and Vanderelst and Winfield [23], the Akratic robot of Bringsjord *et al.* [24], [25] and the Shim's intervening robot mediator in healthcare [26]- are examples of the bottom-up approach of developing AI systems.

Issues and challenges in incorporating ethical considerations in the bottom-up approach are as follows.

- **Bias in input data**- This is a huge challenge to abolish the bias from the input data set. Even Google's image recognition system made the mistake of mapping a human image to a Gorilla because of the bias present in the input set.
- **Coverage of input data**- As a human, we don't need to specify each minute detail for achieving goals. We might skip a few of them, considering them as a part of common sense. For instance- Person A asks person B to get a water bottle from the fridge, but person A won't elaborate on the steps like going to the fridge, opening the fridge's door, taking out the water bottle, closing the door of the fridge, *etc.* as these are all basic steps that any person will perform using their common sense. But, in the case of autonomous systems, we need to specify each and every basic detail in the input details.
- **Explainability**- Without any explainability, decision-making is done using a black-box approach which may not be accepted in some domains, including healthcare. For instance- If a robot makes a decision to perform heart surgery on a patient and gives no explanation or reasons to the family that why this decision of surgery has been taken, then the family members of the patient might get offended and won't allow the robot to perform surgery which in turn might become a danger for the patient.

Some of the bottom-up approaches to building ethical AI systems are as follows.

Motivation Scaffolding: This approach states a method in which small goals are given to the AI with relatively simple final goals that can be represented in AI by means of coding or some other method that is feasible [27]. In this approach, the seed AI is given simple goals, and these goals are replaced with more complex ones. Thus, it would develop into a sophisticated representational structure.

Institution Design: Any task that we perform is not only motivated by our society but also by how this society is organized. For instance, we live in a democratic country; therefore, our will to complete a task might be a composite or average of the wills that lives in our democratic society, whereas a person or a group that is organized in a strong dictatorship society might act as if it had a will of performing a task that is similar to the will of a dictator. Therefore, it might be concluded that the motivation of the AI for performing a task not only depends on the motivation of its constituent subagents but also on how these subagents are organized [28]. Thus, an attempt could be made to shape the motivation of AI by designing appropriate institutions for it.

Hybrid Approach: In a top-down approach, ethics are inculcated into AI systems explicitly through concerns from outside of the AI system. Whereas, in a bottom-up approach, we focus on embedding ethics in AI systems implicitly. A hybrid approach would be the best approach to avoid the problems of designing the ethical AI system as it minimizes the issues and limitations of top-down and bottom-up approaches while maximizing their advantages. Some of the hybrid approaches mentioned in the literature are as follows.

Evolutionary selection: Humans are believed to have evolved with a set of values that are desirable to their livelihood. This provides motivation for the use of evolutionary methods to solve the problem of value learning in AI [29].

This approach seems less promising. A powerful search may find a design that satisfies the formal search criteria but not our intentions. Evolution makes it difficult to avoid mind crimes, especially in the case when one is aiming to create human-like minds.

Associative value accretion: Turing proposed that instead of trying to simulate the adult human mind through programming, we should try to produce a program that simulates a child's mind [30]. He divided this problem further into two parts, i.e., the program which simulates the child's mind and the education process. And these two remain very close. The motivation behind this is that a child learns everything from the initial stage by observing and experiencing things together with the education from where it learns the basic difference between the good and bad. This approach is inspired by the way humans acquire values. It might be considered whether the motivation for the AI system could be built on the same principle. This means that is there any mechanism through which values would be inculcated into an AI system when the same human interacts with the environment? This approach to value learning states a method by which the AI acquires the values through some machinery for inculcating new values as it interacts with the environment.

Limitations, Issues, and Challenges of Extant Approaches

Many extant approaches for developing ethical AI systems lack clarity- on how decision-making is performed. Decision-making in AI systems is a black-box approach which means that the AI system will take the decision, but how that decision has been taken will not be explained. This non-clarity is not acceptable in several domains, including healthcare. Also, what will happen when a previously unknown situation is encountered? For instance- what decision will an eldercare robot will take if it encounters a situation for which it has not been trained yet? What if there is more than one choice for a given situation? With which choice will the AI system will move ahead? The issues and challenges are summarized in Table **1**.

Table 1. Extant Approaches to their Issues and Challenges

S. No	Extant Approach	Description	Issues and Challenges
1.	Using moral stories	Mark O. Riedl and Brent Harrison used Reinforcement Learning to teach values to AI using stories. Reinforcement Learning was used to teach values to AI using stories.	-The technique of learning reward signals is best for the AI machines that have a limited set of goals but need to interact with humans to achieve their goals. -The relationship between the reward function and behavior is complex.
2.	Explicit representation	All the values that are to be inculcated in the AI system are explicitly hand-coded.	-Transferring all the desired human values into an AI system through hand-coding in computer language is not easy. -Seems promising as a way of inculcating domestic values but does not seem to load complex values into ethics systems.
3.	Motivational scaffolding	Small goals are given to the AI system with relatively final goals. These goals can be represented in an AI system by means of coding or some other feasible method.	-It is difficult to develop internal high-level representations that are transparent to humans.

(Table 1) cont.....

S. No	Extant Approach	Description	Issues and Challenges
4.	Institution design	As per this approach, the motivation of an AI system for performing some task does not only depend on the motivation of its constituent subagents but also on how the sub-agents are organized. Thus, ethical AI systems can be created by designing appropriate institutions.	-AI systems might lack many of the attributes that help us predict human-like agents.
5.	Evolutionary selection	The evolution of humans with the desired set of values for their livelihood is the motivation behind this approach.	-Seems less promising. -Makes it difficult to avoid mind crimes in the case when one is trying to copy and create the human mind.
6.	Associative value accretion	This approach is inspired by the way humans acquire values. It might be considered whether the motivation for AI system same principle could be built.	-Replicating the human accretion temperament in an AI system is complex and difficult. -More research is required to make this approach work with sufficient precision.

While overcoming these limitations of an ethical AI system, a developer and/or a researcher has to face a lot of issues and challenges. A few of these are- AI development lacks fiduciary duties and common aims, professional history and norms, legal and professional accountability mechanisms, and proven methods to translate the principles into practice [31]. How human developers and researchers should behave in order to minimize the ethical harms that can arise from robotic systems? Could a machine be ethical? If so, which ethics should determine its behavior? Should society delegate its responsibility to the machines? How can AI systems themselves behave ethically? Developing an ethically aligned machine throws up a list of questions that need to be answered before developing such machines. What does it mean to have artificial intelligence aligned with our own life goals and aspirations? Can it be aligned with one and all at the same time? How to ensure that one person's version of an ideal AI does not make others' life more difficult? How to go about agreeing on human values, and how to ensure that AI understands these values? If we have AI more involved in things like medicine or policing, or education, what should that look like? What else should we, as a society, be asking?

This set of questions has limited the implementation of AGI and, more than that, ethical AGI. Till date, an AI system can perform one or a few tasks. No AI system has been built yet that can perform a set of tasks like we humans do. Every major field of AI seems to solve part of the problem of replicating or even achieving human-level achievement in particular tasks while learning out consideration of wider aspects, even in critical areas. And leaving out these considerations becomes unacceptable when we apply such AI technology in other domains where we expect intelligent agents to act with the rationality and logic that we expect from humans. The most difficult aspects to ensure, as AI systems become more and more autonomous, are as follows, in summary.

- AI systems must follow our norms and values.
- Understand what our desired performance is.
- Do what we desire of them in a given situation.

Eastern Perspectives of Intelligence for Solving AI-VAP

In Eastern Philosophy, human intelligence has four different aspects: mann, buddhi, ahamkara, and chitta (Table **2**). Mann is the importer and exporter of the perceptions from external sources. Buddhi analyses the situations or a situation. Ahamkara is not ego just in terms of egoistic sense. It's the sense of duty and responsibility, sense of identification of the role one is playing at a point in time. Chitta is the unconscious storehouse. It connects us with our consciousness.

In Kathopanishad's perspective, the body is the chariot, senses are the horses, 'mann' (mind) constitutes the reins, 'buddhi' (brain) is the charioteer. If mind

Table 2. The Four Aspects of Intelligence.

S.No	Name	Functionality	Nature
1	Mann	Receives stimuli through organs of perception from external sources	Indecision or doubt
2	Buddhi	Analyzes situations or stimuli received and determines cognition faculty	Decision making
3	Ahamkara	Sense of doership and enjoyership	Ego
4	Chitta	Recollection of past experiences or events	Storehouse or memory

follows the dictates of 'buddhi,' it will be safe; otherwise, senses will run amok. This is a more comprehensive model and provides a window into the workings of the human intellect. More importantly, it provides a good framework for designing AI that has both the quality perspective and the perspective of the value rather than focusing only on the quality perspective in a very narrow interpretation of the term quality.

Proposed Approach

AI development currently focuses primarily on just one part of the four - buddhi (the intellect) or the part that enables the AI system to meet the expectations in terms of performing the task at hand. AI system is designed to make decisions and act based on relevant logic. For example, in the case of game playing, it could be deciding the next move based on the utility value of the move to enable it to win the game eventually. When the domain is very narrow, like playing some game (Chess or Go) in which the only role here is to find the next move, current approaches have succeeded to a large extent because here, the decision-making is in the context of complete and deterministic information and the choices are very limited. But, when we talk about some decision-making systems like autonomous vehicles, wherein there are numerous possibilities of situations that may be encountered, including the presence of unknown unknowns, the methodology is difficult to implement. The decision-making just cannot be expressed in terms of optimizing some or any utility function. For instance, say the passenger asks the autonomous vehicle to take him to the destination as soon as possible. But, in that case, the vehicle cannot just optimize the time duration- it is not just that it has to transport the passenger to the destination in the fastest possible way. It has to follow the traffic rules. This sense of following the traffic rules comes from being a good citizen. It also has to be law-abiding and prevent accidents even if it faces unique or abnormal situations. Therefore, the goal here is not just driving – many other considerations emerge.

Much beyond systems like autonomous vehicles are the AGI systems whose development is being speculated. In this case, there are several roles to be played by the system. One can only imagine all considerations that will have to be programmed when we design an AGI. Provided sufficient memory (Chitta), we may have a good storage of previous actions and responses from where we can retrieve the best match. The question that arises here is - the moment the roles are numerous, how can such a comprehensive situation – response to Chitta be created? How does one integrate consideration of all the aspects of the situation being handled, especially when there is a possibility of unknown unknowns? How does one incorporate these considerations to tackle an interpreted world? The more the number of functions to be implemented, the more the number of roles to be played by the ethical AI system expands. Each role would have its own dynamics and values hierarchy and prioritization according to the expectations from the role being performed. This is the gist of the concept of Ahamkara in Eastern traditions. The approach that emerges as a plausible one is to combine the Dharma/duty, which is related to identity, i.e., ahamkara (ego), and structure to implement the ethical AI system. Ahamkara helps in determining hierarchical relationships between different actions in a dynamic sense. It is important when there are conflicting responses recommended by different values. Treating the AI ethics or values problem as one of either alignment or control is not sufficient. A hybrid approach with both facets would be required. These considerations yield the structure of the system, as depicted in Fig. (**1**).

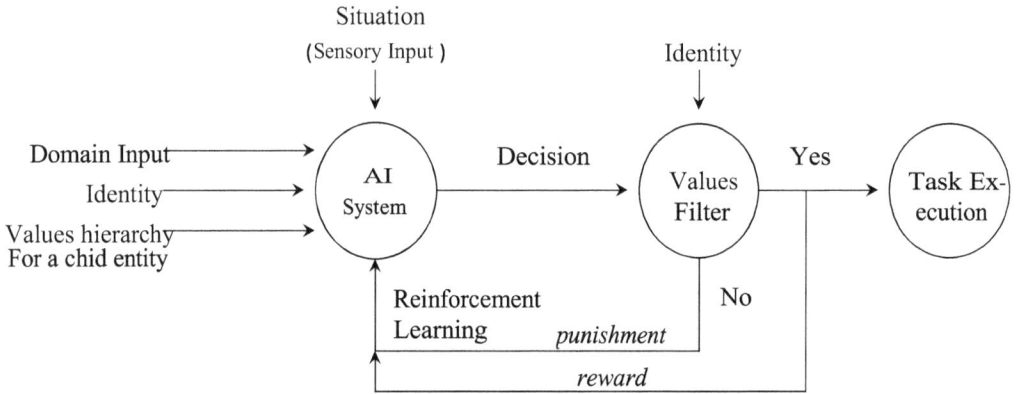

Fig. (1). Proposed architecture for ethically aligned AI system.

CONCLUSION

Aligning values into the AI system is an important problem. The value alignment problem has two aspects- normative and technical. Work done till date in the field of VAP has certain limitations. To overcome these limitations, we can use the concept of the eastern philosophy of intelligence to design the architecture, which can help us in designing and creating ethically aligned AI systems.

Our proposed approach takes care of both aspects- normative and technical-of the value alignment problem. Classification of the role based on the identity takes care of the normative aspect by describing what values are to be followed for a particular given situation, and the technical aspect is taken care of by the rest of the model.

REFERENCES

[1]   M. Campbell, A.J. Hoane Jr, and F. Hsu, "Deep Blue", *Artif. Intell.,* vol. 134, no. 1-2, pp. 57-83, 2002. [http://dx.doi.org/10.1016/S0004-3702(01)00129-1]

[2]   D.G. Wilson, S. Cussat-Blanc, H. Luga, and J.F. Miller, "Evolving simple programs for playing atari games", *Proceedings of the Genetic and Evolutionary Computation Conference,* 2018pp. 229-236 [http://dx.doi.org/10.1145/3205455.3205578]

[3]   D Silver, J Schrittwieser, K Simonyan, I Antonoglou, A Huang, A Guez, T Hubert, L Baker, M Lai, A Bolton, and Y. Chen, "Mastering the game of go without human knowledge. nature. 2017 oct;", 550 (7676):354-9

[4]   D Silver, A Huang, CJ Maddison, A Guez, L Sifre, G Van Den Driessche, J Schrittwieser, I Antonoglou, V Panneershelvam, M Lanctot, and S Dieleman, "Mastering the game of Go with deep neural networks and tree search", *Nature.* 2016 Jan; 529 (7587): 484-9.

[5]   N. Bostrom, "How long before superintelligence?. International Journal of Futures Studies", 1998;2

[6]   S.L. Poczter, and L.M. Jankovic, The google car: driving toward a better future?, *Journal of Business Case Studies,* vol. 10, no. 1, pp. 7-14, 2014. [JBCS].

[7]   K. Bimbraw, "Autonomous cars: past, present and future a review of the developments in the last century, the present scenario and the expected future of autonomous vehicle technology", *In2015 12th international conference on informatics in control, automation and robotics (ICINCO),* vol. 1, pp. 191-198, 2015 Jul 21.IEEE.

[8]   I. Asimov, *Three laws of robotics. Asimov, I. Runaround.,* 1941.

[9]   S. Ogunlere, and A.O. Adebayo, "Ethical Issues in Computing Sciences", *International Research Journal of Engineering and Technology,* vol. 2, no. 7, pp. 10-16, 2015. [IRJET].

[10]   C Shulman, H Jonsson, and N Tarleton, "Machine ethics and superintelligence. C. Reynolds. ", 2009 Oct 1

[11]   N. Soares, "The value learning problem. Machine Intelligence Research Institute", *Technical report,* p. 4, 2015.
[http://dx.doi.org/10.1201/9781351251389-7]

[12]   Q.V. Liao, and M Muller, "Enabling Value Sensitive AI Systems through Participatory Design Fictions. arXiv preprint arXiv:1912.07381", 2019 Dec 13.

[13]   C. Allen, I. Smit, and W. Wallach, "Artificial morality: Top-down, bottom-up, and hybrid approaches", *Ethics Inf. Technol.,* vol. 7, no. 3, pp. 149-155, 2005.
[http://dx.doi.org/10.1007/s10676-006-0004-4]

[14]   A.F. Winfield, K. Michael, J. Pitt, and V. Evers, "Machine ethics: The design and governance of ethical AI and autonomous systems", *Proc. IEEE,* vol. 107, no. 3, pp. 509-517, 2019. [scanning the issue].
[http://dx.doi.org/10.1109/JPROC.2019.2900622]

[15]   F. Rossi, and N. Mattei, "Building ethically bounded ai", *Proceedings of the AAAI Conference on Artificial Intelligence,* vol. Vol. 33, 2019pp. 9785-9789
[http://dx.doi.org/10.1609/aaai.v33i01.33019785]

[16]   CB DeMille, C Heston, Y Brynner, A Baxter, and EG Robinson, *The ten commandments,* .

[17]   HJ Gensler, *Ethics and the golden rule..*Routledge; 2013 May 20. Routledge; 2013 May 20.
[http://dx.doi.org/10.4324/9780203154373]

[18]   M. Anderson, and S.L. Anderson, "GenEth: a general ethical dilemma analyzer", *Paladyn,* vol. 9, no. 1, pp. 337-357, 2018.
[http://dx.doi.org/10.1515/pjbr-2018-0024]

[19]   M.O. Riedl, and B. Harrison, "Using stories to teach human values to artificial agents", *Workshops at the Thirtieth AAAI Conference on Artificial Intelligence,* 2016

[20]   D.K. Elson, *Modeling narrative discourse.* Columbia University, 2012.

[21]   D.G. Bobrow, S. Mittal, and M.J. Stefik, "Expert systems: perils and promise", *Commun. ACM,* vol. 29, no. 9, pp. 880-894, 1986.
[http://dx.doi.org/10.1145/6592.6597]

[22]   AF Winfield, C Blum, and W Liu, "Towards an ethical robot: internal models, consequences and ethical action selection", *In Conference towards autonomous robotic systems,* Springer, Cham., pp. 85-96, 2014 Sep 1.
[http://dx.doi.org/10.1007/978-3-319-10401-0_8]

[23]   D. Vanderelst, and A. Winfield, "An architecture for ethical robots inspired by the simulation theory of cognition", *Cogn. Syst. Res.,* vol. 48, pp. 56-66, 2018.
[http://dx.doi.org/10.1016/j.cogsys.2017.04.002]

[24]   S. Bringsjord, D. Thero, and M. Si, "Akratic robots and the computational logic thereof", *In2014 IEEE International Symposium on Ethics in Science, Technology and Engineering,* pp. 1-8, 2014 May 23. IEEE.
[http://dx.doi.org/10.1109/ETHICS.2014.6893436]

[25]   GM Briggs, and M Scheutz, "Sorry, I can't do that: Developing Mechanisms to Appropriately Reject Directives in Human-Robot Interactions", *In 2015 AAAI fall symposium series,* 2015 Sep 4..

[26]   J. Shim, R. Arkin, and M. Pettinatti, "An Intervening Ethical Governor for a robot mediator in patient-caregiver relationship: Implementation and Evaluation. In2017", *IEEE Int. Conf. Robot. Autom.,* pp. 2936-2942, 2017. [IEEE.].
[http://dx.doi.org/10.1109/ICRA.2017.7989340]

[27]   T. Jurgenson, O. Avner, E. Groshev, and A. Tamar, "Sub-Goal Trees a Framework for Goal-Based Reinforcement Learning", 2020 Nov 21 (pp. 5020-5030). PMLR.

[28]   N. Bostrom, *Superintelligence: Paths, Dangers, Strategies.* Oxford University Press: London, England, 2016.

[29]   F. Liu, and Y. Shi, "Research on artificial intelligence ethics based on the evolution of population knowledge base. International Conference on Intelligence Science ", 2018 Nov 2 (pp. 455-464). Springer, Cham
[http://dx.doi.org/10.1007/978-3-030-01313-4_48]

[30]   "Computing machinery and intelligence-AM Turing. Vol. 59(236):433", *Mind,* 1950.

[31]   B. Mittelstadt, "Principles alone cannot guarantee ethical AI", *Nat. Mach. Intell.,* vol. 1, no. 11, pp. 501-507, 2019.
[http://dx.doi.org/10.1038/s42256-019-0114-4]

## CHAPTER 15

Cryptocurrency Portfolio Management Using Reinforcement Learning

Vatsal Khandor[1,*], **Sanay Shah**[1], **Parth Kalkotwar**[1], **Saurav Tiwari**[1] and **Sindhu Nair**[1]

[1] *Dwarkadas J. Sanghvi College of Engineering, Mumbai, India*

Abstract: Portfolio management is the science of choosing the best investment policies and strategies with the aim of getting maximum returns. Simply, it means managing the assets/stocks of a company, organization, or individual and taking into account the risks, and increasing the profit. This paper proposes portfolio management using a bot leveraging a reinforcement learning environment specifically for cryptocurrencies which are a hot topic in the current world of technology. The reinforcement Learning Environment gives the reward/penalty to the agent, which helps it train itself during the training process and make decisions based on the trial-and-error method. Dense and CNN networks are used for training the agent to taking the decision to either buy, hold or sell the coin. Various technical indicators, like MACD, SMA, *etc.*, are also included in the dataset while making the decisions. The bot is trained on 3-year hourly data of Bitcoin, and results demonstrate that the Dense and CNN network models show a good amount of profit against a starting balance of 1,000, indicating that reinforcement learning environments can be efficacious and can be incorporated into the trading environments.

Keywords: Actor-Critic, Bitcoin, Cryptocurrency, CNN, Portfolio Management, Reinforcement Learning.

INTRODUCTION

Cryptocurrency is an asset that is digital and is considered a medium of exchange. No physical form exists from cryptocurrency, like that of money, which is in the form of paper. They exist in the form of different types of coins. Some examples of coins are bitcoin, Ethereum, Cardano, Polkadot, *etc.* These coins are obtained by a process called mining.

* Corresponding author Vatsal Khandor: Dwarkadas J. Sanghvi College of Engineering, Mumbai, India; E-mail: khandorvatsal@gmail.com

Gyanendra Verma & Rajesh Doriya (Eds.)

The ownership records of each coin individually are stored in a ledger that exists in the form of a computerized database. Since the transactions of these coins need to be secured, it is stored using strong cryptography. Also, strong cryptography is used to verify the transfer of coin ownership, and the creation of additional coins is controlled as well. Central authorities do not issue cryptocurrency. Cryptocurrencies typically use decentralized control for getting issued. When it is created, or rather in crypto terms, when it is minted prior to its issuance or before it is issued by a single issuer, that is, that coin belongs to that particular user; it is generally considered centralized. Cryptocurrencies work on blockchain technology, which is decentralized. The crypto transactions are managed and recorded by many computers onto which the blockchain technology is spread.

Hence, blockchain as a technology is preferred due to its security. Portfolio management is the control of an organization's projects and programs. Selection and prioritization are also made under portfolio management in line with the capacity to deliver for the company and its strategic objectives. The final goal is the maintenance of business as usual and to balance the implementation of change initiatives while optimizing ROI (return on investment). In simpler words, it involves a technique of analyzing and selecting a group of investments that meet the long-term financial objectives of a client, a company, or an institution. Also, risk tolerance is taken care of. Some of the fundamental objectives of portfolio management are capital appreciation, risk optimization, protecting earnings against market risks, ensuring flexibility of portfolio, allocating resources optimally, maximizing return on investment, and improving the overall proficiency of the portfolio, as demonstrated in [2]. Also, different types of portfolio management are active, passive, discretionary, and non-discretionary portfolio management. A portfolio can be managed in three different ways. The first is asset allocation, in which the investors put money into assets. These assets are both volatile and non-volatile. Money is put in such a way that, at minimum risk, we get substantial returns. The second one is diversification, wherein the portfolio of the investor is well-balanced. Also, the portfolio is diversified across different investment avenues. In doing so, the collection of the investors is revamped significantly by achieving a perfect blend of reward and risk. This, in turn, helps to generate risk-adjusted returns over time and also helps to cushion risks. The third method is rebalancing, in which investors rebalance the ratio of portfolio components to yield higher returns at minimal loss.

Reinforcement learning is a subset of machine learning where it is concerned with how intelligent agents will take actions in an environment so that the cumulative reward is maximized. It basically focuses on taking a suitable action that would, in turn, maximize the reward in a particular situation. Reinforcement learning is employed by various software and machines to find the best possible behavior and the best path which should be taken in a specific situation. Reinforcement learning is one of three basic machine learning types, the other two being supervised learning and unsupervised learning. The environment is typically stated in the form of a Markov decision process (MDP). The different types of reinforcement learning are associate, deep, safe, and inverse. Also, the different reinforcement learning algorithms as in [1] are Q-Learning, DQN (Deep Q Network), DDPG (Deep Deterministic Policy Gradient), A3C (Asynchronous Advantage Actor-Critic Algorithm), *etc.*

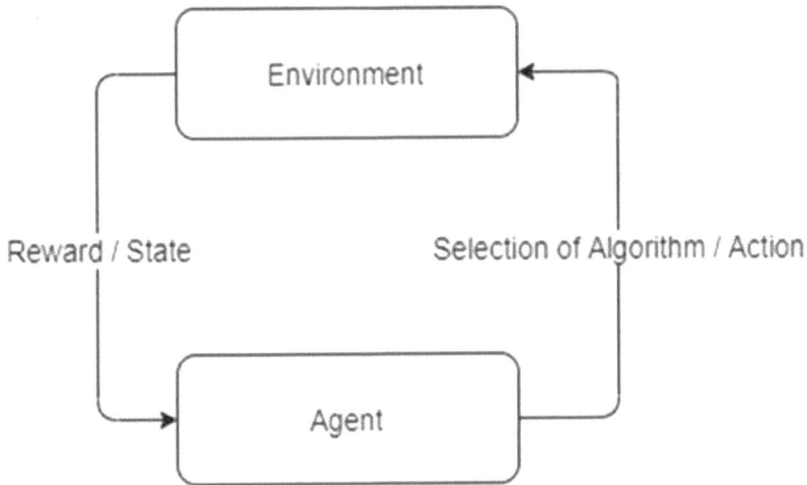

Fig. (1). Basic Block for Reinforcement Learning.

RELATED WORK

Various different machine learning techniques to perform algorithmic trading are observed. Author [1] proposes a novel trading approach that uses a Markov Decision Process (MDP), and to improve the performance of Q-learning, the author augments MDP with an estimate of current trend information and sentimental analysis of news articles. The implemented system performs sentimental analysis using Word2Vec and finds the trend analysis using Neural Networks, and they formulate the statement as an MDP and solve this MDP using Reinforcement learning. Though, the evidence on the use of a live dataset is still widely debated since the author uses only a 5-year historical price dataset. And for the sentimental analysis model, the author uses 10-years news articles obtained from Reuters. The author concludes the result based on the term "Sharpe ratio." The author also captures the current trend information and formulates the augmenting trend information into an MDP. The author also uses 6 different technical indicators: SMA, Moving Average, Stochastic K, Stochastic D, RSI, and

Larry William's R% and scale them and then input them into the neural network to predict the trend for the stock.

Researchers in [2] have used DQN, T-DQN, and Double-DQN algorithms. They insisted on using random samples since past experience being sequential would be largely correlated, and such randomizing technique would help break this behavior. TensorFlow has been used to build the 4 hidden layered neural networks. Normally, the closing price is a parameter used in the datasets, but here they used an adjusted closing price because it would accurately reflect the stock value after accounting for any corporate action. The strategies used here are to maximize gain with minimum risks. The authors [2] used other than standard metrics like Huber loss and Adam optimizer to make the model more robust and adaptive methods to eliminate sensitive learning rates. FIFO methodology was used to buy and sell stocks and used checkpoints in the dataset to make sure that the data did not overfit. Their result concluded that Double-DQN performs the best than the other two algorithms because it uses two separate Q-value estimators.

The researchers evaluate the performance of the Convolutional Neural Networks [3], which is compared with three benchmarks used and the other three portfolio management algorithms and achieving positive results. The data is split into 3 parts: train, test, and cross-validation sets. However, the authors make a point that this process could be improved since the training set was small. The paper also differs from conventional Reinforcement Learning because it does not have an explicit mapping relationship with the reward. The strategy applied for Portfolio Management is a "Uniform Constant Rebalanced Portfolio," and the CNN trader achieves a significantly lower risk, resulting in a higher Sharpe ratio than PAMR. It also showcases a discussion on "The Expiration Problem" and the "Dilemma Between Performance Evaluation and Hyperparameters tuning."

Similar to [2], researchers in [4] have concluded that Double Deep Q-learning Networks are the most suited and profitable approach for the trading of bitcoin. The agent defines the stop loss and a take-profit to the wallet. The authors also considered the exploration-exploitation dilemma, and for this purpose, the agent could take a random action. The researchers from the preliminary analysis concluded Sharpe D-DQN is the best trading system.

Few Machine Learning approaches have been studied to get an understanding of the effect of traditional machine learning techniques in the field of cryptocurrency portfolio management. In [8], a framework consisting of four machine learning algorithms is used with the aim of generating higher returns and lower risks. To achieve this, the original time sampled data is resampled on the basis of the closing values of the cryptocurrencies. Further, an unweighted ensemble classifier along with four machine learning algorithms, namely Logistic Regression, Random Forest, Support Vector Classifier, and Grading Tree Boosting, is used to obtain the results.

In [5], Carlos *et al.* provide a means to create a trading method with a dynamic number of assets. An actor-critic architecture, based on Deep Learning techniques, is used to provide better results for a dynamic number of assets. Additionally, a novel algorithm, which uses Linear Programming techniques, is used to minimize the transaction costs. To encounter the problems of limited data [6], Kim *et al.* studied three reinforcement learning-based methods to maximize profits. A combination of a deep learning regressor and a deep Q-network to predict the number of shares to trade, analysis of Q-values to enhance profits, and a transfer learning approach is used to encounter the problems of limited financial data. In [7], Park *et al.* propose a portfolio trading strategy using deep Q-learning. Feasible action space is created using a mapping function. Further, a Markov decision process model is used for the trading process, ensuring a practically feasible approach.

In [9], a framework for deep reinforcement learning is applied. This framework has been applied to cryptocurrencies for market making (DRLMM). The agents selected are two advanced policy gradient-based algorithms. They are required to interact with the observation space. This is done through limited order book data and order flow arrival statistics. Within the experiment, the function approximator is emulated by the forward feed neural network. Consequently, two reward functions are compared. The daily and average trade returns are used to evaluate the performance of each combination of agent and reward functions. This paper demonstrated the effectiveness of deep reinforcement learning in solving stochastic inventory control challenges faced using the DRLMM framework.

In [10], the approach applied to the general portfolio management problem is a full machine learning one. This is done by completely letting the algorithms observe and learn from the market history. Also, no prior knowledge of the financial market is assumed, and no model is made. The management actions of the market and the portfolio vector are directly outputted. The trading algorithm is tested in a crypto-currency exchange market, and a set of coins chosen by the previous trading volume ranking are considered in the portfolio selection.

In [11], the placement of limit orders at cryptocurrency exchanges is optimized using deep reinforcement learning. A proximal policy optimization has been found to reliably learn superior order placement strategies when compared to deep double Q-networks and other benchmarks. Some important features are queue imbalances and current liquidity costs, where the former is interpreted as predictors of short-term mid-price returns.

Authors in [12] have proposed an automated bot performing swing trading using deep reinforcement learning and leveraged sentiment analysis, unlike [13], to get the trend and sentiment of the stock from the economic news, which is supposed to be enhancing the accuracy. The reinforcement learning is implemented using the deep deterministic policy gradient (DDPG) based neural network. The authors have used RCNNs for the classification of the sentiments of news, which leverages the advantages of both – CNN and RNN. The authors have implemented a binary classification indicating a positive or negative trend of the stock based on the news headlines. The authors trained the agent on 30 days of data on NASDAQ-GE stock and on 5months of data on NASDAQ-GOOGL stock and compared the stagnant and R.L. bot asset value and concluded that the bot-based asset was always higher than the stagnant value. The authors have demanded the use of a master complex network for multiple stocks in contrast to the single stock at a time used by them in this work.

The authors in [13] have proposed giving a recommendation to the traders to either buy, sell or hold their cryptocurrencies. Authors have performed their testing on the hourly historical data of Bitcoin, Ethereum, and LiteCoin. They have used the following trading strategies while giving input to the agent– Double Crossover Strategy, Swing Trading, and Scalping Trading. Unlike [12], the authors here have used Neural Networks to decide the action to be taken by the agent. The authors have compared the percent change in net worth using the aforesaid strategies for the three coins. They concluded that, in the case of Bitcoin, there was a 114.4% return on the principal amount that was invested within one month; in the case of LiteCoin, there was a chance of an increase in the initial fortune by 174.6%, and in the case of Ethereum it would lead to 41.4% net returns.

DATASET PRE-PROCESSING

Reinforcement learning environments are a popular way to address the highly erratic and volatile cryptocurrency markets [4]. However, outstripping these markets and implementing automated trading strategies requires a lot of backtesting, which in turn demands a lot of historical data and computational power. There are a lot of exchanges providing historical cryptocurrency data; however, the majority of them are paid and are not very cheap, and those who provide free data give low temporal resolution data or provide limited-time period data. In our work, we have used the API provided by the Bitfinex Exchange. We used the public API endpoints of the Bitfinex API for fetching the historical data.

It returns a list consisting of the date, open, close, high, low, and volume values of the cryptocurrency mentioned. 'Bitfinex-tencars' is the library in python that is used for getting the data from Bitfinex Exchange API, which can be easily downloaded using pip. The parameters to be passed to the API instance are as follows:

- Symbol: cryptocurrency symbol, default: BTCUSD.
- Interval: the temporal resolution of the data, *e.g.*, 1m for 1 minute, 1h for 1 hour of the data, *etc.*
- Limit: number of data points to be returned.
- start: start time of interval of data desired (in milliseconds)
- end: end time of interval of data desired (in milliseconds)

The data returned in the form of a list is converted into a data frame and saved into a .csv file format. The historical data in the .csv file is used for training the agent to make decisions of either buy, hold or sell. In this work, we have used 3 years of historical bitcoin data with an interval of 1 hour for training and testing purposes.

No trader or investor will prefer making blind trades without any fundamental or technical analysis, and everyone must be using some technical indicators, as in [14]. There are many technical indicators that are used by analysts while analyzing a particular stock for an uptrend or downtrend. These indicators can be applied to cryptocurrency markets and charts as well, which will embellish the learning of the agent and generate more profit. The technical indicators used in our work are as follows:

Simple Moving Average

This is the most widely used technical analysis measure, where data points can be analyzed on the basis of time. For instance, a 20-day moving average gives us the average of different data values with a gap of 20 days. Bollinger Bands: Bollinger Bands is an analysis tool represented by a group of trend lines 2 standard deviations (positive and negative) away from the SMA indicator of a particular asset, however, which may be modified according to the user. Bollinger Bands are specifically used for getting to know the market conditions – whether the market is overbought or oversold. It is quotidian for traders that if the prices are near the upper band, then the overall condition is overbought, and the prices closer to the lower bound indicate an oversold market condition.

Moving Average Convergence/Divergence

MACD is a momentum indicator following a particular trend, displaying the correlation between the two exponential moving averages of the market's price. The long term and short-term exponential moving averages are 26-day periods and 12-day period moving averages, respectively. However, the strategy can be changed and customized. The long-term EMA is subtracted from the short-term EMA representing the MACD line, and it is plotted on the chart. A positive MACD indicates a positive uptrend which occurs when the short-term moving average is more than the long-term moving average. Similarly, a negative falling MACD indicates bears coming into action. Along with the MACD line, a nine-period EMA of the MACD line called the signal line or trigger line is plotted on top of the MACD line and acts as a trigger for buying or selling signals. Traders perform buy orders if MACD crosses this signal line and might short or sell if the MACD line goes below this signal line. This is demonstrated in [8].

Parabolic Stop and Reverse

The parabolic SAR indicator is used by analysts and traders to identify the trend directions and reversal in the prices. Entry and exit points in an asset are determined by the indicator using the trailing stop and reverse method, hence 'SAR.' Parabolic stop and reverse, parabolic SAR or PSAR are the different notations of the indicator by traders and analysts. The PSAR indicator is represented on the chart in the form of dots either above or below the candlestick. The dots below the bar represent an uptrend in the market, indicating bullish behavior, and the dots above the candlestick represent the bears coming into action. This indicator generates buy or sell signals depending upon the movement of dots. For example, if the dots move from above the candlestick to below, a buy signal is generated and vice versa.

Relative Strength Index

RSI is a momentum indicator used in technical analysis for getting the market conditions, whether it is oversold or overbought. It is an oscillator, moving between two extremes, having a reading of 0-100. Traditional usage of RSI shows that a value above 70 indicates that the market is overbought and might face some correction. On the other hand, an RSI of less than 30 indicates the market is in an oversold condition, and an uptrend can be expected. RSI is a quite popular tool used by traders and analysts, and usually, it is plotted separately below the chart.

The 'ta' library in python is used for evaluating the values of the aforementioned indicators. The values are integrated into the dataset, and 9 more features are added to the dataset contributing to the technical indicators' values. The indicators are plotted using matplotlib using the Plot OHCL function. After the addition of these indicators, the data is divided into training and testing, which is used in a Reinforcement Learning Environment where a CNN and a Dense Neural Network Custom model are trained upon it in Fig. (**2**).

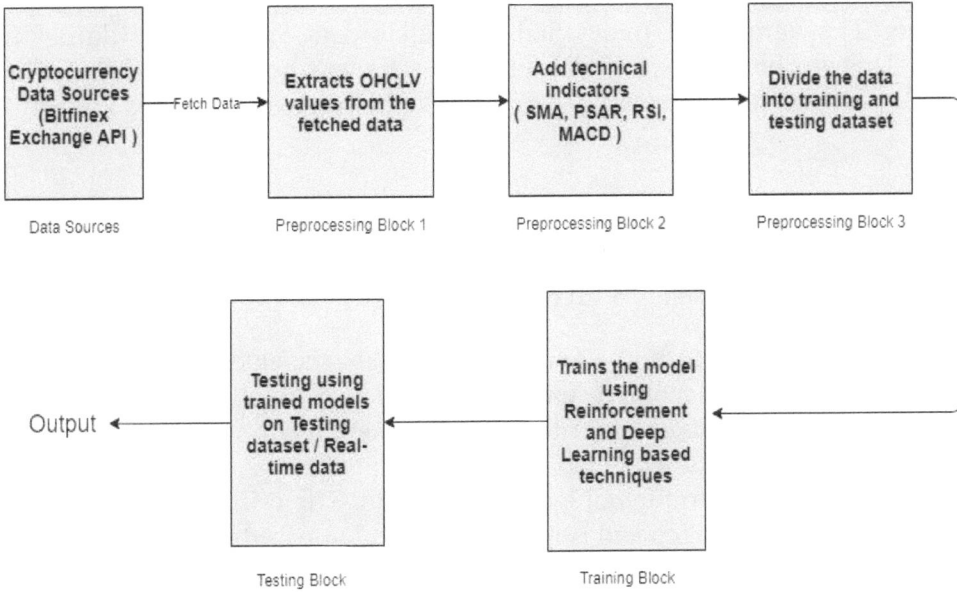

Fig. (2). System Flow Chart.

The diagram proposes an explanation of the system's working. The data is extracted using the bitfinex API using a Python script. Information about different features is needed for more accurate analysis. The following features are used for Bitcoin: Open, High, Close, Low, Volume (OHCLV).

OHCLV is an aggregated form of market data that is represented in the form of candlestick charts. These charts are in the form of a candle having a wick and have different time intervals from 1 minute to 1 day. The 15-minute candle is used extensively by traders and analysts. OHCLV stands for Open, High, Low, Close, Volume, and each of these terms is explained below:

Open: This represents the opening price for that particular time interval.

High: The highest price reached during the specified time interval is represented by this attribute. The upper wick of the candle indicates the high price for that interval.

Low: The lowest price reached during the specified time interval is represented by this attribute. The lower wick of the candle indicates the low price for that interval.

Close: This represents the closing price for that particular time interval.

Volume: The number of trades and buy/sell orders taking place during that period. This attribute is very important from a trader's point of view as it allows one to look deeply into the market structure and helps grasp processes that move a price.

As mentioned previously, technical indicators are added to the data frame in the pre-processing stage before dividing the data into train and testing sets.

MODELING AND EVALUATION

For the reinforcement learning environment, we use the actor-critic method as in [6]. In this actor-critic method, the value-based and policy-based methods are fused together into a single algorithm. This is done using two neural networks, which basically are the actor and the critic. The actor controls how an agent behaves and is related to the policy-based method. The critic is used to measure how well the action is taken and is related to the value-based method. We train the critic model that approximates the value function. This value function replaces the reward function of a policy gradient algorithm like reinforcement learning and calculates rewards only at the end of the episode. It enables the temporal difference (T.D.) updates along with reducing variance and speeding up learning. In the class critic model, we have defined the proximal policy optimization function (PPO) to calculate the value loss. We are using K means for this. Proximal policy optimization is an algorithm that comes under reinforcement learning. A reinforcement learning environment is used to train and test the data with Convolutional Neural Networks and layered Dense Network. The following specifications were defined for the reward and the penalty for the agent in the system: A small reward when the net worth is multiplied by 0.00001 was added to the net worth. And similarly, for a penalty, the same multiplied number was subtracted from the net worth. The entire system is trained on the Google Cloud Platform, which ensures the availability of a GPU.

Convolutional Neural Networks (CNN)

There are three layers in a Convolutional Neural Network as illustrated in Fig. (**3**), which is a deep learning algorithm. A convolutional layer, a pooling layer, and a fully connected layer. Performing a dot product between two matrices is the basic function of the Convolution Layer. The output of the network is replaced by the pooling layer by deriving a summary statistic of the nearby outputs. The most popular process is max pooling, which gives the maximum output from the neighborhood [10, 11]. The fully connected layer aids in mapping the input and output representations.

Dense Neural Network Model

It is a basic convolution neural network model used, which consists of a total of seven dense layers. Two similar dense neural networks are used for the actor as well as the Critic model. Each of which consists of three dense layers. A single dense layer is shared between the actor and critic model, which proves to provide better results. In each model, the input obtained from the shared dense layer is passed into a flatten layer. Further, three more dense layers are attached to the flatten layer, which consists of 512, 256, and 64 neurons, respectively. Relu activation function is used, which helps to overcome the vanishing gradient problem. It also enables the model to learn faster and provide accurate results, as in [14].

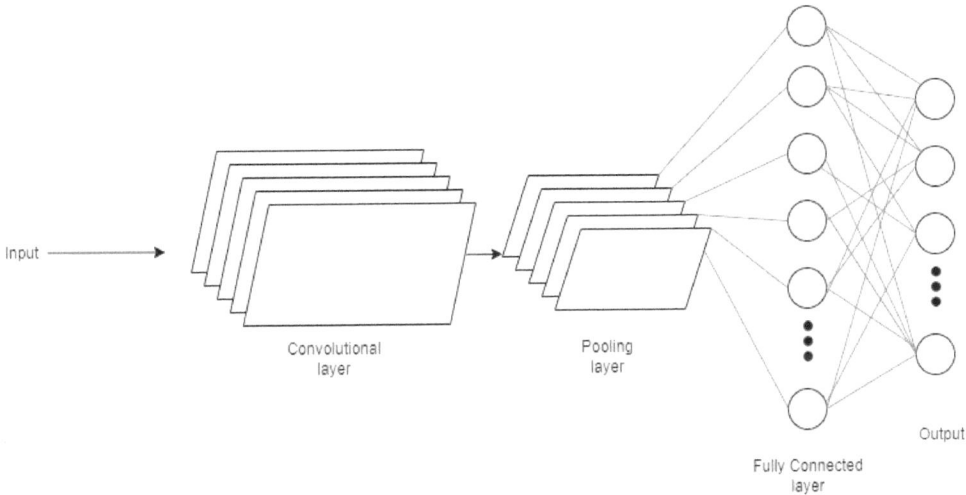

Fig. (3). CNN Architecture diagram.

For training the agent, different parameters like lookback window size, learning rate, number of epochs, optimizer, batch size, and the model instance are described for the agent. The various parameters which are used for training the agent have their respective values in turn. One of the parameters used is the lookback window size. There is no specific value for it. The second parameter is lr which is logistic regression. Logistic regression is a technique borrowed from the field of statistics by machine learning. It is the go-to method for binary classification problems. It's a supervised learning classification system for predicting the likelihood of a target variable. The value for the logistic regression parameter in our case is 0.00001. The next parameter is epoch. An epoch is a term that refers to the number of rounds the algorithm has made across the full training dataset. Batches are commonly used to group data sets. The number of epochs equals the number of iterations if the batch size is the entire training dataset. The number of epochs here is 5. The fourth parameter is the optimizer. The optimizer is a mechanism for reducing losses by changing the properties of our neural network, such as weights and learning rate. These strategies are responsible for providing the most accurate results possible. The optimizer value is Adam. The optimizer Adam involves a combination of two gradient descent methodologies. The penultimate parameter is the batch size. It refers to the number of training examples used in one iteration. The batch size is of three types. Batch mode, mini-batch mode, and stochastic mode are the three options. The batch size here is 32. The final parameter is the model. A model is a file that has been taught to recognize specific patterns. When a model is trained on a collection of data, it is given an algorithm that it may use to reason about and learn from that data (Fig. **4**).

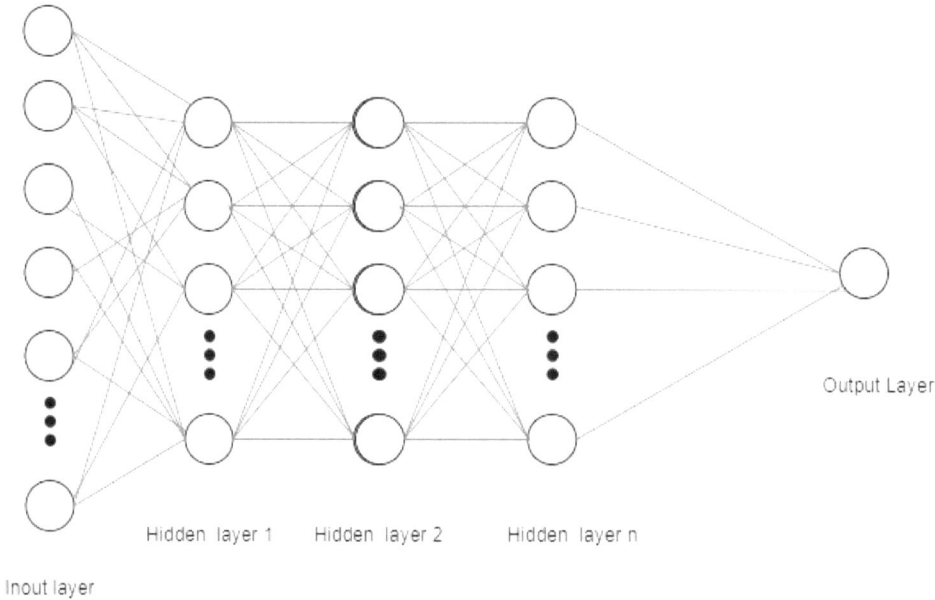

Fig. (4). DNN Architecture diagram.

Depending on the model specified, the agent then creates a training environment on the training data frame, and there are parameters used for training the agent. The first testing parameter is the 'training environment.' This environment is created prior. In reinforcement learning, the environment is the agent's world in which it lives and interacts. The second parameter is "visualize." The value of this parameter is false. The third testing parameter is the "training episodes." The episode comprises all the states that come in between an initial state and a terminal state. The number of training episodes is 10000. The final testing parameter is the "training batch size." The number of training batch sizes is 500.

The values used for the parameters are given in Table **1**.

Table 1. Training Parameters and Values

Parameters	Values
batch size	32
optimizer	Adam
epochs	5
lr	0.00001
lookback window size	lookback window size
model	Dense/CNN

Depending on the model specified, the agent then creates a training environment on the training data frame, and the parameters used for training the agent are given in Table **2**.

Table 2. Testing Parameters and Values

Parameters	Values
train env (Environment created prior)	train env
visualize	False
training batch size	500
train episodes	10000

Table 3. Testing Results

Initial Balance	Model Type	Final Net Worth	Profit%
1000	Dense	1371.04	37.14
1000	CNN	1136.42	13.64

The initial balance for the model Dense is 1000. The final net worth for this particular model type is 1371.04. Thus, the profit, which is basically the difference between the final net worth and the initial balance, is 37.14%. Correspondingly, the initial balance for the model type CNN is 1000. The final net worth for this particular model type is 1136.42. Thus, the profit is 13.64% in Table **3**.

CONCLUSION AND FUTURE SCOPE

In this work, it has been demonstrated that reinforcement learning can be a solution and can cater to the ever-increasing needs of getting maximum profits in this competitive financial world. After training the model on historical data and testing on the current data, we conclude that reinforcement learning can be used to get lucrative returns without any human involvement, and the entire process can be automated. Also, as the topic of cryptocurrencies is very notorious in today's modernized and digitized world, it has proven to be giving massive returns to investors and hence developing an automated system that can handle all the trades by just running a program without having the need of supervising it by a human, is the need of the hour. Similar to positional trading, it is important for a cryptocurrency to be bought and sold at the right time. A system like this can thus help manage the portfolio leading to maximum returns.

There have also been many obstacles during this work that could not be addressed due to the lack of resources and verifiability. The veracity of the source of historical data was a major problem faced during the development of the model since cryptocurrency is a topic of concern in the current world of technology. Also, there were limitations of computational power. It would have taken months to train different types of models on the total amount of data available. As the sentiments of the market also play a crucial role in determining the prices of the currencies, sentiment analysis could also be incorporated and integrated along with the historical data, which would give promising results considering the current trends. Better decision-making strategies involving financial knowledge could help the agent perform even better.

REFERENCES

[1]   S. Kaur, 2017. Algorithmic trading using sentiment analysis and reinforcement learning. positions. http://cs229.stanford.edu/proj2017/final-reports/5222284.pdf

[2]   J. Patani, S. Nair, K. Mehta, A. Sankhe, and P. Kanani, "Financial Portfolio Management using Reinforcement Learning", IJAST, vol. 29, no. 05, pp. 9740 - 9751, May 2020. http://sersc.org/journals/index.php/IJAST/article/ view/19442/9885

[3]   Z. Jiang, and J. Liang, "Cryptocurrency portfolio managementwith deep reinforcement learning", In 2017 Intelligent Systems Conference (IntelliSys), pp. 905-913. IEEE, 2017. [http://dx.doi.org/10.1109/IntelliSys.2017.8324237]

[4]   G. Lucarelli, and M. Borrotti, "A deep reinforcement learning approachfor automated cryptocurrency trading", *IFIP International Conference on Artificial Intelligence Applications and Innovations,* pp. 247-258, 2019. [http://dx.doi.org/10.1007/978-3-030-19823-7_20]

[5]   C. Betancourt, and W.H. Chen, "Deep reinforcement learning for portfolio management of markets

with a dynamic number of assets", *Expert Syst. Appl.,* vol. 164, p. 114002, 2021. [http://dx.doi.org/10.1016/j.eswa.2020.114002]

[6]   Jeong, G. and Kim, H.Y., 2019. Improving financial trading decisions using deep Q-learning: Predicting the number of shares, action strategies, and transfer learning. Expert Systems with Applications, 117, pp.125-138. https://doi.org/10.1016/j.eswa. 2018.09.036

[7]   H. Park, M.K. Sim, and D.G. Choi, "An intelligent financial portfolio trading strategy using deep Q-learning", *Expert Syst. Appl.,* vol. 158, p. 113573, 2020. [http://dx.doi.org/10.1016/j.eswa.2020.113573]

[8]   T.A. Borges, and R.F. Neves, "Ensemble of machine learning algorithms for cryptocurrency investment with different data resampling methods", *Appl. Soft Comput.,* vol. 90, p. 106187, 2020. [http://dx.doi.org/10.1016/j.asoc.2020.106187]

[9]   J Sadighian, "Deep reinforcement learning in cryptocurrency market making", https://arxiv.org/abs/1911.08647v1

[10]   Z. Jiang, and J. Liang, "Cryptocurrency portfolio managementwith deep reinforcement learning", *2017 Intelligent Systems Conference (IntelliSys),* IEEE., pp. 905-913, 2017. [http://dx.doi.org/10.1109/IntelliSys.2017.8324237]

[11]   M. Schnaubelt, *Deep reinforcement learning for the optimal placement ofcryptocurrency limit orders.,* 2021.http://hdl. handle.net/10419/216206

[12]   A.R. Azhikodan, A.G. Bhat, and M.V. Jadhav, Stock trading bot usingdeep reinforcement learning.*Innovations in Computer Science and Engineering.* Springer: Singapore, 2019, pp. 41-49. [http://dx.doi.org/10.1007/978-981-10-8201-6_5]

[13]   O. Sattarov, A. Muminov, C.W. Lee, H.K. Kang, R. Oh, J. Ahn, H.J. Oh, and H.S. Jeon, "Recommending Cryptocurrency Trading Points with Deep Reinforcement Learning Approach", *Applied Sciences,* vol. 10, no. 4, p. 1506, 2020. [http://dx.doi.org/10.3390/app10041506]

[14]   R. Balsys, and R.L.B.T. Bot, https://pylessons.com/RL-BTC-BOT/

SUBJECT INDEX

A

Agent, chemotherapy 38
Alphabet and numeric signs 131
Anderson's GenEth system 224
Arabic sign language (ArSL) 108, 112, 114
Artificial Intelligence 5, 16, 20, 21, 24, 75, 76, 92, 93, 113
  techniques 113
  neural networks (ANN) 5, 16, 20, 21, 24, 75, 76, 92, 93
Atelectasis 29
Audio recordings 149
Automatic segmentation methods 112

B

Balanced two-stage residual networks 66
Barcode 207
  based inventory management systems 207
  detection methodology 207
Batch normalization techniques 118
Bayesian regularization neural network 50
Bayes theorem 95
Blocks 41, 65, 66, 67
  image reconstruction 67
  residual convolution 67
  residual network 65, 67
Boltzmann Machines 8, 9, 16
Box recommender systems 194
Breast cancer 29, 30, 35, 74, 75, 77, 82, 89
  datasets 75, 77
Breast cancer detection 29, 75
  by mammography screening 29

C

Cancer(s) 30, 35
  genome 35
  kidney 30
Cardiotocograph 91

Cardiotocography 91
Cellular-level morphological factors 38
CF-based recommender method 191
Chest 26, 47
  lung X-rays 47
  X-ray images 26
Computer-aided design (CAD) 26, 29, 35
Computer vision 105, 208
  and image processing 208
Computerized tomography (CT) 29, 47
Computing tools 69
Convolutional recurrent neural network (CRNN) 131

D

Deep 9, 16, 67, 237, 240
  deterministic policy gradient (DDPG) 237, 240
  forward neural networks (DFNN) 9, 16
  recursive convolution network (DRCN) 67
Deep Learning 4, 9, 27, 33, 50, 112
  in medical imaging 27
  methods 27, 33, 50, 112
  networks 4
  neural network 9
Devices 117, 131
  wearable 131
  web camera 117
Drug-protein Interaction 3
Dynamic sense 231

E

Education 168, 169, 171, 180
  ecosystem 168
  system 169, 171, 180
Electronic fetal monitoring (EFM) 91
Embedding generation system 197
Ensemble-based classification technique 97
Epenthesis movements 106, 107, 113

www.ingramcontent.com/pod-product-compliance
Lightning Source LLC
Chambersburg PA
CBHW050820220326
41598CB00006B/269